JOY OF THE FRONTIER

An Exciting New Account of Adventures in the San Juan Mountains and New Mexico in the 1880s

By
William
Flewellyn
Saunders

WESTERN REFLECTIONS PUBLISHING COMPANY®
Lake City, Colorado

© Copyright 2020
Western Reflections Publishing Company

All Rights Reserved

ISBN 978-1-937851-44-6

Cover and Text Design by Laurie Casselberry
Laurie Goralka Design

Introduction and Epilogue by Steven G. Baker

Editors—
P. David Smith
Jan M. Smith
Lyndon J. Lampert

Western Reflections Publishing Co.
P. O. Box 1149
951B Highway 149 North
Lake City, Colorado 81235
www.westernreflectionspublishing.com
westernreflectionspublishing@gmail.com

Preface

I WAS GIVEN THIS MANUSCRIPT by Marvin Gregory, an Ouray historian, in 1982 as information that I might be interested in for *Mountain Mysteries*—my first book which I did together with Marvin. It had been given to him earlier by one of Saunders's relatives and unfortunately all Marvin could remember was that the relative lived in Salt Lake City. I used it as a reference mainly in my second book, *Ouray: Chief of the Utes,* for information on the Ute Rebellion of 1879 and the Meeker Massacre. Later, when my wife and I founded Western Reflections Publishing Company, I made several unsuccessful attempts to contact members of the Saunders family that might give us permission to publish the book. Later I discovered that Steven G. Baker of Montrose also had a copy of the book which he used for information in his extensive research on the Utes. He had successfully found Saunders's son or grandson in Salt Lake City, Utah. He corresponded with him about helping with the publication and research for all or part of the book, but no final agreement on the details was reached. Then all communication stopped.

Around 1990 Western Reflections also tried to contact Saunders's relatives, but with no luck, and eventually we gave up. In 2019 Lyn Lampert began working as an Associate editor in the Western Reflections office, and I began to show him manuscripts that had been submitted to us that we might reconsider for publication. This manuscript was one of those, but I explained that I had checked the copyright out several times in the 1990s and that looked like the book might still be in copyright. Lyn really liked the manuscript and did some copyright law research that showed that I had been right at the time I did my research, but that the copyright law now provides that the copyright expires seventy-five years after the death of the author on unpublished manuscripts. He also discovered Saunders died in 1935, so the copyright had expired in 2010.

The only copy that either Steven Baker or Western Reflections had was typed on a manual typewriter with many mistakes and type overs over mistakes or corrections, as well as almost illegible handwritten notes, and the manuscript had been copied on an early model copier that did not reproduce well. In addition, one of the pages was missing. We knew that the manuscript was important and contained a lot of new information that had never been published. Jan, Lyn, and I edited that copy for Saunders's mistakes in spelling and grammar and for words, towns, or events that might not be easily known by the reader today, but tried our best to keep the "flavor" of the original. This included leaving in some vocabulary that readers might find distasteful or racist—but it is the way it was written almost 100 years ago. If you are offended we apologize. Lyn, Steve and I also added footnotes to correct a few of Saunders's historical mistakes (he was writing fifty years after the events happened). Although he made these mistakes, we have checked his presence at the events and feel that he was either there at the events mentioned or he gathered the details later as a newspaper reporter. Baker's close colleague, Dr. John P. Wilson, an archaeologist and ethnohistorian from Los Cruces, New Mexico is also acknowledged for his comments and assistance in locating old newspaper articles that proved pertinent to this tome.

In all, we have spent months polishing the manuscript, and we hope that you will find it as enjoyable as we have working on it.

P. David Smith, Publisher

Table of Contents

		Page Number
Preface	. . . .	. 3
Introduction by Steven G. Baker	. 7
Chapter 1	The Circuit Rider Life in a Alabama Village	15
Chapter 2	The First American School in a Foreign Country	34
Chapter 3	Growing Up on the Waterfront in Old Norfolk	43
Chapter 4	College Life in South Carolina and Virginia	51
Chapter 5	Journalism with Walter Hines Page	63
Chapter 6	Denver—Wicked and Unashamed.	71
Chapter 7	A Gold Mining Camp Fifty Years Ago	77
Chapter 8	A Hunt with Chief Ouray and Chipeta	87
Chapter 9	White River Massacre and Rescue of the Women Captives	101
Chapter 10	The Knife Vote for Peace or War	131
Chapter 11	My Duel on the Santa Fe Plaza	143
Chapter 12	Lew Wallace, Ben Hur and Billy the Kid	151
Chapter 13	General Ulysses S. Grant Pans Gold with Me	161
Chapter 14	Surveying on the Plains	167
Chapter 15	Albuquerque Raw and Turbulent	184
Chapter 16	A Lady Gambler Double-Crosses Us	194
Chapter 17 Back in Colorado, No Longer a Hero		203
Epilogue by Steven G. Baker		210
Index	. . . .	215

Introduction
by Steven G. Baker

FOLLOWING THE END OF THE CIVIL WAR in 1865, a young Alabamian, William ("Willie") Flewellyn Saunders (1858-1935), was but one of the multitude of Americans and newly arrived foreign immigrants who began flocking to the Rocky Mountains in Colorado. People were then coming west in multitudes in order to observe the wonders of the ever-evolving American frontier. The vast amount of land acquired from Mexico in the Mexican-American War were then rapidly giving way to civilization, but there were still places where men's dreams of financial fortune and a better life were popularly thought to be achievable. There were also exciting and often exotic places with magnificent scenery, colorful indigenous Native American cultures, and a "wild and wooly" lifestyle. Writings about these frontiers became very popular genres in a massive "Western" literature of the time.

That literature is often filled with fiction, but there are also non-fiction personal accounts and reminiscences of those who ventured westward and saw the frontier with their own eyes. With the advent of railroads and the "boom time" discovery of gold and silver in the Rocky Mountains, Colorado soon emerged as a popular destination both for those seeking their fortunes and those whose curiosity made them simply tourists wishing to observe nature's wonders. The tourists were almost always well-rewarded by seeing first-hand the many wonders of the West, but few fortune seekers struck it rich on the mining frontier of Colorado. This tome by William Flewellyn Saunders is a previously unpublished personal reminiscence about his youth and early formative years in the South and as a young adult on the western frontier in Colorado and New Mexico. Such personal accounts are common in the literature of the time but were typically prepared to commemorate an individual's participation in or witnesses to some major historical event, such as the Civil War, the Indian Wars on the Plains, or traveling the Oregon Trail. These spurred many to pick up their pen and paper and commence writing. Such writings are very common and were often the only thing that the writers—who were usually neither professionally trained nor well-educated like Saunders—ever produced.

In comparison to so many of these personal accounts, this manuscript stands apart as somewhat unique. Early in his life W. F. Saunders was a smart and well-educated young man who not only had graduated from college but was an aspiring newspaper man who was a good observer and writer. At the still formative age of only twenty, he was already employed in that profession. For the next few years he worked at newspapers from Louisville, Kentucky; the nascent mining camp of Ouray, Colorado; and then on to Santa Fe and Albuquerque, New Mexico. His time in Colorado and New Mexico placed him directly on what were then the outer margins of the western frontier, where he personally observed a number of historic events and met some of the major figures in the history of the United States and the local regions. In short, he was well-trained and well-placed to experience a host of first-person memories of the people and places about which he wrote and published in the papers. At a regional scale, such as his memories of the 1870s events surrounding the Ute reservation on Colorado's Western Slope, are important and rare reminiscences of considerable value to historians, ethnohistorians, and archaeologists. They greatly enrich our knowledge of its regional history.

Internal details indicate that Saunders prepared this manuscript around 1925-1931. He likely did it over a period of time when he is known to have been living and working in Mexico. The internal structure and some word choices/transcriptions in the typewritten document have led me to believe that he was dictating to someone else. He also may have had copies of some of his original published news stories before him. The events he describes from the 1870s and 80s were many decades old by the time he wrote and he sometimes gets his dates a bit confused. One thing he did not do—as writers of remembrances often do—is to fictionalize by casting himself as a central player or hero in the events that he describes. This volume is his story and is certainly about him and his life on the western frontier; but it is told in a way that is mostly convincingly accurate. He is, therefore, certainly a central character but not necessarily the major one in the events described. His accounting of the shooting prowess of Chipeta ("White Singing Bird," the wife of Ouray ("The Arrow") [1833-1880], who was the legendary leader of the combined Tabeguache and Uncompahgre Ute Indian bands (variously known by either name) may, however, be a bit "overblown." Saunders seems to have been a bit infatuated with Chipeta. He obviously at least admired her greatly. Still, however, there is no overt reason to doubt that she may actually have been a remarkable shot of such uncanny ability as he relates.

Both P. David Smith and I have spent much of our lifetimes researching the history of the San Juan Mountains and the Utes, and especially their reservation years on the Western Slope. We have raised only minor questions relative to Saunders's narrative of the events of the late 1870s in and about the reservation and the mining camp of Ouray. Some of these may simply be due to memories that had faded from Saunders's mind over the years. These were critical times in the history of the Utes and the desire of the Whites to have them permanently removed from Colorado. With a Ute war threatening the Western Slope settlements, any news about the agency and Ouray was of utmost importance. Since he was a reporter in Ouray—which was only twenty-five miles from the Ute agency—he was ever attentive to any news involving it and the Utes. He frequently visited the agency and knew Ouray, Chipeta, many other Utes, the employees of the agency, and ultimately he became personally acquainted with the government men, both military and civilian, who had dealings there. His remembrances—such as his account of his participation in the dramatic rescue of the captive Meeker women, are thus critical ones for gaining better understanding about the events involving the Utes in their last years in Colorado. He even provides one of the only good descriptions of the interior of Ouray and Chipeta's home, which was located near present Montrose. His articles on the Ute situation were then picked up by papers in Denver and elsewhere in the nation. His accounting of the Utes constitutes one of the outstanding contributions of Saunders's writing.

This volume is broken into what is essentially three major parts. The first deals with his childhood memories of growing up in Alabama as the son of an itinerant Methodist circuit preacher. This consists of interesting and credible vignettes of life during Civil War reconstruction in the post-bellum South, including the advent of the KKK. It also includes an accounting of his four years in college and start as a cub newspaperman soon after the end of the war. The second major portion deals with his travels to Denver and on to Ouray, Colorado, where he certainly did find the "frontier" at a critical time in its evolution. This includes his extensive remembrances of Ouray, Chipeta and the Utes, which make this a very rare and important document.

The third portion of the volume speaks to his years in New Mexico where he also worked both as a newspaperman and a laborer on a government surveying crew. There he met and reported on the famed outlaw, "Billy the Kid" (Henry McCarty 1859-1881), and gives an excellent accounting of life on a survey crew, including a description of how the difficult work was carried out under often adverse conditions. I personally found this to be very interesting as I had never before seen anything written like this by a direct participant in such everyday but then common work.

One of the more interesting aspects of the entire work is how Saunders opens up his personal life and relates the extreme depths of alcoholism that he sank to once he arrived in Denver as such a young man. Drink was constantly present in quantity on the Colorado and New Mexico frontier. It was a big battle for him and he, with great candor, reflects on how it was destroying him and just how difficult it was for him to "stay on the wagon." He describes this at several places and makes no bones about his problem with it. What we do not know is how he fared with his alcoholism following his return eastward from the Colorado frontier. As Alcoholics Anonymous affirms, you never quit being alcoholic even if you are not drinking.

In 1878 Saunders was a twenty year-old recent college graduate and cub reporter working in Louisville, Kentucky with Walter Hines Page (1858-1918) who was then editing the *Louisville Age*, which did not long survive. Page emerged an important figure in the history of American journalism and became the U.S. Ambassador to the United Kingdom during World War I. The young reporter also became well-acquainted with the noted theologian and linguist, Crawford Howell Toy (1836-1919), before he became a professor of languages at Harvard. Toy was a progressive thinker and became rather famous as a theologian and heretic within the Southern Baptist Church, which he ultimately disavowed. Saunders credits both Page and Toy as important influences in his professional development. Toy actually married Saunders's sister, Nancy, in 1894 and remained in the Harvard area till the end of his life. There, he and Nancy became friends of Woodrow Wilson and his wife. There are entries for them being friends listed among Wilson's Papers in the Library of Congress and elsewhere. When the *Age* folded in 1878 or thereabouts, Saunders did not know what he should do next, then noticed a sign suggesting that folks should "Go West" to the new mining frontier in and around Leadville, Colorado. He determined to head there and try to better his situation.

He arrived in Denver and then went on to Lake City, Colorado by train and from there traveled via stagecoach to Ouray, arriving there in

1879. His father and friends had encouraged him to go on west to Ouray rather than dallying in Denver, which he details in his remembrances. He well-describes the booming little mining camp where he quickly found work as the lead reporter for the *Ouray Times*. While in Ouray he reported details of the regionally notable Cuddigan lynching of a pregnant woman and its aftermath. His close proximity to the reservation was advantageous because he was able to watch, follow, and report on key personalities involved in the then pending and greatly feared potential Ute War and the actual Apache War of 1879 and the aftermath of the related events.

Saunders left Ouray and traveled back to Denver but did not stay long. By the spring of 1880 he was working as editor of the *Santa Fe New Mexican*. General Hatch, who had helped investigate the Ute troubles the year before, had invited him and helped him secure the post. Saunders wrote candidly about Santa Fe, which he believed to be one of the wildest towns in the country. He described his interaction with the famed pioneer archaeologist, Adolph Bandolier and other local personages, as well as his own personal six-gun duel on the plaza in Santa Fe. Though he does not brag about his action, he claims he had to shoot a man who was threatening him there.

During his time in New Mexico he met many new people via his editorship of the paper. These included "Billy the Kid," one of the most famous desperados in United States frontier history. He wrote an interesting account of an extended interview that he had with him that appears in this volume. While still editing the paper in 1880, at but twenty-two years old, he even had occasion to meet the former U.S. President, General Ulysses Grant, and to travel and prospect with him while he evaluated mining properties in the region. Saunders gives us some interesting details about Grant and his personality.

Saunders's run as editor was, however, not to last very long as he had become a heavy drinker. He was indulging to the point that he said his nerves were shattered within a year and he could not even eat breakfast without first having a drink. His struggles with the bottle were what led him to give up his newspaper work and sign onto a government surveying crew as a lowly "chain and mound man." He knew such hard work would keep him in remote areas where he could not obtain liquor, and he thus felt it would help him sober up and lead to restoration of his health. His remembrances of this grueling work are detailed and interesting as such accounts do not appear to have ever been commonly produced. He many months—May to December—surveying in the harsh desert country of southern New Mexico where his party had to deal with many hardships, including a lack of potable water and hostile Apaches. He also recounts how bad the work was, how the surveying parties were outfitted and operated, and how he acquired the nickname of "Soapweed Saunders."

His strenuous time with the surveying crew served its purpose. It had toughened him, restored his health, and cleared his head. Returning to Santa Fe, he found that the *New Mexican* had been sold in his absence and a new editor appointed. When he showed up in December to see his "legion" of old friends, the *New Mexican* (week of Dec. 16, 1881) reported on the event. It particularly noted that his time out surveying had left him looking scruffy and like he had "been out with Jules Verne," (noted 19th century science fiction writer and author of *From the Earth to the Moon*) and "fired from a cannon to the rugged steeps of the moon." He looked so different that his friends played a joke by introducing him to some of his old acquaintances about Santa Fe as a "Mr. Robinson." These people did not recognize him until the crowd finally began to laugh!

He soon obtained a post in Albuquerque running a new paper, the *Albuquerque Review*. Soon, however, he fell off the wagon again and was drinking heavily. He tried once more to save himself and abruptly resigned from the *Review* and went prospecting for a time. Ultimately he settled for a position of less responsibility with the *Albuquerque Democrat*, but his beat took him into the gambling houses and saloons where he could easily drink all the time. He quickly quit that job and signed on briefly as a laborer in a silver mine. Still unsettled and drinking, he decided to return to Ouray in 1880. He made a difficult trip back to Ouray where he spent the winter of 1880-1881. There he was able to obtain all the whiskey he wanted, but held no real job.

As part of his newspaper work in New Mexico he wrote a famous tale known as the "Ghosts of the Pecos" that dealt with army officers in New Mexico from the time of the American occupation to the coming of the Atchison, Topeka, and Santa Fe Railroad which brought about the "new era of rapid progress and forgetfulness of 'ye olden times.'" This was retrospectively reported in the *Santa Fe New Mexican* on June 11, 1907. This story was apparently quite popular among army officers but no copy has yet been located.

During his original New Mexico sojourn Saunders became an ardent opponent of gambling and started the first anti-gambling crusade in the Southwest. According to the *Santa Fe New Mexican* (June 11, 1907) the city was then full of gamblers and "their useless associates." Although they "ruled the roost" and had about everything under their sway, Saunders was said to have been courageous with much nerve and force managed to keep up the anti-gambling fight for a year. His efforts ended, however, when the *New Mexican* folded in 1881. This description is—in spite of his own "devil in the bottle"—fully in keeping with his "high minded" nature and the memories of people in St. Louis who noted that he was a "political idealist."

> *During these two [sic] years—parts of 1880-1881—quite often Mr. Saunders carried his life in his hands, so to speak. He was threatened several times with lynching, with being smashed up, with having the office of the paper burned and other choice occurrences, through which a man mi ght go once, but not two or three times. However, he did his duty by the people and by his employers, but did not succeed in eradicating gambling and running it out root and branch as evidenced by the fact that it still exists and flourishes like a green bay tree and will do so until the first of January of the coming year, when the anti-gambling law passed by the 37th Legislative Assembly will go into effect.*
> (*Santa Fe New Mexican* June 11, 1907)

By spring of 1882 Willie Saunders had gone back to Denver where he reported for the *Times* and the *Republican*. While he made a decent living, he admits that he was never sober. After a time, which he does not define, he went to St. Louis, Missouri and found work there with the *Chronicle*. Saunders ended his remembrances with his arrival in St. Louis. What is known of his subsequent life there is outlined in the Epilogue to this volume.

I believe anyone interested in the old western American frontier and particularly the history of Colorado and the Ute Indians, as well as all the other accountings in this fine book, will find Willie Saunderses' volume to be both very interesting and a credibly informational "easy read."

Steven G. Baker, M. A.
Director, Uncompahgre Valley Ute Project
Centuries Research, Inc., Montrose, Colorado

CHAPTER 1

The Circuit Rider Life in a Alabama Village

My father's early life and training... religion in the Deep South... Camp meetings in the Piney Woods... the marriage of my father and mother... the Girl's School in Tuscaloosa... my father goes to war.

THE CIRCUIT RIDER was a valiant figure in the South of early days.

My father was one of them.

Robert Milton Saunders was the name given to him when he was born in the little village of Rome, Georgia, in 1830. Robert, because that was his father's name, and Milton because his mother, backwoods woman though she was, read whatever books she could get hold of, and loved *Paradise Lost* next to the Bible.

From the time of my father's birth, his mother planned to make him a preacher. She was a fervent Methodist, as were all the rest of the family.

His father was a farmer. He raised cotton and tobacco, and was able to give his son a good common school education, which Robert Milton made good use of.

When he was sixteen, he was admitted to the ministry and was assigned as a circuit rider to four churches in the woods, the nearest seven miles away from Rome and the others from fifteen to thirty miles distant.

He was seldom at home. He served his churches on horseback and carried with him his Bible, a hymn book, a meager outfit of clothing and a few simple medicines in his saddle bags.

He would preach one Sunday morning in one church, spend some time talking to the congregation, who always had many problems to submit to him, sitting under the trees, or informally on the benches of the church. Then he would go home with some family for dinner, and in the afternoon ride on for services in the next church and spend the night with some family of that congregation.

The following Sunday these two churches would go without services and he would minister to some other two.

In the early 1880s, the United States was mainly agrarian and Circuit Riders provided ministers for rural churches. Three or four churches split the minister's salary yet they were still overseen by a minister from their denomination.

Illustration from The Circuit Rider: A Tale of the Heroic Age by Edward Eggleston.

When he began preaching he was six feet three inches tall, and weighed two hundred pounds, was very muscular and alert in his movements. Although his journeying took him into many lonely places, he never went armed, for he was very quick to anger and did not trust his self-control.

But he had many fisticuff fights with rowdies who would come to the night meetings in the woods and try to break them up by turbulent behavior. When this happened my father would stop the services, and calling on some of the deacons to help him he would have the disturbers thrown out of the church, put on their horses or into their buggies, with a stern warning to keep away from that vicinity in the future. The men of the Lord were so uniformly victorious in these battles that word went around to the farms and turpentine camps that the churches of Parson Saunders were good places to stay away from and after the first year of his ministry he had no more trouble.

His first sermon was preached in a little frame church in Rome, holding about three hundred people. The chancel and the steps leading up to the pulpit were carpeted but the floor of the rest of the church was bare. The pews were all straight-backed and most uncomfortable, of course, because true religion was thought to be incompatible with comfort. The sermons were usually very long, sometimes two hours. A sermon only an hour long was received with great dissatisfaction by the congregation.

At the side of the chancel was a special bench on which sat the deacons and other prominent members of the church, never any women. Visiting preachers sat behind the pulpit rail, with the officiating preacher.

1 | The Circuit Rider Life in a Alabama Village

A melodeon[1] at the side of the chancel provided the accompaniment for hymns as the preacher lined them out, two lines at a time, the congregation then singing them as best they could.

The melodeon player was considered a most distinguished person.

Revivals were held whenever it seemed to the preacher and the elders of the church that interest in religion was waning in the community. Sometimes they were held in a church in town but the most successful ones were held in the woods in some open space where there was plenty of room to put up tents to accommodate the crowds that always came to these camp meetings. If there was a church in the clearing, well and good, but if not, the preachers held forth in the open air and everybody liked that better, for the churches were small and stuffy.

July and August was the time when the big camp meetings were held. The weather was settled then and the farmers had some leisure. The camp meetings were looked forward to all the year—by the older women as a season of religious refreshment and gossip, by the men as an opportunity to meet their friends from afar off, and talk about crops and business, and by the young people as a time for sweet hearting.

The camp meetings lasted for a week—sometimes ten days. Often there were moonlight nights, which the young folks took full advantage of. The girls had much more liberty than they had at home, for in the crowd it was often impossible for families to sit together, so it was an easy matter for a young couple to slip off and go love making into the surrounding woods.

About a month before the time set, the preachers of all the churches round about would announce from their pulpits the names of the preachers who would be there, the date of the opening and the place of the meeting.

These were all regular ministers, not evangelists, like those who officiate at revival meetings in these days. The evangelist came into the field when the regular preachers began to lose their fervor and enthusiasm, but in these early days of the church, when my father rode his circuit, every preacher was an evangelist, full of fire and an ardent desire to save souls from the flames of Hell.

About a week before the opening of the meeting the families who were going to attend began to come to the clearing and set up their tents. Those who came first got the best places of course. People came from

---

[1] There were several types of melodeons, but this melodeon was probably a type of reed or "American" organ that is a small keyboard instrument that looks a little like today's keyboard instrument but made music by reed vibration. They were very popular in the 19th century because of their portability but they could be played like a small piano.

fifty miles away, in wagons, in buggies and on horseback. The women had side saddles, and wore long riding skirts over their regular skirts. A woman in the riding togs of today would not have been allowed to come into the church. Often they rode double, two on a horse, the man in the saddle and the woman behind him, clinging to his waist, sometimes holding a small child in her lap.

All the year the housewives had been planning meals for the camp meeting, each one wishing secretly to make a little better showing than anyone else and many good things have been prepared and put away for this time—preserves, jellies, apple butter, sausages, smoked hams, pickles and relishes of all sorts.

There were cooking tents where fried chicken, biscuits and coffee could be prepared and long tables of boards on trestles, where, if the crowd was great they ate in relays.

Every housewife vied with the others, bringing their best table linen—this of course was long before paper table cloths and napkins were invented, and there was nothing canned, except sardines imported from the North.

Usually there were five or six preachers at these meetings—relieving each other for the sermons, of which there were three every day. They were full of the soundest Biblical doctrine. There was a physical Heaven, where those who had been Christians in life lived forever and happiness after death, and a physical Hell, where the wicked endured torture forever ... no faltering, no quibbling, no doubt.

This is an engraving from a Methodist camp meeting in 1819, but it would have looked pretty much the same in the 1850s. Note the tents in the background as the meetings could last for days.
                Artist - Jacques Gerard Milbert, Courtesy of Library of Congress.

Most of the families who came to the meeting were well-to-do, and brought slaves with them to do the cooking and other work.

The slaves were housed in two large tents, one for the men and one for the women, places far enough away from the tents of their masters to dull the noise of their singing and laughter, which usually lasted long after the white folks had gone to bed.

The souls of the Negroes were not neglected. They had their own religious revivals after those of the white folks were over. They had their own churches, in town, or on the plantation or in the country, and they had their own preachers, though very often, as a special favor to them, a white preacher would go to one of their churches and conduct services for them.

The slave owners believed that religion was a good thing for the Negroes and looked indulgently at their services, but I imagine that most of them never thought for a moment that the slaves would be allowed to consort with the white people in Heaven.

In the Negro churches the intense emotionalism of the black race developed the hymns which were the beginning and the foundation of the Negro spirituals, as they are now called. In these revivals the religious ecstasy was much more violent than in the white churches and the converts in the frenzy of the regeneration would leap from the mourners' bench and push their way through the congregation embracing friends and enemies alike.

As I write, there comes to my mind a story told to me by my mother when I was a boy.

Our cook, a big yellow woman named Alice, said to her one morning, "I got religion las' night, Miss Molly." "Oh, did you, Alice" answered my mother gently, "I suppose you will make better biscuits now." "Yes'm, Miss Molly. And when I got up from the mourners bench, with my eyes jus' stream' with salvation, there was that good-for-nothin' black Rosa, what got Joe away from me an' married him, grinnin' all over, an' I just went up to her an' threw my arms aroun' her an' shouted, 'Sister, we's goin' to Heaven together!,' an' I hugged her so tight that bran' new hat Joe give was smashed all the pieces. You ought to seen her face Miss Molly!"

But that does not mean that the religious exaltation of the Negro was not sincere—it usually was. Alice was human—and ingenuous.

There was a special tent, set some distance away from the others, where the preachers slept and met for consultation between services. They ate with one family and another of the congregation, and the tents where the preachers were guests acquired high dignity on the camp grounds. Even the darkeys who served these tents felt superior to the other slaves. The wives of the married preachers were the welcome guests of some family of their home congregation.

In their own tent the revivalists relaxed from the strain of the exhausting church services. They lay down and rested, told stories or smoked. A few of them chewed tobacco but no one smoked or chewed in public. Not that they would have denied the habit, but among people they were expected to set an example to the young.

My father, by the way, did not learn to smoke until he went into the army.

These backwoods preachers and circuit riders were all deeply religious men, of all ages, from sixteen to fifty. All of them believed that they had received "a call from God" to go out among people and preach His word. Some of them would even tell how they had been wakened at night and heard the voice of God telling them to leave everything and go preach the Gospel. Compared with modern standards most of them were profoundly ignorant. They did not have to be educated or even highly intelligent to preach.

To be accepted as the mouthpiece of God it was necessary only to be fervently religious and fluent in speech.

Few had any money, yet they had no difficulty in finding wives and raising families. The people of their congregation provided them with a home and with a small salary. Often during the year there were donation parties when quantities of food and clothing were taken to the parsonage.

It is hard for the generation of the present to understand—impossible for them to sympathize with—the respect and even veneration felt by the people of the old South for the circuit rider or the preacher in the small towns, cut off as they were from all the centres of large interests. He was looked upon as one who was in daily communion with God. When he visited a family it was looked upon as a very high honor, except, to tell the truth, by the children who felt dreadful apprehension of long prayers and short rations. I myself, to this day, have a predilection for chicken necks, the result of childish years when the necks and backs would be all that was left after the bountiful meal prepared for the visiting preacher. We children, of course, always ate at the second table.

Ethical questions were always submitted to the preacher for decision and the neighbors were always invited to come in and bring their difficulties, religious or otherwise, for his advice.

Every politician who aspired to office sought the favor of the preacher, who was without exception, the most influential man in the community. So you can see that the preachers had few spare moments during the camp meeting.

The camp meeting grounds were lighted at night by great torches of lightwood, set up all around the grounds and along the paths leading from the tents to the church, if there happened to be a church, the tents were lighted by large candles, homemade and much larger than those bought in the shops. If there was a church it was illumined by large oil lamps with reflectors.

These lighting effects made the nights much more impressive and soul-stirring than the days, and the result was that the services in the evening were more fruitful of conversions than those during the day. The preachers knew this and vied with each other in securing assignments to preach at night.

It usually took about a week for the crowd to be worked up to the point of great emotionalism, and the evening services for the last week were devoted to the intensification of this religious ardor. The most stirring hymns were chosen and at the close of the sermon the preacher would invite all those who were ready to accept Christ and be forgiven for their sins to come forward and kneel at the mourners' bench.

There was always a throng of penitents, who would kneel, bury their faces in their hands and wait for the touch of the preachers hand upon their head and his whisper that their sins would be forgiven if they would accept Christ and resolved to lead a better life. There were always several preachers inside the chancel to encourage and exhort the sinners.

The men at the mourners' bench moaned and groaned and sighed, the women sobbed. Now and then a mother, a sister or a wife watching the soul in travail at the altar, would leave her seat and going forward, would kneel at the altar with the penitent and whisper words that she thought would help him.

The preachers could no longer line-out the hymns—their attention was all on the mourners.

Someone in the congregation would burst out into a revivalist song that everyone knew:

> *There is a fountain filled with blood*
> *Drawn from Immanuel's veins*
> *And sinners plunged beneath that flood*
> *Lose all their guilty stains.*[2]

---

[2] From *Praise for the Fountain Opened* by William Cowper.

Or another,:

> *Jesus paid it all,*
> *All the debt I owe,*
> *Sin had left a crimson stain*
> *He washed it white as snow.* [3]

Men and women in the congregation would join in with fervor and the coldest there would feel the emotional stimulant. A man or woman kneeling at the altar would suddenly arise and shout, "I am saved! I am saved! Jesus has forgiven all my sins!"

And while "Amens" and "Hallelujahs" rose from the congregation in sympathy, the leader of the singing would change from a melancholy chant to something joyous like,

> *Hallelujah 'tis done!*
> *I believe on the Son*
> *I am saved by the blood*
> *Of the crucified One.* [4]

The mourners at the bench who had thus declared that their sins were forgiven were said to have been "converted." "We had twenty converts last night," a preacher would say in the rest tent to the others who had not been present.

This emotional upheaval in the minds of the converts was always sincere—for the time anyway. I have never known hypocritical conversions at these revivals. The change in the behavior of the convert would be marked for days. The man or woman would go about calm and gentle, looked on with awe by those not converted, as one set apart. Sometimes the convert would backslide into the ways of the unregenerate; a change that was received with sorrow by the family, but with scarcely repressed exultation by the ribald. But most often the conversion was the beginning of a new life of purpose and usefulness to the community.

My mother, Mary Jane Toomer, came of old Virginia stock. Her family were ship builders in Deep Creek, Virginia, a little seaport town near Norfolk. Her grandfather James H. Toomer built the privateer schooner, *The Seven Sisters*, which during the war of 1812 gave a good account of itself, taking seven prizes.

---

[3] *Jesus Paid It All* by Elvina M. Hall.
[4] *Hallelujah 'Tis Done* by Phillip P. Bliss was published in 1874 after the time frame in Saunders's manuscript.

1 | The Circuit Rider Life in a Alabama Village

After this war was finished, the Toomer family moved to Portsmouth, across the Elizabeth River, and as time went on developed into a family of educators, whose descendants are to be found in schools and colleges through Virginia, North Carolina and Georgia and even as far north as Harvard. My mother for many years held the chair of Modern Languages in Randolph-Macon Girls' College and was the first woman to receive the Carnegie Teachers' Pension.

My great-grandfather must have been a delightful old gentleman and I have often wished that the records of the Toomer family which I found in the old courthouse of Portsmouth had told more of his early life, which from the meager details I found must have been full of interest.

His will showed his unconventionality. He left small bequests to his children, leaving all the rest of his estate to his wife and ending with the words, "I leave also to my beloved wife, Sallie, my own private still, that she may hereafter brew her own drink." His most cherished possession! Not that my great-grandmother was a toper,[5] but I am sure that great-grandfather felt that the still made a bond between them that death could not break.

My mother was a cultivated woman, of brilliance and great initiative. She was very active in the society life of Portsmouth and I do not know how it happened that she left her home and her family when she was still quite young and went to teach school in the small town of Wetumpka in Alabama.

It was there that she met my father, who was conducting a revival meeting there. I believe the courtship was a wildfire affair. My mother was deeply religious in her youth and apart from the spiritual appeal, my father must have been a rather splendid young man, with his magnificent build, his aquiline features and his mass of wavy dark hair.

They were married very soon, my father got a permanent church in Wetumpka and they settled down there and began raising a family. All of us children were born there, I, my brother Jim and my sister Nancy.

But my mother was dissatisfied there. She felt the pressure of poverty very keenly and she was sure they could lead a broader life somewhere else. In the end she persuaded my father to buy the Woman's [sis] College in Tuscaloosa, (I have no idea where they got the money) and from the first year of their management the experiment proved a financial success.

My father managed the business and taught some of the classes though my mother, with one or two assistants, did most of the teaching.

---

[5] A "toper" is a drunk.

They brought Crawford Howell Toy, a young fellow of twenty, "Cousin Crawford," of whom I shall have more to say later, from Virginia, to help with both management and teaching, and everything went well.

They were both satisfied with their lives, believing that they were doing good and prospering at the same time. My mother often visited Mobile and Montgomery, where she found wider fields of activity, while my father, whenever he pleased, could make a round of country churches preaching.

Then the war came.

My father went into the Confederate Army as Chaplain, and Cousin Crawford enlisted.

That left the responsibility of the Woman's [sic] College entirely on my mother, but nothing ever daunted her.

She rallied to the emergency, sent to Portsmouth for two of her sisters to come to her aid and the Woman's [sic] College went on without interruption during all the long years of the war.

Very quietly most of the time for Tuscaloosa was off the beaten track of the firing—far from Georgia, where the battle raged unceasingly and equally far from the Mississippi River where the fighting was continuous.

Most of the time we did not even have news of what was going on.

LIFE IN AN ALABAMA VILLAGE

It was a glorious morning in late September 1864. The sun was shining brightly, there was not a cloud in the sky and the air had an exhilarating tang. In the little Alabama town of Tuscaloosa the children were playing hopscotch on the wooden sidewalks or rolling hoops in the unpaved streets. In front of the shops in the centre of the town were farm wagons, driven, all of them, by women, who sat bargaining with the shop keepers, who had come out to see if they wanted anything from the wagons. All the able-bodied men being in the army, the farms were managed by the women aided by the loyal slaves.

When the women were unable to sell their produce to the shopkeepers, they drove about town, from house to house, bartering with the housewives. Little money was exchanged. There was nothing but paper and the Confederate bills were looked on with distrust. The farm women prefer to exchange their wares for tea, coffee, sugar, drugs and dry goods.

I was a boy of five and I was playing with a group of children in front of the College. In spite of the absence of my father and Cousin Crawford, the routine of the school had not been interrupted. Classes were heard reciting monotonously through the open windows, exercises were being played on several pianos and vocal pupils were running scales.

Suddenly, interrupting the shouts and laughter of the children in the street, faintly in the distance arose the slow, dull beat of drums.

The children stopped playing and were still, as they saw that the grown people were all listening.

Then there appeared soldiers in grey, marching in fours, dusty, dispirited and bent with fatigue.

They were the men of Hood's army, retreating before Sherman's devastating march from Atlanta to the sea.

As the first soldiers came in sight, all business was suspended and everybody rushed to the side of the road to see.

"Camp here and we'll feed you," called out one woman.

"Can't do it," shouted an officer on horseback, "but bring out what you've got and hand it to the men as they pass along."

That was done. Everything edible in the farm wagons was handed to the soldiers. Coffee, such as it was, made mostly of chicory and parched corn, was hastily boiled and brought to the side of the road in big pots, and the women in every house hurriedly made sandwiches and sent them by the children to the marching soldiers. Then a soldier struck up:

> *Oh, I'll eat when I'm hungry,*
> *I'll drink when I'm dry,*
> *If the Yankees don't kill me,*
> *I'll live till I die.*

The tune was a dolorous one and dragged. It was taken up by one file of the retreating Confederates after another, and presently, for a mile, we could hear the chant. Ten thousand of these beaten men went through Tuscaloosa before noon that day.

I was one of the boys who carried sandwiches to the soldiers. The scene made an indelible impression on me. On one of my trips back to the house for sandwiches which my mother and many busy young women were making, I found an officer on horseback talking to my mother, and I heard him say to her, "I'm afraid we're on our last legs. They have too much money and too many men for us. We ought not to be running away from Sherman, but our food and ammunition are giving out. A lot of the men marching along there with us are wounded, but we have no hospital facilities."

"Oh," said my mother, "How can God permit such things! Do you mean that we will have to surrender?"

"I wouldn't dare suggest such a thing, but you all should prepare for the worst."

As the last of the soldiers trudged past the spectators, who lined the road, all the food that could be prepared quickly having been distributed, an officer, with a half healed scar running across his face, rode to the group that seemed thickest, and called out, "The Yankees are about two days behind us. Burn that bridge. That will hold 'em a while."

We did burn the bridge, that same day, but when the Yankees came it didn't hold them very long. The Black Warrior River was very low and fordable, and although the few able-bodied men left in Tuscaloosa and some youths made a feeble defense, the blue-coated soldiers easily crossed the river and after an exchange of a few shots drove the defenders to their homes. One of our boys, severely wounded, was brought to the Woman's [sic] College and there nursed. Several, on both sides were killed by the first and the only volley of shots fired from the banks of the river and by the advancing invaders.

The Yankees swarmed all over the little town, officers quartered in the homes of the people, and the soldiers camping in tents in the streets. The people of the town were panic-stricken. There was no looting nor burning of houses, but soldiers walked into shops and took what they wanted without pay. No one appeared on the streets except soldiers. Neighbors who visited each other did so by the backyards.

Children slipped into the streets and went around the tents curiously. I did this with my brother. In one tent a soldier said to us, "We are hungry, can't you get us something to eat from your house!" and he added, "I'll give you this pistol for some bread and meat."

We knew that our mother had gone to a neighbor's and stealing into our house we brought the soldier a whole pan of biscuits and took his pistol in exchange.

That night the biscuits were missed and we were questioned. We confessed and produce the pistol. The family was horrified. We had been trafficking with the devil. The next morning we were forced to return the pistol and we were threatened with the most awful punishment if we even spoke to one of the invaders.

My uncle, Sheldon Toomer, who was with the Confederate army, owned a horse and buggy. The horse, a beautiful bay, he was riding, but the buggy was in a shed, open to the street, a low paling[6] fence across

---

[6] A "paling" is a type of low pointed stake fence.

the front. Three officers road up to the front door of our house and one of them dismounted and clattered the big knocker.

"That's a nice buggy you have there," he said to my mother, who came to the door. Where's the horse?"

"My brother is riding it, fighting you Yankees," answered my mother, spiritedly.

"Ah, then we'll confiscate the buggy," he said. "Let us in there."

"Wait a minute," she said, and shut the door in his face.

Calling her two sisters she ran with them around to the shed and the three women, with an axe and hatchet and a stick of wood, broke out the spokes of the wheels of the buggy, while the three officers, mounted on their horses sat outside and looked on laughing.

"Crash," went a spoke under the axe of my mother. And "smash" went others as a hatchet and stick of wood fell.

"God help us," prayed the women.

It would have been easy enough for the cavalry men to have jumped over the fence, overpowered the women and taken the buggy, but they really didn't want the vehicle very much and they enjoyed the spectacle of three pretty southern women in a rage, so they let them go until every spoke in the wheels of the buggy were broken.

In the background stood all the children of the family, struck dumb with horror at the scene. They had never seen their parents in such a white heat of anger.

Presently all the spokes of the buggy wheels had been beaten out by the women.

"There," said my mother to the laughing cavalrymen, as she straightened up defiantly and threw away her axe. "You may take the buggy and much good may it do you."

This is just one picture of the life we lived during the Civil War. For three years before that and for a year after, the people of Tuscaloosa, like those of all the small towns, had almost no communication with those of the outside world. We got the Mobile papers occasionally, but they had little definite news. Now and then a wounded soldier came back from the Army, brought in a wagon. If he died, then everybody in town went to the funeral. If he lived, he helped his family with the chores around the house. The Woman's [sic] College was a sort of hospital, and several of the crippled soldiers were nursed there. My uncle came without one leg, which he had lost at the Battle of Malvern Hill, and he busied himself painting headboards for the graves of the soldiers in the town cemetery. The studies in the college went on, classes in mathematics, French, German and English literature, as well as in music.

We had plenty to eat, very plain food, of course, because we could get nothing. We seldom had coffee or tea, and we made a beverage out of parched corn, which tasted like the substitutes for coffee we have nowadays. We had a lively community spirit in the little town. Whenever a family had to do something beyond the power of the family itself or of that of the slaves attached to the family, we gave a party and invited everybody and they all came and helped with the things to be done.

Very important was the making of the tallow candles which furnished most of the light for the long winter evenings. Kerosene was expensive and was not always to be had, even if one could afford to buy it, so, as soon as the hot summer weather was over the women started to prepare their stock of candles to be hung up in great bunches in the store rooms and taken out very sparingly, for the task of making them was long and tedious.

I well remember the tubs of smoking hot tallow and the women hastening from the tubs to the racks where they hung the rods, each one two feet long, with twelve cotton wicks hanging from it. These were dipped over and over again into the liquid tallow until the successive layers had made them fat and round.

It took fifteen or twenty minutes to cool the tallow between each dipping and the time had to be calculated to a nicety, for if they were dipped too soon, the previous layer would be melted off and if left too long the candle might crack. Each woman could manage ten or fifteen rods.

These candle-making parties were usually begun in the evenings, in the front or back yards of the houses, and the work was finished the next day. During the evening, there was dancing, either in the yards or the house, to the music of a Negro fiddler or a piano played by one of the girls of the college.

Even during the most wretched days of the war, when the people were poorest and the news from the battle fronts the worst, Christmas was observed with the making of gifts, such feasting as we could provide from the depleted larders of the households, and parties with music.

The Fourth of July was never observed, and indeed, that day has never been celebrated heartily in the south as it is in the north. I have wondered if the southerners did not have a vague idea that the Fourth of July was a northern affair, and had nothing to do with the south.

I remember that Blind Tom, with his master, came to one of these Christmas parties of ours. Blind Tom was a Negro, then a youth, of very low mental capacity but a musical phenomenon. He had never been taught to play on any musical instrument, but he could sit at a piano and improvise melodies, some of them very simple and pleasant to hear

1 | The Circuit Rider Life in a Alabama Village

After the Civil War southerners tended to romanticize plantation life and often represented slaves as children that needed guidance and discipline.
      Currier and Ives lithograph 1872, Courtesy of Library of Congress.

and some of them weird and barbaric. This was wonderful enough to be done by one with no musical training whatever, but he had an accomplishment even more unusual. He would listen intently to a symphony, a fugue, a nocturne or any composition by Beethoven, Bach, Chopin or some other composer, something that would take fifteen minutes or so to play by note, and then he would sit at the piano and play the composition exactly as if it had been played, with the same expression, missing no notes and adding nothing. It was a phenomenal feat of memory. Blind Tom was a great favorite with his audiences. While the piece he was to imitate was being played, he would listen close to the piano, with his head bowed. Then, when his master said, "Now, Tom," he would go to the piano. When he had ended his playing, he would leap from the piano stool and applauded himself vigorously. Of course his audience would join in. After the war, when Tom was freed, the court placed him in the charge of his former master as his guardian, and this man took him around the country, showing him in theatres and making a good deal of money, on which he and Tom lived.

   One of Tom's compositions he called the Battle of Manassas, and he composed it a after he heard a narrative of the fight from a returned soldier. It was the first descriptive musical composition I had ever heard, and it made a deep impression on me. The Negro's mentality was about that of a three-year-old child. He would sit at the piano and begin to play, describing in a chant the thing he was imitating on the keys.

> "First there was the drum and fife, playing Dixie! The Confederates advance to the charge!" Tom would shout. "Then the drum and fife playing, Yankee Doodle; the Yankees come to meet 'em.
> "Then the rattle of the small arms, and the boom of the heavy guns; the Confederate yell and the Yankee hurrah, which Tom would imitate with zest; the retreat of the Confederates, when the piano would become mournful; then the rally of the Confederates and their charge.
> "The Yankees are running; the Confederates are chasing them," and Tom would break into Dixie played on heavy chords, while he shouted the rebel yell of victory."

He would work up to this climax with great vigor and enthusiasm, and when he got up from the piano and began to applaud himself the audience would join him with a thunder of approval.

I have heard since then many descriptive musical compositions, but none have so thrilled me as that Battle of Manassas.

My uncle, Chapel Ross, owned one of the largest plantations in Alabama, about ten miles out of Opelika. He had 130 slaves and raised cotton, corn, hay and every kind of garden vegetable. He had horses, mules, cows and hogs and was quite well-to-do, with no mortgage on the farm and a good bank account. When the war began, he took all his money out of his bank and kept it in his house, in gold. Cash was the word on his plantation, except with his neighbors in poorer circumstances, many of whom he helped with loans, for which he would take no interest, and with the services of his plantation hands. A severe physical disability had prevented him from going into the army. We children often visited his family, since there were cousins there of our own age, and Tuscaloosa was very near Opelika.

My Aunt Sallie delighted in having a large brood of youngsters trailing at her skirts and was always glad to see us when we visited her. She wore a girdle at her waist, with an enormous bunch of keys dangling from it, big and little.

There was the key to the cellar, where the liquors were kept; the key to the springhouse, quite a good little cabin, built around a gushing spring, with shelves all around it, for the butter, milk and cream were placed and kept as cold as ice; the key to the smoke house, where the meats were; and other smaller keys without number. I often wondered how in the world Aunt Sallie would know those keys apart. When she wanted one, she would grope for an instant at her girdle, without looking and then choose with unerring precision.

Those on the plantation lived on what it raised all through the war. They bought nothing except coffee and sugar. The cotton and the corn and the vegetables that could be spared were sold, and some of those things were traded to neighbors.

Chapel Ross had the reputation of being one of the mildest and gentlest of slave-owning masters; yet he believed in flogging slaves.

I remember once standing with the other children, my brother and sister and my cousins, in an enclosure near the slave quarters, away from the house, watching the whipping of a stalwart Negro. He wore nothing but cotton drawers and his wrists were tied to a post above his head. My uncle took the overseer aside before the whipping began and I heard him say to the man, who was drawing the blacksnake whip through his fingers, "Hurt him so he'll feel it, but don't draw the blood, I don't want him sick. I want to work him today."

As each lash came down on the back of the slave, he would shudder and cry out, "Oh, my Lord, Massa. I won't run away no more. Don't let him whip me no more, Massa; I'll be good."

We children watched fascinated and dumb as the whipping went on. It lasted about ten minutes, and then the overseer untied the hands of the slave and ordered, "Now, you get back to the quarters and after your dinner get out in the field with the rest."

Of course, we children should not have been allowed to watch this brutalizing spectacle, but the whipping of slaves was such a commonplace that it was not thought an improper sight for children.

Some of the beatings given as punishment to black slaves were horrible and drew blood such as shown in this engraving.
Artist: Henry L. Stephens
Courtesy of Library of Congress

In these days the parent spares the rod and spoils the child. In those days the children of the south were subjected to the severest discipline, not only by the parents themselves but by the Negro mammies to whose nursing they were entrusted; and they grew up obedient and respectful and so fearful of their elders that they were not frank and open in their behavior but furtive very often. We had to be seen and not heard at the dining table; we had to ask permission to do anything unusual, and had to defer to our elders in everything without argument, whether we thought they were right or wrong.

The punishment for an offense was not one planned to fit the crime—it was just plain hard whipping that left marks on the body. My father, who was a very kind man, used to command me to go up to the garret[7] when he felt it necessary to punish me. You would come in with a bundle of peach tree switches, which he had cut himself, big and little, would lock the door and make me strip stark naked. Then he would make me put my head between his legs; hold it as tight as a vice, and belabor me with the switches all over the body, from head to foot, paying not the slightest attention to my yells.

Then, and not before the whipping, he would lecture me, pointing out the gravity of my offense and would leave the room, leaving me to dispose of the instruments of punishment.

Of course my screams aroused the whole house and must have made everybody very uncomfortable. Usually when I emerged from the garret, clothed again, with face contorted and tearful, I would find one of the Negro servants waiting to sympathize with me and wanting to do something to comfort me.

It never occurred to me to resent these whippings. I knew that I had deserved them.

And my black mammy, sympathetic though she was, did not spare me when I deserved punishment. I shall never forget one bit of her discipline.

I was four years old. My mother was giving an afternoon party and was probably a little flustered by the last-minute arrangements.

It was almost time for the guests to arrive and I, dressed in my best white suit, was bubbling over with excitement and anticipation. Perhaps it was the excitement—but suddenly occurred one of those unmentionable childish accidents. I was overwhelmed with shame, my mother was aghast, and suddenly guests began coming up the drive.

---

[7] "Garret" is another name for an attic.

My mother called, frantically, "Mammy Lou, take this child and give him what he deserves!" and I was hustled out through the back hall and down the kitchen walk too frightened to resist.

What Mammy Lou meant to do I do not know, but she caught sight of the rain barrel beside the summer kitchen and, making the punishment fit the crime, she plunged me, soiled trousers and all, into the rainwater barrel. The water came up to my neck. I clung to the side of the barrel and shrieked, believing that I had been brought there to be drowned like an unwanted puppy, while Mammy Lou, whose heart was rent with pity for me, but whose conscience insisted on the punishment, stood by in grim silence—for years, it seemed to me. Of course it was only a minute or two—then she reached in, lifted me out of the barrel, wrapped me in her apron and with consoling words took me to bed where I sobbed myself to sleep.

CHAPTER 2

The First American School in a Foreign Country

Frightful domination of the Negro in the South after the Civil War... the true story of the organization of the KU KLUX... how the name was chosen... my parents establish a college for American girls in Berlin... my short career in a German boy's school...the simple life in a German hamlet near Berlin.

WHEN THE CIVIL WAR ENDED, the people of the South feared that the country was falling into chaos. Martial law governed the principal towns. The Negroes, just freed, naturally were unable to restrain themselves, and were defiant and insolent toward their former owners. Their attitude was becoming more violent. Dishonest politicians from the northern states were laying their hands on the offices of control. They were called "carpetbaggers" because some of them, seeing the rich plunder of the south, rushed down there with no baggage but a carpet bag.

The prospect seemed dismal and fearful, and the southerners seemed helpless.

In this emergency arose the famous Ku Klux Klan. Who suggested the idea I do not know, but I do know how and where the Klan began its work and how it got its name.

The first meeting of Klansmen was held in Pulaski, a small town in Tennessee, and a center of southern feeling, in the house of J. B. Childers, a leading merchant of the place. The meeting was held at night, with closed blinds and only one lamp burning in the room, and that turned down. Yankee soldiers were quartered in the town and there was need for secrecy.

There were eleven men at the meeting and only one woman, Mrs. Childers. The subject of the meeting had been talked over by those present before, and when they met they went at once to business. It was decided to organize a secret society which should so intimidate the

2 | The First American School in a Foreign Country

Negroes that they would behave, and it was the unanimous sense of the meeting that if the leaders of the Negroes didn't scare they should be killed.

A thorough program of ways to frighten the Negroes was laid out, and the pointed hoods with eye holes, and a long white robe, were chosen as the costume the Klansmen should wear.

It was hard to agree on a name for the society. These names were suggested:

"The Southerners.

Defenders of the South.

Knights of the Golden Horseshoe. (The name of an old organization)

The Cavaliers."

None of these names seemed to please everybody. Then one man asked, "What are some of the names of the Greek letter societies in the colleges?"

Several were given, in the Greek words for which the letters stood were spoken and repeated as their sound was tested.

"Kappa alpha," said one of the conspirators.

"Kuklo's Adelphown."

"Kuklas what?" asked another.

"Kuklos, kuklos, kuklos," repeated one after another, as they all seem to find an agreeable sound of ferocity in the word, and then one man lifted out of his chair with force of his idea.

"Here it is," he cried, "Kuklos—Kuklux—sounds like the rattling of bones. We'll call it the Ku Klux and have the emblem of a skull and bones painted on the front of the robes. That name and the picture will scare the niggers to death."

The name was adopted unanimously, and it certainly served its purpose. It did sound like the rattling of bones. Mrs. Childers made the first fifteen robes herself, and they were used on the first Ku Klux raid, when three Negro leaders were called out of their cabins in the county, met by fifteen specters in ghastly gowns and hoods, tied to trees, and so whipped with blacksnake whips that they disappeared from the vicinity.

The news of the organization of the Ku Klux Klan in Pulaski and its scheme went all over the south in a month, and soon there was a complete organization, with branches in every county of every southern state.

Very few Negroes were killed by the Ku Klux. Some were. But usually it was found that the troublesome ones could be cowed by a midnight visit of the Klansman to their homes, and a show of gleaming hood and robe and hands, made to shine by phosphorus, this accomplished by a pretense of drinking a whole bucket of water brought out by the Negro, the water being poured into a rubber bag inside the Klansman's robe. If the Negro was not cowed, there was another visit and a whipping that was serious.

I know, of course, the several accounts of the origin and the purpose of the Ku Klux have been written in magazine and in books, quite different from this.

But this story of the Klansman, which I believe is true, was told me by Mr. Childers himself, with Mrs. Childers sitting by and adding detail now and then.

The government tried to protect the Negroes from the Ku Klux, and the whole south was in a turmoil. Many Southerners who could lay their hands on money left the country to stay away until tranquility returned. Those who remained and had wives and daughters did not fear so much for themselves as for their women.

One book I have read, giving a history of the Ku Klux, and written by a southerner, says that the Ku Klux was organized in a lawyer's office in Pulaski, and that its purpose was purely one of social diversion. It was well enough to give out that story during the years when the government was ferreting out the leaders of the Ku Klux and trying to punish them, but there is certainly no reason why the real purpose, and known all over the south, should be concealed now. There seem to be a necessity for the Ku Klux then, to terrify the unruly Negroes, and it developed out of that necessity. When it had done its work it disappeared.

Out of these dreadful conditions came the organization of the first American school ever established in a foreign country. My mother, who was a born leader, persuaded my father to call a conference of the patrons of the Tuscaloosa College in whose judgment she had the most confidence. When they came she said to them: "It is going to be a long time before the South settles down to safety and quiet. We will take the girls whose parents want to send them with us, to Berlin, and teach them there until things look better here."

The plan seemed good to everyone in the group.

"You have relieved our minds greatly," said the father of two girls in the college. "We have been much troubled, and we have entire confidence in Mr. Saunders and yourself. I will send one of my daughters, and keep the younger one at home."

Money was very scarce in the south then, but the plan of a foreign school met with great favor, and in enough money was found to finance it. There was a great deal of correspondence, and within three months the party assembled in the old Astor house on Broadway, in

New York—there were seventeen young women from Alabama, Georgia, Tennessee and the Carolinas.

Crawford H. Toy, who had been associated with my parents in the Tuscaloosa College, met us there, as well as the girls who did not accompany us from Tuscaloosa. Mr. Toy had left Tuscaloosa College early in the war and had fought with the Norfolk Light Artillery Blues. He was captured at Gettysburg, and had been imprisoned until the close of the war. He was, years after, Professor of Hebrew in the Southern Baptist Theological Seminary in Greenville, South Carolina, and in Louisville, Kentucky; and was senior professor of Oriental languages in Harvard University, when he died. [8]

Howell Crawford Toy was an early American Hebrew scholar, who in 1880 became a professor of Hebrew and oriental languages at Harvard University and a Dexter lecturer of biblical literature.
Courtesy of Wikipedia.

There were twenty-three of us in the party that sailed from New York for Hamburg, my father and mother, Mr. Toy, the seventeen girls, and we three children. I was six years old; my brother, James, was three years older, and my sister, Nancy, one year younger than I.

The Civil War feeling was still running high, and there were many southerners on the ship, although most of the passengers were from the north. In the salon one evening, one of our girls was playing the piano, and several youths from the south were hanging over the piano and singing to her accompaniment. Suddenly she broke into Dixie. They all sang one stanza with great enthusiasm, and when they came to the part of the chorus,

> "By Dixieland, I'll take my stand,
> To live and die for Dixie,"

---

[8] Crawford Howell Toy was a renowned scholar of Hebrew at Southern Baptist Seminary, but was dismissed in 1879 over his liberal views of scripture. Later, he taught at Harvard University and became a practicing Unitarian.

Some man, sitting in the salon, listening, hissed loudly. One of the young men at the piano turned around, saw who the hisser was, and without warning leaped on him, dragged him off his seat on to the floor, and a rough and tumble fight followed.

The ship's officer separated the combatants, but the southerner was mad with rage.

"Put us ashore! Put us ashore!" he shouted, "And let us fight it out."

As the ship was hundreds of miles from shore, everybody in the salon roared with laughter, and the strain was relieved.

Before my father found a house where he could install his American School in Berlin, we lived in the Hotel de Rome, on the corner of Charlotten Strasse and Unteren den Linden near the Palace of King William the first, of Prussia. There were twenty-five of us altogether in the party. One morning there was a great commotion about the hotel. The victorious Prussians, returning from their triumphant war with Austria, were to March through Berlin that afternoon, and we stood on the verandah for hours watching the troops come by with bands playing and banners flying, some of the soldiers carrying Austrian flags captured in battle. The whole air was filled with the joy of the victor.

We remembered that just a few months before, so short a time that the scene was fresh in our minds, all of us had stood on the streets of Tuscaloosa and had seen the Confederate soldiers marching through, ragged and footsore, discouraged and ill-nourished, retreating before Sherman's advance, some of them singing, in the effort to keep up their spirits,

> *I'll eat when I'm hungry,*
> *I'll drink when I'm dry,*
> *If the Yankees don't kill me,*
> *Then I'll live till I die.*

The contrast was saddening and some of the girls cried.

This American School in Berlin was very well organized. Only languages, music and social accomplishments were taught. We had a very large house of three stories, with servants, and my father engaged the best German teachers of languages in music that could be got in Berlin. My brother and I went to the public school and my sister was taught at home.

This school went on for three years. Every six months my father would go back to the United States, taking home some of the girls and bringing back to Berlin others.

During these three years, there were altogether thirty southern young women in this American School. They came from the best and most aristocratic families of the south; with a few exceptions they were graceful, good-looking, and highly intelligent, excellent representatives of southern society. In those days there were very few Americans or English in Berlin, and so our party of foreigners was conspicuous.

Every evening there were callers for the ladies, mostly German army officers and they went out frequently to theater parties and dinners and balls. But not one of the girls was married over there, and I have often wondered at that. No doubt there were love affairs—in fact my mother has told me of several—but there were not even engagements to marry.

One reason for this was the infinite tact of my mother, who knew well that the parents of the girls back in the United States would not like their daughters to marry or to become engaged to a German until they had first seen the man and judged him; another reason was that many of the girls either had been engaged to marry some southern soldier who had been killed in the war, and were still grieving too sincerely to entertain so soon thought of another sweetheart; and a third reason was that the German men, with intention to become suitors, very soon discovered that these southern visitors were really not rich and indeed had no background of money. However, the social life of the pupils of the school was lively enough, and the atmosphere of the house was never dull.

On Sundays, my father took all of the school family who had church habits to a Lutheran church. On Sunday afternoons, we went to a beer garden, heard good music, and drank beer. The pastor of the church who had preached in the morning often came and sat with us at our table and drank beer with us. Or we spent the afternoon riding and walking about the city, strolling in the parks, visiting Charlottenburg and Sans-Souci.

I heard my first opera in Kroll's theater, one Sunday evening, with Pauline Lucca, the prima donna. It was "Der Freischutz." Afterwards I heard her, too, in "Il Trovato Re." That was one of the times the pastor of the Lutheran Church was with us. The audience sat at round tables and drank beer, as they listened.

There was a church near Sans-Souci, I remember, the walls of which were hung with the flags which the Prussians had taken in battle. Even to my childish mind, this sanctification of war seemed incongruous with the tranquil religious atmosphere of the church.

All three of us children went to a kindergarten, and during two summers my brother and I were taught in a vacation public school. I enjoyed myself hugely during those two periods of four months each. There were many more applicants for these desks than there was room, and all the boys whose parents wanted them to go to this school were examined for entrance, but the examinations were easy. I think elementary mathematics like the multiplication table, and both of us boys were received, even though we were foreigners.

Our lessons were easy, but great attention was paid to our physical training. We sang for half an hour every day, and there were two periods of outdoor instruction in the gymnasium in a large yard, and that gymnasium was the cause of my undoing finally.

On Saturdays all the boys in the school, big and little, were taken for hikes in the country. How far we walked I don't remember, but I think that the whole trip was about ten miles.

At noon, we always stopped in some suburban garden, where the older boys were drilled in calisthenics, and we all ate the lunches we had brought with us and drank "Weiss Beer," [9] which we had to buy.

I became very fond of this gymnasium work, and one day toward the close of the second summer I spent in the school, I remained on the bars, practicing something, after the other boys had obeyed the bell and had gone into the school room. A boy was sent to call me in and I refused to go. A teacher came out and summoned me roughly and I spoke impudently to him and was there upon hauled by him, kicking and struggling, into the school room.

I was yelling loudly, "Lass mich los, du schweinhund! Lass mich los! Ich bin nicht Deutscher! Ich bin Amerikaner!"

The rest of the boys were horrified at such insubordination and insolent language, and gazed in amazement. I had short shrift, as became my offence. All school proceedings were stopped while I was sternly lectured and formally expelled.

My father sent a proper apology to the principal of the school for my conduct, but he made no effort to have me reinstated and instead got me a tutor. That was punishment enough. Instead of the jolly companionship of those cheerful German boys I had to sit for hours every day, with two other boys, at a desk in one room, studying or pretending to study.

For the first time in my life I realized what a penalty there might be for lack of self-control.

Two of our three summers in Germany we spent in Berlin. One spring and summer the school was moved into the country, to a village called Tegel, about fifty miles from Berlin. It was a settlement of two hundred people, which had grown up about a dam and locks, built to aid navigation on a little stream that bore flat boats carrying grain and

---

[9] Weissbeer, also spelled weisbeer, is a dark brown beer made from barley rather than wheat.

lumber down to the River Spree. A great forest, almost virgin, ran nearly up to the village on one side, so full of game that the King thought it worthwhile to maintain foresters to guard it against poachers.

These foresters were most vigilant. My brother and I spent much time in the forest, playing with the German boys, and we thought it would be fun to snare some birds and have them as pets. So we set up several snares in the woods. Most country boys know this kind of snare. It is made of a bent bough, with the noose string and a little stick holding the noose open. The bird is lured by a cluster of berries hung just in front of the stick, perched on the stick to peck the berries, and springs the trigger of the elastic bough which flies back and draws the noose tight around his legs.

We examined these snares twice a day, and one day we caught a bird and were taking it out of the noose when we were hailed by a forester. We were in the densest part of the woods and he had no business being there, we thought, but he was, and had caught us.

"Don't you know there is a fine of ten thalers for this?" he asked, sternly, "or you can go to jail and work it out," he said.

We thought of our angry parents, of jail, of the whippings that surely would follow the report of our crime, and our burst of tears was torrential. The forester seemed placated by our dismay, and released both the bird and us—but you know how careful we were afterward to venture into that forest only in the most circumspect way.

Life in the little place was communal. There was a flour mill on the stream which was kept busy grinding grain for the people in the vicinity, pay being taken in grain, and there was a blacksmith; but there was not a single shot in the settlement, and there was no special mechanics. Every man was a mechanic of some sort. When a house was built, which happened once while we were there, the bricks were made in kilns right there, and the neighbors helped the one building the house in making the plans and in doing the actual work of putting it up.

When the walls got up higher than the heads of the men laying the bricks, ladders were laid, and the children, mostly the boys, were placed on the ladders with their backs to the rungs, and passed up the bricks from one to another, hand-over-hand. For this work, we got at noon and at evening all the coffee we could drink, and we thought ourselves well paid.

The people were most sociable, and we entertained and went out frequently. It was most interesting to dine with a family. The simplicity of the housekeeping was astonishing. The furniture of the cottages—only three or four were large enough to be called houses—was all homemade, and so were the carpets. There was meat and game and plenty of vegetables, and good, well-baked bread. All of this came from the country nearby, and was not bought, but bartered. We had no butter, but used goose grease instead. Coffee had to be bought, and it was the very cheapest that Brazil exported, but at that it was as good as much of the coffee now on the market sold under flashy names and often called Mocha and Java.

Sugar was bought in large sacks and came to the table in big lumps. One of these lumps was tied to a string and suspended from a rafter above the table, and one who wanted sugar would seize the swinging string and knock off a piece of sugar with his knife.

The "dunking" of bread and sweet cakes and coffee was the only way in which it was eaten. I have heard violent controversy on the propriety in salubrity of dunking, but let me say it was certainly adds a delicious flavor to the bread or the cake.

There was no brewery in this village of Tegel, but seven miles away there was one in another small settlement, and weiss beer was brought to Tegel in huge casks. I never heard of "lager" beer there. Weiss beer and coffee were the beverages.

By the time that 1870 came, the people of the South had concluded that the bottom was not going to drop out of things, and my father began to get letters from his principal patrons, suggesting that he close the Berlin school and bring the girls back to the United States. He did so. The pupils were all met in New York by parents or guardians, and escorted back to their southern homes.

CHAPTER 3

Growing Up on the Waterfront in Old Norfolk

How Virginia boys made pocket money... catching and selling crabs and picking strawberries... swimming in the docks. The only boy in a girl's school. I am destined to ministry.

MY PARENTS DID NOT RETURN to Tuscaloosa. Instead, they built a college for young women in Norfolk, Virginia, on a larger scale.

At this time, in 1869, there were few experienced educators of young women in the South, and the reputation of my father and my mother filled their college in Norfolk as soon as it was open. There were always nearly a hundred girls in the school, between fifteen and twenty years, and they were taught English, a little mathematics, French and German, music and deportment.[10] I was then nine years old[11] and my brother was three years older. We were the only boys in the school. My brother stayed in the school for only three years, and was then sent to a boys' school in Norfolk, but I remained in the school for seven years. I have often wondered what effect on my character this intimate association with girls for so long a time had. I studied with them; played with them during recess; ate lunch with them and sang with them during the half-hour given to school singing every day. During all the time when I was in this school I went barefooted, except Sundays, when I had to wear shoes I hated, with those horrible brass-bound toes, to prevent the shoes from being kicked out.

When I was fifteen I was taken from this girls' school and sent to a private school for boys taught by Richard Galt. This school was regarded as the best in town. It had only one room, a very large one. The pupils sat at desks around the wall and Mr. Galt sat in the centre of the room,

---

[10] "Deportment" is proper conduct or behavior, perhaps a class that should still be offered and made mandatory today.
[11] Saunders was actually eleven in 1869.

where he could see everything going on. There were no other teachers. The classes, as he called them, sat around his chair in a semicircle. He was very thorough and had no patience with dullness or laziness. He had only one punishment. The spelling lesson, with which the school began each morning, was a page in Webster's dictionary, and when a boy misbehaved, Mr. Galt would look at him and say, "You may have eight times for that."

That meant that the offender had to copy the words on the page of the spelling lesson eight times on a slate or paper—just the words spelled, not the definitions—and show them to Mr. Galt before he could go home after school. Quite often several boys would be given the same punishment, and when that happened, a common practice was the selling of a slate full of words by one culprit to another. Mr. Galt was unsuspicious and after one boy had shown him a slate full of words that seemed enough as he glanced at it, it was easy enough to hand the slate to another boy.

During all my school days in Norfolk, my father, while he taught in the Women's College, kept up his preaching, serving several churches in the country.

Once, when I was fourteen years old, my father took me to a camp meeting in the country, near Virginia Beach, and overcome by the tremendous wave of religious ecstasy sweeping over the church, I went forward to the mourners' bench and surrendered to the emotional elation. I wept and quivered and presently, on the urging of the preacher, declared myself a convert to Christianity, and rising, made my way to a pew. My father, who had been sitting inside the altar rail, came to me and putting his arms around me said, "Son, do you really believe that you want to be a Christian?"

"Yes, I do."

When we left the church, he drove down to the ocean, and stopped the horse on the beach, and there he talked to me as he had never talked before, affirming his belief in God and in Jesus Christ and admonishing me to be sure that I understood what I was feeling. I did not, but thought I did, and I declared that I wanted to be a Christian and would try to lead a Christian life.

After that, my father began to cherish the idea that I should be a preacher, and while he never broached the plan to me, gradually the family and friends in various ways showed me that I was regarded as one set aside for the ministry. My father then took me with him whenever he went into the country to preach.

On the Saturdays before these Sundays, I blackened his shoes; washed his buggy carefully; groomed the horse and went over the harness thoroughly, testing all the straps and buckle. Usually there were two services. He would preach in the morning, a sermon about an hour and a half long; go to the home of some farmer for dinner and then drive seven or often ten miles to another church, where he would preach the same sermon or another. These Sunday dinners in the homes of the deeply religious Methodist were a horror. It was thought wrong to do any cooking on Sunday, so everything had to be eaten cold, even sweet potatoes which lie like lead in the stomach when cold.

But this companionship with my father was good for me. As a child, when I had gone to camp-meetings with him in Alabama, I had been impressed with the religious fervor of the people, and now, grown older, I learned to respect their simple faith, and their belief in the fundamentals of the Bible.

When my father had no engagement to preach in the country, he insisted that I should attend all the church services. He did not direct the religious life of my brother, who he thought was going to be a lawyer. I had to go to Sunday school on Sunday mornings; to the Bible class in the afternoon, and hear both morning and evening sermons. My father would take me into the chancel with him and I sat there, by his side, in full view of the congregation. If I went to sleep at night, as I often did, he would, while listening to the preacher intently, take a pin from his coat and stick it in my leg to wake me.

My father did not impress on me the idea that I was destined to be a preacher. I think he was waiting for me to feel a call from God as he had, but somehow the word passed around among the Negroes of the household, and they began to treat me with enormous respect as one anointed with the oil of sanctity. I was too young to be sent to any theological seminary, but my father saw to it that I should be religionized. He taught me to say grace before meals, as the phrase went—some call it asking a blessing. I had to read the Bible through every year. By reading three chapters every day and five every Sunday, I read it through five times, long genealogies and all the rest of it.

I was sitting one day on the back steps, going through my daily stint of three chapters, when the mulatto servant, a comely woman, with her sleeves rolled up to her shoulders, ventured to interrupt me, and she did it with great hesitation.

"Master Willie," she said, "When you gets through studyin' won't you please help me pick up some of these here locusts lyin' all over the yard. They'se millions of them and I make some good beer out of them."

The locusts she meant are sometimes called honey pods in the South. They are long pods, with a back of sweetness that makes a delicious taste.

I was intent then on the story of Samson and I paid Alice no attention. She came back after a few minutes and renewed her request. I was angered and I had an open knife in my hand. I threw it violently at her and it stabbed her through the fleshy part of her upper arm. She cried out and went away. I was horrified by what I had done, but Alice said not a word to my parents. When I saw her again, later in the evening, she had her sleeves rolled down covering the wound.

I got her off to one side, "Alice," I said, "please forgive me, I didn't mean to do that."

"Lord, Master Willy, said Alice, "that ain't nuthin', I oughtn't to come in on you like that when you was reading the Bible. I guess it was the debble that made me do it."

But the refining association with the girls in the school, and the chastening influence of my religious reputation did not make me gentle. I was mild enough in the presence of my parents, but away from the house, I sought companionship of the boys of my own age.

Norfolk and Portsmouth are separated by the Elizabeth River, a mile wide; ten miles north this widens in to Hampton Roads and Chesapeake Bay. So, very naturally, our sports were largely aquatic. I learned to swim with the other boys on a beach known as Fort Norfolk, which was where the cannons were planted that troubled the British fleet when it shelled Norfolk in the war of 1812. This beach was shelving, with no undertow, and one could wade half a mile out before the water got six feet deep. After I got so that I felt at home in the water, I would go out in a boat to a buoy marking the channel. We would moor the boat to it; put our clothes on it and dive off it and swim around it, watching the tide very carefully, for fear of being taken out to sea.

Getting permission of the captains, we would climb on the bowsprits of ships anchored in the harbor and dive off the tips. It was a delight to swim in the docks at night. The water was very deep and there was no tide to disconcert the swimmer.

One moonlight night, a party of us was swimming off a dock naked, our clothes heaped on it, when there came a hail from the side of the dock, "Here, you boys come out of there and go up to the police station with me. You know you can't swim here naked."

The police! And arrest meant that our parents would pay our fines and we would be punished at home certainly. All of us except one, scrambled up the side of the dock opposite to the threatening voice and fled through the back streets of Portsmouth to our homes. Passers-by on these streets who were startled by the white skinned figures that flew past them and had strange tales to tell at the breakfast tables next morning. We climbed into windows at our homes and went to bed with dreadful apprehension of the next morning when our parents would find out what we had done. But the one courageous youngster who had faced the music and had gone to the police station with the officer had carried with him all our clothes and being dismissed with a reprimand by the chief of police he lugged the big bundle of apparel from house to house and by the loyal connivance of our servants saved us from exposure.

Few of us had any money. None of us had an allowance from her parents. That practice was not known the in the South. We had to build our own boats. We did this at a place called Ghent, which was then a little shanty town in the suburbs of Norfolk, on a creek. I have helped to build many a rowboat and even cat boats[12] there, and in these we used to make long trips out towards the sea, down to Virginia Beach and Newport News, which were then unsettled.

Most of our sports were out-of-doors. We rolled hoops, played marbles and pecked eggs. In that season of egg pecking, every boy sallied from his house in the afternoon with several eggs in his pocket, carefully picked out for the hardness of their shells, which was tested against the teeth, and the shout went along the streets, "Who's got an egg?"

Presently there would come the answer, "I got an egg."

The two boys would meet and arrange for the terms of the egg combat. Then one would hold his egg enclosed in his hand until only the tip showed and the other boy would strike the tip with the end of his egg, until one or the other broke. The broken egg would go to the owner of the unbroken one. Many a skillful egg pecking boy kept the larder of his family full of eggs for three or four weeks.

There was a marsh near my house where tall and stout reeds grew. When we felt particularly inclined to belligerency, we would go there, two sides and pull up the reeds, roots and all, and then stationing ourselves about fifty feet apart, we would hurl the reeds at each other until the boys on one side or the other took to their heels. This was a dangerous sport. The heavy roots of the reeds made the javelin fly straight and strike with force, and sometimes the bodies of an unlucky combatant would be covered with bruises. We had no shields except our hands, but a boy with a quick eye could turn aside a flying reed. Once a reed struck me squarely in one eye. The eyelid closed before the reed hit but the shot knocked me down and made me faint, and I have gone through life as a result of this blow with the sight of my right eye twice as strong as that of the left eye.

---

[12] Cat boats are sailboats with a single mast set well forward in the front of the boat. In the mid-1800s they were used frequently for transporting freight (they could be loaded from the back as they usually had no keel) and often were used for leisure.

I got my fill of reading as I grew up. There was a good library in Norfolk, and my mother saw to it that there were always the latest books in the house, in English, French and German. I read voraciously, with little direction, but my father insisted, when I was with him, that I should read what he thought were good books. *Plutarch's Lives* he thought well of, and he liked to see me with one of the big volumes in my arms. Now, I thought Plutarch was interesting, but not always, and so I took one of the volumes and with a sharp knife cut out a deep square in the leaves, so I could put a dime novel inside, and appear to be reading Plutarch while I was really feeding on the frontier exploits of bad men.

Some of us made pocket money by crabbing, both for hard and soft shell crabs. When our mothers were giving a party and wanted deviled crabs, we would be sent out to get the hard shell ones. A big market basket, a stout line and a piece of meat was our equipment.

We would go over to Ghent or some other Creek, when the tide was coming in and catch the crabs with the meat tied to the line. A crab will clutch a piece of meat and hold on until he is in the basket. A hard shell crab, by the way, cannot nip you if you hold him by a flipper behind, or put your fingers over his eyes without holding the flippers. I always wondered why a crab couldn't nip unless he could see.

We usually came home with three times as many crabs as were needed for the party, and the rest of them we sold to the restaurants for ten cents a dozen.

But we could get twenty-five cents a dozen from restaurants for the soft shell crabs, and the hardier of us went in for that kind of purveying. With trousers rolled up to our thighs, a bag tied around the waist, and a long stick we waded into the deep mud of a creek, and when the tide was out, leaving hundreds of holes a foot or so in diameter, where the young crabs hide, waiting for their shells to grow. Struggling through the mud, we would poke the stick into each of these holes, and feeling a crab we would reach down with our hands, seize it and put it in the bag. If the crab were a peeler; that is, just peeling off his hard shell, or a paper shell, the crab whose shell had already begun to harden, we will throw it back. It was very hard work and I have never got more than two dozen crabs in a day's excursion. But fifty cents was a fortune in those days.

There were several other ways in which we made pocket money. Norfolk then had no water works, and so no running water in the houses. All our water was got from cisterns in the yards, filled by rain water, and every few months these cisterns had to be cleaned of mud. We boys would contract with the neighbors to clean the cisterns for a dollar and four of us would do the job in a day, two going down in the cistern, and sending up the mud in buckets to the two above who would dispose of it by piling it in the yard, in a fence corner.

Then, too, we had another way. Sloops and schooners would come from Maryland and lay up at the wharves with watermelons and their masters would sell these for three dollars a hundred. Several of us would get together the three dollars in one way or another, and would buy a hundred watermelons at the wharf. We would pay a Negro twenty five cents to haul the melons to the house of one of us, and piling them on the sidewalk near the front porch, we would sell them to passers-by for five cents apiece, or sometimes, if the melons were very big, for ten cents. We usually sold our stock in two or three days, and made a little money, while we all had the pleasure a feeling ourselves merchants.

But the thing we especially liked to do was picking strawberries in May and June. Norfolk has always been a great strawberry growing part of the country, and every afternoon, at six o'clock, ships left the Norfolk wharves loaded with crates of berries for New York. The strawberry fields were about ten miles from town, and the one, where we picked, employed more than two hundred pickers, mostly Negroes. We got three cents a quart for picking the berries, and we could pick forty or fifty quarts a day, by beginning early and working until four o'clock, when the picking had to stop, so the berries could be crated and rushed to the boats.

So, at four o'clock a long line formed in front of the paymaster shanty to cash the tickets which the pickers had got as they delivered the berries to the craters, which they did every hour.

Four or five hundred dollars was paid out in an hour to the loaders, the craters and the pickers. Some of the Negroes, whose wives and children helped, drew five or ten dollars.

As the first of the pickers turned away from the window with his money, several gamblers, white and black, appeared, having driven out from Norfolk in buggies.

Their equipment for fleecing the Negroes was very simple—just an oil cloth with numbers from 1 to 6 painted on it and a dice box and dice. You put your money on a number, after the oil cloth had been unrolled and laid down on the ground, and if you drew the number you got two for one. If you didn't throw it you lost your money.

The odds were greatly against the player, and if he kept at it, making small bets, he was sure to go broke, but now and then a plunger, would break the bank which usually had about ten or twenty dollars in it. When that happened, a shout of enthusiasm went up from the Negroes, and the playing would double in vigor.

But on the other hand, I have seen a whole Negro family, wife and several children, standing behind their father begging him to stop playing with their money, as they saw he was losing it.

"Ben, if you don't give me half of the money," I heard one woman say, "none of us ain' never goin' to pick no more for you, and I'm goin' to stan' right up in church nex' Sunday, and tell de congregation why we can't pay what we owe the church."

CHAPTER 4

College Life in South Carolina and Virginia

After four years of religious training I find that I will not fit the Pulpit… Lanterns and hair oil for courting collegians… Selling Bibles to the mountaineers in the vacations…[13] *Poe's Lenore smokes a pipe.*

I CAME TO THE AGE OF FIFTEEN, in 1874, with a somewhat ragged mental development. I knew French and German, and in the girl's school I had become unusually well read in the literature of English, but I was entirely ignorant of the practical things of life, and could hardly add a column of figures without counting on my fingers. We had no vocational training in those days; no business colleges; no agricultural schools. I had not been taught to think of the future. Physically, I was sturdy—a good runner, swimmer, oarsman and sailor, but because I was very near-sighted, I could not play ball.

My father felt that I was not in the religious atmosphere he wanted for me, and that I spent too much time around the wharves of Norfolk, making friends of sailors and listening to their tales of the sea. So, for the next four years, until I was nearly twenty years old, I was placed under religious influences. First I was sent to Furman University, in Greenville, South Carolina, a Baptist institution, and put in the charge of Mr. C. C. Toy who had been with us in Berlin, and now had the chair of Hebrew in the Southern Baptist Theological Seminary there. I went to that University for two years, associating with students in the theological seminary, earnest and intent on their preparation for the ministry, and with the youths of the university, many of whom intended also to go into the ministry.

Greenville was an ideal college town, of about one thousand people. On three sides farmers tilled rich soil, and on the other side there

---

[13] A "vacation" at this time meant a large, basically unoccupied section of land.

Richard Furman Hall at Furman University, originally called "Old Main" was built in 1854 in downtown Greenville, South Carolina. It was renamed "Richard Furman Hall" in 1921.
South Carolina Digital Library

loomed the mountains of the Blue Ridge, Asheville and the famous Toraway country being only about forty miles away; but every foot of the roads rough going. There were two cotton mills, which employed mostly the people from the mountains.

There was a well patronized school for youths, as well as a boarding school for girls. None of the streets were paved, and the sidewalks were wooden, some of them in very bad condition, rotten and full of holes. The streets were unlighted, and people going out at night carried little lanterns, swinging by a chain from the hand. The pupils in the girl's school were allowed to see visitors only Friday and Saturday evenings, and one could see, approaching this school after dark on these evenings, many of these dancing lanterns, looking like fireflies, signs of the youths, coming a-courting.

These were the days when young man used hair-oil, in meeting someone on the street on visiting night, one could tell by the smell approaching that a beau was on his way to the school.

Greenville had not suffered from the ravages of the Civil War, as other towns of the South had. It was too far away from the paths of the armies. But the state was under the carpet bag rule still, and because of the fear of the Ku-Klux implanted in the minds of the Negroes, blue-coated soldiers were always on guard at the polls whenever there were elections in the town.

The war had impoverished the people, of course. There were no rich in Greenville; no attempt made by anybody to maintain style. Dressing for formal occasions meant merely putting on a clean shirt and collar, blacking one's shoes and brushing one's hair, adding the hair oil, if the frog was going a-wooing. I never saw a student with a new suit of clothes, except the son of a carpetbag office holder of some sort, down in Columbia, the capital of South Carolina, who entered Furman University. He wore the most fashionable clothes, silk neckties and patent leather shoes, the first I had ever seen; and a diamond ring on his third finger. He smoked cigars. All the rest of the students, if we smoked, made our own cigarettes or smoked pipes, with leaf tobacco.

This young man, I learned, had been sent to Furman University to ingratiate himself with the farmers' sons there and advance the political plans of his father. He got two rooms in the best boarding house, as it once began to make advances to the other young men there. He got the cold shoulder everywhere, and when he contrived an introduction to one of the girls at their school, she cruelly arranged for a dozen of her friends to come to the door of the parlor and peep in at him as if he were a curiosity. Not being a fool, he stood this sort of ostracism only a month, and then one evening asked several of us to come to his room after supper. We did.

"I live in Pennsylvania," he said, "and my father came down south with his family to live. But you fellows don't want me to live with you, do you?"

One of the students, the President of one of the two literary societies, answered,

"Your father is a black Republican, and he is trying to teach the Negro that he is just as good as the white man and is making us farmers all sorts of trouble. We want nothing to do with him nor his family. But we have not treated you impolitely, and I don't see what you have to complain of."

"Well, why don't you ask me to join one of your fraternities? I'll give a new set of furniture to the one that does."

There was dead silence at that. He did not know it, but for a student to be asked to be admitted to a secret college fraternity was an unpardonable breach of etiquette, something never done.

The young man picked up the box of cigars that lay on the table and pass them around. No one accepted a cigar and no one lighted his own pipe or cigarette. The Columbia youth thought the other students were pondering his request.

"Now, my father has a lot of influence with the legislature," he went on, "and he has asked me to make a report on things at this university, because the state gives the university an appropriation every year. My report could do a lot of harm or good."

"Good night!" said our spokesman, and we all filed out and assembled in another room.

"Do you think that fellow can hurt the university?" asked one of us.

"I don't know," said the president of the literary society; "I'm going to tell President Furman what he said tomorrow morning."

I never knew what President Furman said. The young man from Columbia was not asked to join a fraternity, and he went back home after he had been three months in Greenville. At the next session of the South Carolina legislature a bill was introduced and passed abolishing all fraternities and colleges that receive subsidies from the state. That included our university. The reason given was that the sons of poor families were not asked to join these fraternities and were humiliated by this slight.

We always thought that the young man who couldn't get in had got his revenge in this way.

While I was in Greenville, the Baptists had a great revival of religion, and for the second time, I went through a racking spiritual upheaval, from which I emerged chastened and thoughtful, but quite sure that I did not have in me the stuff that preachers are made of. I felt that I was not made of fine enough clay. Yet those two tremendous emotional shocks, which I had felt in this revival, and in the former one in Norfolk, no doubt came at just the right period, that of adolescence, to save me from plunging into uncleanness, made restless as I was by the vigor of my body.

This second conversion to religion was just at the end of the college session, and I was just in the mood to accept the proposition of a New York publishing house, that sent an agent to Greenville, enlisting the students to sell Bibles during the summer. These were very large family Bibles, with blank pages in the front for the names and the history of members of the family, two brass clasps and a medallion on the outside for a monogram. They sold for ten dollars, and the dollar I collected with the sale was my commission. The house in New York collected the other payments. I chose the mountains as my territory and no money was lost on my subscribers. Mountain people as a rule were honest.

I sold twenty Bibles in July. I visited only the cabins near the roads, walking and carrying a sample Bible in a strap. I would address the woman who always opened the door. The man never came to the door and was usually invisible when I went in.

"May I read you a chapter from the Bible?" I would say.

Always the woman was glad to hear. Then I would ask if it should be the life and the miracles of Jesus Christ in the New Testament, or the story of King David or that of Samson, in the Old Testament. That being decided, the woman would call in the others of the family to listen. Sometimes she would go to the back door and shout and bring in men with guns and dogs.

When I had read an hour or more I would bring forward the offer to sell the Bible, and if there was any money in the house, I would make the sale. If there was another cabin near this one I would call on two in one day, but usually I would spend the entire day in this one, having my meals with the family and sleeping in the loft.

When August came, I found that I had in my pocket nearly twenty dollars from the Bible sales, also fifty dollars which I had received before I left Greenville as the prize in a composition for Greek scholarship, sponsored by the governor of the state, in his desire to make himself popular with the students of the South Carolina colleges. This money took me home to Norfolk and bought me some new clothes which I needed badly.

This short experience in selling Bibles to the mountain people had attached me greatly to them. They were simple, direct, and appreciative of little acts of courtesy and kindness. But, until the stranger made it plain that he was to be trusted, he was treated with coolness and downright suspicion. Many years after my college days in Greenville, I went back there, on a sort of sentimental journey, and called on Dr. Davis Furman, the son of the President of Furman University, who had been one of my intimate friends when I was a student there.

He was now a successful physician in Greenville, and he would get up in the middle of the night and ride ten miles out into the mountains if a woman was about to have a baby. The mountain people simply idolized him.

"I want to get a horse and buggy, Davis," I said, "and ride out through the mountains where I sold Bibles, with a Negro driving, and I may want a drink now and then. Suppose you give me a letter of introduction to some of the principal men of the mountains, so they won't shoot me for a revenue officer, hunting for moonshine whiskey."

Dr. Fuhrman laughed. "I won't give you a letter of introduction. I'll give you something better that'll introduce you as all right. But don't call it moonshine. The mountain people don't know the meaning of the word. Moonshine is a literary word. The mountain man calls it blockade whiskey, and a man who makes it is a blockader. But the word blockade is enough. You don't have to add 'whiskey.'"

Then he took a prescription pad and drew on it sketches of himself and of me, very rough but good likenesses, both of them. We were looking at each other and smiling broadly.

"You show that to anybody in the mountains and he'll take you right into his family," said Davis, as he handed the drawing to me.

I tried the picture on the first day of my drive, in the foothills of the mountains, just before we reached the winding ascent that led up to the bluff known as Caesar's Head. There was a country store there, with hitching racks all around it and several horses standing by them. A low veranda ran all around the store, let up to by three steps. Fifteen or twenty men sat on the steps or were perched on the railing of the veranda, some chewing tobacco or smoking cob pipes, some with guns leaning against the railing. My Negro driver said, with some apprehension, "Boss, I don' wan' no drink, you go in."

I made my way to the door of the store and looked in. There was no one inside that I could see.

"Good afternoon, gentlemen," I said, "Where can I find the owner of the store?"

No one answered, but one man got off the rail and went in the store, and a youth turned his face and said something to the man next to him that made him grin. I began to be a little nervous. The lack of response to my salutation disconcerted me.

I looked around at the unfriendly faces.

"Doctor Davis Furman sent me here," I said; "I am a friend of his, and I have a note from him here."

I drew this sketch from my pocket. The man who had gone into the store appeared at the door.

"Come in here," he invited me.

I went in and handed him the sketch Davis had made.

"That's enough," he said, and the atmosphere changed miraculously. "Where are you going?" asked the storekeeper.

"I want to see the mountains and the people. I used to sell Bibles out here, twenty-five years ago."

"You did. Now I remember. You sold my wife one and we've got it yet."

He brought out some peach brandy, which we drank then filled a quart flask and gave it to me. And he told me the names of the people I should visit.

He walked with me to the buggy, and the men on the veranda, now cordial, waved their hands at me and some of them called out, "So long!"

This sketch of Davis was really magical. It was not only a passport to the hospitality of the mountaineers but to their hearts. The friend of Dr. Davis, as they called him, was a man to be trusted.

With no other introduction I traveled with my negro driver all through those mountains, wherever there was a passable road, to Hendersonville, and the little village of Brevard, into every little of settlement in the country about Lake Toxaway, adding to my vocabulary some delicious bits of the mountain vernacular, into the box in the buggy several bottles of whiskey, and old fruit brandies. The scent of the Laurel comes to me strongly as I recall that travel. There were families in the country where I was who were always on the edge of a bloody feud but that made no difference to me. The name and the sketch of Dr. Davis were a talisman.

Davis Furman died while I was writing this book[14] and I am sure that his death will be mourned by those mountain people for years.

Before I leave Greenville, I want to say a little more about "Cousin Crawford," who had been my guardian there, and who, indeed, was a potent influence in my life from the time that I was a child in Tuscaloosa until I was twenty years old.

Dr. Crawford Howell Toy, I should begin to say, for he was already recognized in educational circles as an authority on Oriental languages, and was later to achieve eminence in that field in which he had specialized since he was a very young man.

The Southern Baptist Theological Seminary was a narrow field for a man of his research and ability but he was absorbed in the work there. He gave liberally to his students from his great fund of knowledge—many things which were not in the curriculum in which no doubt went entirely over their heads, and even though he was much occupied, lecturing to his classes, correcting their papers and working on his book, *The History of The Jews,* he was never too busy to receive them in his little study, talk to them and advise them.

These students were of many kinds. Some were raw young men from the farms roundabout, a few were from the cities, and a number of them were men of middle-age who had fought through the war, had been sobered by the experience and felt a call to go into the ministry. All of them looked up to him greatly and valued his counsel.

He entered into their pursuits—went quail hunting with some of them on Saturday, watched their games, discussed personal problems with them. Sometimes with a few words he would clarify a question that had been tormenting one of them for days.

With me he was always patient and forbearing, sparing rebuke, even when I knew well that I deserved it. I must have been a great trial to him—and rambunctious lad of sixteen or so, just released from the restraints of home life and none too ready to take advice.

But he was always ready with helpful suggestions when I could bring myself to accept them. It is due entirely to his encouragement that I began to develop a small talent for writing which he was the first to

---

[14] Dr. Davis Furman died November 25, 1931; so Saunders was writing this manuscript at about seventy-three years of age.

discover in me. He persuaded me to bring my little screeds[15] to him for criticism, which was always to the point. He told me that he thought I would do well in newspaper work, and if I have made any success along that line, I feel that I owe it all to Dr. Toy, who turned my mind in that direction at a time when I was mentally at loose ends.

And I was at loose ends. I remember that just before my second conversion to religion, when any sort of restraint was particularly galling, I craved companionship of a rougher kind and I joined the Volunteer Fire Department of Greenville, spending much of my time in the engine house.

Dr. Toy understood, I think, and he did not remonstrate as he might well have done for I am sure my manner deteriorated greatly—he only grumbled now and then when I would get up at night at the alarm of fire and upset the furniture as I dressed and dashed out of the room.

Davis Furman, by the way, was one of these volunteers too, and we were looked upon by the other students of the University as rowdies.

But Cousin Crawford must have given a fairly good report to my father, for when I came home at vacation time, my father took me down to his study in the Methodist Church and talked to me for the first time in my life practically, as man to man.

"I am going to send you to Randolph-Macon College," he said, "to complete your education. Being the son of a Methodist preacher, you will have no tuition to pay there, but you will have to live very cheaply. Your board and washing will cost you $22.99 a month and I will allow you two dollars for your other expenses."

Of course that was very little money, even for those days, and it would be enough, and I would be glad to go to Randolph-Macon. It was a larger college than the one in Greenville, and Ashland was a larger town, and I thought I would like it though the people there were even poorer than those of Greenville. It was only seventeen miles from Richmond but the atmosphere of the city had reached it. There were no theaters, no billiard rooms, no temptations to spend money—except on the girls, and the girls had learned to expect nothing from the college boys, except an escort to church, a moonlight walk, or now and then a dance in the country.

Before the war, Ashland had been a bustling little village, the center of a rich farming and stock raising community. It had been the home of Henry Clay, and the country around it was full of Virginia tradition, most of the families being of old Virginia stock, entirely impoverished by the ravages of the war.

---

[15] Screeds are small bits of scribbled writing.

Once I took an Ashland girl in a buggy to a dance six miles out in the country. The dance was to be in the long living room of the household. At one end was an enormous fireplace that took up nearly the whole end of the room, and it was piled with logs whose heat warmed the whole great room. In one corner of this fireplace, on a little wooden seat, was an old woman, bent, with white hair, and she puffed in her toothless mouth a short stemmed clay pipe.

While the girl I had brought went to talk to a group of her friends, I went to the fire and warming my hands greeted the old lady.

"It's very cold this evening."

"Yes, but hearts may be warm in memory," she answered.

I looked at her more carefully; then, I was struck by the fineness of her face and the sweetness of her mouth, when the pipe was not disfiguring it.

I went to the group of girls and greeting my hostess with them, I said, "That is a lovely old lady there. Who is she, may I ask?"

Very tender and a little melancholy was the look of my hostess as her eyes went to the solitary figure in the chimney corner.

"That is my grandmother," she said.

"She is the Lenore of Edgar Allan Poe, and she thinks of him constantly. Her father would not let her marry him because he was such a drunkard and he never had enough money even to buy a wedding suit. She seemed to have put him out of her mind, but when my grandfather died, she began to live in the past again."

Looking back on the four years I spent in those two typical southern towns, just a few years after the war ended, I have wondered often why the directors of the two colleges, Furman University and Randolph Macon, did not take more interest in the lives of the students outside of the college buildings. Here were 700 youths, preparing to meet the problems of the world, utterly unequipped and floundering, willing to accept advice from their elders. Yet their elders gave them none. The members of the faculty of both colleges were men who taught well in the class room, but away from it they were aloof and seemingly without interest in the recreations or occupations of their scholars.

No member of the faculty of either college seemed to link the things he was teaching with the things the student would have to know to make a living. In both colleges great stress was laid on higher mathematics, Greek and Latin—in Greenville even astronomy and navigation were taught—but French and Italian were taught casually, simply as a romance language and Spanish, the most important language of all commercial tongues, was never taught at all in either college.

Most of the students in both the South Carolina and the Virginia College were thinking vaguely of going into professions, at times when they thought at all—only a few intended to go into farming or into business—and that only because they wanted to follow the footsteps of their parents. In Greenville, the students thought of the ministry mostly, because they were religious and because the ministry appeared to them to be the dignified occupation of a gentleman.

But, both with the teachers and the students, this apathy was no doubt that the benumbing influence of the Civil War. All these students have been brought up in good circumstances, in families where there were slaves to do the work, and looking forward to lives at ease, getting married when they were old enough, as their fathers had done, and sure of a competence.

Now, they were not even sure of an education, and indeed, many of us had to leave college before we were graduated, and start out in the world to make a living.

When I returned to Norfolk, after two years at Randolph-Macon College, my father, I think, had definitely resigned the hope of seeing me in the pulpit. He had got reports from the President of Randolph-Macon that show him I was not inclined to the ministry. He said nothing of his thought to me, and allowed me to do pretty much as I pleased during the next year.

I could find nothing to do in Norfolk. For what was I qualified? I could play the guitar and the piano a little and sing, and I found that I could write for newspapers but I could get no money for that. The town was full of youths of my age, living on their parents, and making no living themselves.

It was thought unworthy for people of gentle birth to work with their hands. Negro labor, men and women, was still plentiful and cheap, sometimes to be had merely for their keep, as in slavery days.

Girls were not taught to cook nor to do housework; if they set the table they were doing quite enough; young boys did chores about the house and the yard to earn pocket money, such as sawing wood or cleaning out cisterns, but when they grew to be fifteen or sixteen they were not expected to do menial work such as could be done by Negroes. If their parents could afford it, boys and girls were sent to college, the cheaper the better, and if the parents could not afford it they simply idle around town, supported by their fathers.

I had a cousin, whose mother came to Virginia from Alabama, when her husband died, and taught in my uncle's school for girls. He was a lusty chap of seventeen, whom idleness irked, and as he grew older and the urge for courting attacked him he became impatient of his dependence on his mother and eager to make some money for himself.

He could not get a place in any of the shops, where young man were working for thirty dollars a month often—I have known a man to get married on that pay—and he went down on the wharf and got a freight hauler to give him a job driving a truck. Now, driving a truck in those days was not what driving a truck now is. A truck was a stout car, drawn by one horse, with two heavy poles projecting out behind. The driver of the truck usually stood up, although he had a seat. When the truck stopped, the two poles behind tilted with the body and came down to the ground, so that barrels or boxes could be rolled or slid on them into the truck. It was heavy work for the driver, who usually was a brawny Negro.

My cousin was overjoyed to get this job which was going to pay him $1.50 a day and one evening, he came to our house and announced it proudly. There were visitors at the table, ladies, and when Jim told them that he was going to be a truck driver, one might have thought, from the expression on their faces, that he had declared his intention of committing suicide.

My father was the only one at the table who heartily approved. He leaned over the table and patted my cousin on the back.

"Good for you, my boy," he said, "You have the real stuff in you. Any work is dignified. Don't mind what people say."

But he had to mind when the girls began to give him the cold shoulder, and after sticking to his guns for several months until he was convinced of his social ostracism, and went to Newport News, just then becoming a shipbuilding town and a busy one. He got a job there driving a truck and when I again saw him many years after he left Norfolk, he was owner of a fleet of trucks, had settled definitely into a middle-class life and was quite scornful of aristocratic social distinctions.

But the lines of caste were crudely drawn in Norfolk, and it was with some hesitation that, having left college I applied to the School Board for the place of Principal of the Public School. The best families of Norfolk did not send their children to the public school. That was regarded as low. The public school was patronized by the children of mechanics and laborers and those who worked on the wharves. The town was full of private schools for boys. The college managed by my father and mother was the principal one for young women and girls. But it happened that there was no vacancy in any one of these and the school board was looking for a Principal for one of their schools. I thought, owing to the educational reputation of my family I would have no difficulty in obtaining the post. I saw all the Directors, many of them intimate friends of my father and got much encouragement.

But greatly to my disappointment the Directors elected a one-armed Confederate Colonel for principal, a handsome old fellow who made no pretensions to scholarship, but told the directors that he would guarantee to keep order in the school.

Greatly chagrined I went to the President of the School Board for an explanation.

"Colonel Taylor needs the job," he said. "You are young and can wait. Besides we don't need a diamond to cut a paving stone."

However, it is probable that, from the force of association, I would have settled down into some sort of teaching job, for which, I am sure, I had no vocation, but the day after this ambition to become a teacher withered, came a letter from Dr. Toy which changed the current of my whole life.

The Southern Baptist Theological Seminary had been removed from Greenville to Louisville and Dr. Toy wrote me from there, saying if I would come to Louisville he was sure that he could help me to find employment on some newspaper.

And so, hoping to begin to make my own living, I bade my parents and all my kinsfolk goodbye, and started off cheerfully into the real world.

It was many years before I saw any of them again.

CHAPTER 5

Journalism with Walter Hines Page

The ambitious Page strove to realize in the Louisville age and why he failed ... I write book reviews and solicit business ... A Kentucky boarding house, its epicurean table and the clever conversation of Page and Dr. Toy. I decide to seek fortune in the mining camps of Colorado.

BUT IT SEEMED IMPOSSIBLE FOR ME, even with the influential introductions of Doctor Toy, to get on the staff of a Louisville newspaper. Leg reporters at that time were being paid $8 a week in Louisville and the very best could be got by the city editors for twelve or fifteen dollars. I went to every newspaper office in town and was told everywhere that the paper had all the experienced men it needed, men who knew the town and would not have to be trained.

I seem to be up against it, and was sitting disconsolately on the front steps of my boarding house one Spring evening, rolling a cigarette and wondering what I should do next, when a slender, keen faced young man about twenty-five years old, with a small dark mustache, came out of the house, and sitting down beside me, lighted a cigar.

It was Walter Hines Page,[16] a young man almost as obscure as I was at that time, but who rose to great distinction in later years, among other things representing the United States as Ambassador to Great Britain during the World War of 1914.

I had known him at Randolph-Macon but had lost sight of him since then and was very glad to meet him in Louisville and renew the acquaintance. Indeed, Dr. Toy had spoken to him of me before I came and it was no doubt due to Dr. Toy's recommendation that he sought me out this evening.

---

[16] Walter Hines Page served as U. S. Ambassador to the United Kingdom during World War I and was editor of the *Atlantic Monthly* from 1896-1899. In 1900 he helped found Doubleday, Page & Co., which became one of the nation's largest booksellers of the twentieth century.

He had no doubt noticed my despondency for the last few days, and he began without preamble, "How would you like to work with me on the *Age*?" he asked.

I knew that the *Louisville Age* was an aristocratic literary journal and I was struck down by the flattering offer. After I found my voice, I said that I would like it very much and then he told me something about his plans and aspirations.

"You know the *Nation*, don't you?" he said. "Well, I want to make the *Louisville Age* the kind of magazine for the South that *The Nation* is for the North. The South needs the influence of the North to develop it—in its material reconstruction as well as its general advancement in culture. We got off the track during the war—we are floundering. This generation of young people is bewildered by the sudden plunge into poverty after the years of luxury and indolence in which they grew up. We need the hard commonsense of the North—their vigor, their initiative. If we can work up the subscriptions to the *AGE*—if we can interest the people, I can do the rest and I am going to do it."

Walter Hines Page was an American journalist and publisher who was a famous newspaper reporter of his time, then was editor of the Atlantic Monthly *and an owner and editor of Doubleday, Page & Co. book publishers. He was later appointed ambassador to Britain by Woodrow Wilson. Photo Courtesy of Library of Congress.*

I was beginning to be a little alarmed. "What will you expect me to do," I asked. All that I wanted to do at that time was something that would put me into a literary atmosphere and give me some experience in writing. I would gladly have swept out the office to have a place on the staff of *The Age*—but would I be able to do anything that would supplement the ambitions of Walter Hines Page.

"We will talk over your duties tomorrow," he said. "The important thing is to work up the subscriptions, but the *Age* must be built up a little first." And with that he left me.

5 | Journalism with Walter Hines Page

The next morning I reported at the office of the *Age*.

"Now," said Page. "I have written all we need this week, except two book reviews. You can write those. Hunt around these books here and review any that strike you. I'll go out and see some people and maybe get some advertising. I hate that and I'll have you do the soliciting hereafter, as well as the book reviews. I'll pay you five dollars a week and half of the money we get for the advertising you bring in. Is that all right?"

"All right?" I was in the seventh heaven.

The first book review I wrote for the *AGE*, was *Airy, Fairy Lillian*, by the then greatly admired author, "The Duchess."

I don't blame you for laughing, but at that time the book was a bestseller, and it struck my fancy. Mr. Page made no censure of my choice but of course he thought the book was too trivial, and after that he selected the books for me to review, George Cable, George Eliot and Thomas Hardy.

For the next few weeks I trod on air. The writing was to my taste and Paige was a stimulating editor. He did not cut my stuff too severely and his interpolations always strengthened my idea. I got some advertisements to and the commission on those, with my five dollars a week, paid my board.

The publication of the *Age* was the first real professional entry of Page into journalism, although he had written a good deal while at Randolph-Macon and Johns Hopkins.

He was teaching in a boy's school in Louisville, when some Louisville men, who had started the *AGE*, and found they had bitten off more than they could chew, came to him and asked him to take it off their hands at his own terms.

He thought he saw there an opportunity.

The *Age* was a very good-looking little publication. Sixteen pages, long primer type, with four pages of advertisements.

I wrote two or three pages of book reviews and Page wrote all the rest of the magazine.

His articles were all short, often tinged with humor, but never flippant nor superficial. He wrote thoughtfully of politics, national and international, but never touched on local matters unless they had some special significance. The reader would hardly have known that the *Age* was published in Louisville.

But something—I think it was the magnetism of Walter Page—made the *Age* office the favorite dropping-in place of Louisville men who had no particular business, of which there were many.

Old river men used to drift in and talk with the editor of the dwindling of the river trade, merchants with not enough business to keep them occupied, plantation owners whose plantations were no longer profitable since the war. One of our almost daily callers was Will S. Hayes, at that time editor of the river column of the *Courier-Journal* and the author of many Negro songs with a river motif. The songs of Hayes never approached the melody or the real sentiment of those of Stephen Foster, but they were simple, sincere and pathetic, redolent of the darkie of the levees.

I listen to these with all my ears. I have never known river life before and though it was fast disappearing it was still fascinating. It was Hayes who interested me the most but Walter Page got something from everybody.

The office of the *Age* was down near the River—the Ohio—for rents were low there— but it was an easy walk from there to the business part of Louisville, where advertisements were to be had. We had two rooms, on the second floor of an old building—a "walk up"—of course. In the front room Walter Page sat and did his writing, in long hand, naturally, since there were no typewriters in those days. He wrote furiously, smoking always, stopping now and then to read over to himself, aloud, what he had written. He wrote with a pencil and his handwriting was the most legible I have ever seen in a newspaper office.

I had a desk in the back room and on the floor of that room were piled newspapers, magazines and books, some still in their wrappers and some opened. There was a janitor in the building but we demanded little of him and got less. Both of us looked after our own desks and kept them in order—beyond that we did not care.

In this atmosphere of dust and disorder we did our brain work, but in the evening we came home to peace and order and quiet.

The boarding house, where we lived, was an unusual place. It had the real Southern home atmosphere. It was managed by the widow of an impoverished Kentucky plantation owner, with three Negro servants, all of whom had been her slaves and had stayed with her after the war. The cooking was delicious—all the Southern viands that could be procured in the Louisville markets were served in old plantation style profusion.

For breakfast we always had country sausage, steak and eggs, Sally Lunn[17], beaten biscuit, waffles with honey and coffee, whose aroma filled the house in the morning and delighted our nostrils as we came down the stairs in the morning. For dinner there was Brunswick stew, fried chicken and gumbo, stuffed ham and the most delicious desserts.

---

[17] "Sally Lunn" is a large English bun, sweet bread, or tea cake but always made with yeast dough that includes cream and eggs.

5 | Journalism with Walter Hines Page

Did you ever eat stuffed ham or do you even know what it is? I think it is almost unknown outside of the South. It is too much trouble to make. First, you must have a large ham, of perfect curing and flavor—and that is hard to get in these days. Then you must make a thick dressing, perfectly flavored as if you were preparing it for a turkey. Next with a wooden skewer, pierce deep holes in the ham, all through it, and stuff the holes tight with the dressing. Then bake the ham. Some say that it can only be properly baked with a wood fire, but that may not be so.

When finished you have something that must be eaten with prayer and meditation—never in a hurry. When the ham is sliced, each slice has twenty or thirty little islands of taste, flavor bearers to the ham, which enrapture the tongue and the palate.

The boarders to whom these gastronomic delicacies were offered for appreciation were not many, about twelve, I think. Besides Cousin Crawford and Walter Page, there were several Louisville merchants with their wives, a wealthy Kentucky distiller, who was also a horse breeder and more over a very well-educated man, a bachelor doctor of large practice and an artist of sorts.

The conversation at the dinner table, led always by Doctor Toy and Walter Page took a very wide range. Both of them kept a close watch on current affairs and while their viewpoint was often widely different, that made it more interesting and instructive for the rest of us, who like to be led in such matters. Both of them had a keen sense of humor. Page was fond of stories, and told them well, often using one to point his argument with telling effect. Dr. Toy excelled in a kind of dry wit, and an appreciation of all kinds of humor, a characteristic which was to stand him in very good stead in the course of the next few years as I will explain. It is an interesting story and one for which it is worth digressing.

Dr. Toy had felt for some time that his religious views were too unorthodox to please the Faculty of the Theological Seminary. The necessity of holding himself in check continually chafed him and he was sure that sooner or later he would find it necessary to disclose his ideas, so making an unpleasant situation, and he had decided that it would be better to resign, the sooner the better, rather than run that risk.

And so, towards the end of the year, he carried out that resolution, a little more precipitately than he had intended, but with confidence that he would be able to find some congenial employment in New York—something that would give him time to work on his books, *Judaism and Christianity*, and *The History of the Religion of the Jews* both of which he had been working on for many years.

His thoughts had been turning to New York and the opportunities there for a long time, but when he finally reached the city he had many disappointments. He could find no position such as his qualifications entitled him to, and finally, in default of anything else, he turned to newspaper work, which had always interested him.

But there too he met with little success. Competition in the Great City is keen and the New York touch is not to be acquired in a day. He finally got a job as a columnist on one of the dailies and it was here that his sense of humor came into play. His joke column was such a success that a real career opened up before him. But things were to turn out quite otherwise.

He read in his newspaper one evening—a paper that he might never have read if he had not been working for it—an article on some abstruse Oriental subject—Sanskrit, Chaldean, Assyrian, I do not know which—which was so full of errors that Dr. Toy was moved to sit down immediately and write, from his enormous store of knowledge, a refutation of this article.

The paper was quite willing to publish it and Dr. Toy went on compiling his column of jokes and thought no more about it.

But a few weeks later came a letter from the Faculty of Harvard University offering him the chair of Oriental Languages at the University!

Needless to say, he accepted the honor and held the position until his death many years later.

It is not often that one sees such a striking example of the recognition of great merit.

Not long after he went to Harvard, Dr. Toy astonished the whole family—or possibly I was the only one astonished—by marrying my sister Nancy. It was a May and January marriage, but a most successful one. Nancy had inherited my mother's brilliant mind and her social gifts. She had a charming personality, a ready wit, infinite tact, so that she was equally at home with the college students and the most erudite of professors and quickly made a place for the Toy ménage[18] in the rather exacting social life of Cambridge.

Dr. Toy was naturally very modest and retiring—Nancy helped him to bear the honors which otherwise he would hardly have known what to do with, she protected him from imposition which he would have been too kind-hearted to resist, she supplemented him in every way and made his life tranquil and, I imagine, free from care.

She was of great material help too. While working on his books, he was attacked by writer's cramp, and Nancy wrote the manuscript of both

---

[18] "Ménage" means "household."

5 | Journalism with Walter Hines Page

books in longhand (this too, was before the time of typewriters) working hour after hour, correcting, erasing, rewriting.

No one but a writer can understand what it means to have an amanuensis who is thoroughly in sympathy with what is being done, whose cooperation is so close that it amounts to inspiration.

A most fortunate marriage.

After Dr. Toy left Louisville the boarding house table seemed very dull but we were so busy we hardly had time to miss him otherwise, but hard as we worked we did not seem to be getting anywhere.

The *Age* barely made a living and if it had not been for the interest in the work I should have thought that we were wasting our time. It was always hard to pay the printer and when rent day came around our efforts to get together the necessary cash were superhuman.

One day Page said to me, "The Southern Baptist Conference opens tomorrow. I have arranged for you to go to the church where the conference is to be held and talk to the preachers and try to get subscriptions. The conference will last two days. You ought to be able to work up a good deal of interest in that time. Those people ought to see what I'm trying to do and support us. They could talk to the people in their own towns when they got home and that ought to bring in subscriptions."

I took a big bundle of *Ages* up to the church the next morning and tackled preachers going in and coming out, selling and giving away the magazines, and soliciting bravely. I didn't see Page until the two days were over.

Then I went to the office and handed him $6.40. "One subscription," I reported, "and the rest is for magazines at five cents a copy."

"Keep it." said Page, "I reckon the *Age* is a failure. I talked to some of those men too, and while they don't like to see me give up the *Age*, they seem to think we can't get support for this kind of magazine in the South. I suppose that is true. However, I am going to see Henry Watterson and see what he thinks."

His air, as he spoke, was not dejected but thoughtful.

The conversation with Watterson must have been discouraging, for Page did not tell me of it that evening. I felt so strongly that the end had come that I did not go back to the office after that day, and he seemed to take that as a matter of course. We talked of other things when we met at the dinner table—not of our plans, for neither of us had any.

I was completely at a loss. There seems to be nothing for me to do but to go home. Cousin Crawford had spoken of sending for me to come to New York, but that project had gone glimmering. (This was before the Harvard offer.) I had lost confidence in my ability and felt that I would never make a place for myself in the literary world—and what else could I do?

I was walking down the main street of Louisville, feeling very much depressed, when the red and blue colors of a huge railway poster struck my eye.

HOW TO GO WEST, it said, in letters nearly a foot high. Then followed a short description of the riches coming out of the mines in Leadville, and I felt that I had found my guide.

The fare to Denver which was the hub of the gold rush was ten dollars.

I had twenty dollars.

Within an hour I had bought my ticket and was back at the boarding house packing my bag and saying hasty goodbyes to my associates there.

The artist who lived there insisted on taking me up to his room, when he heard that I was going out West, and showed me some photographs, framed and tinted on the glass so that they made the effect of an oil painting.

"This is a new thing," he said, "and it will go like wildfire out there in the West. You can set up a little studio in Denver and make money hand-over-fist. I did. Everybody is crazy about it in Louisville."

To my uneducated eye the photographs were beautiful, the idea fascinated me and I paid him two of my remaining ten dollars for the outfit of paints, brushes and sample photographs, and felt that I had something to begin with in Denver.

Page and I shook hands at parting and his handclasp was hearty.

"If you find a rich mine, let me in on it," he said with a smile.

I never found the rich mine, and I never saw Walter Page again but the months of my intimate association with him live in my memory as one of the most valuable episodes of my life.

CHAPTER 6

Denver–Wicked and Unashamed

The gateway of the mining camps of the Southwest where everything was wide open... faro, poker, roulette.... "keno!" shouts one player and "O hell" groans the others... broke and hungry... luck and my guitar help me along the way to Ouray... "Fate cannot harm me, I have dined today."

I TRAVELED TO DENVER in an emigrant car, and when I got there I jumped into the first omnibus I saw and with my trunk went to a hotel.

I got there at night, and after supper for which I did not have to pay, since the hotel was on the American plan, I went out to look over the town.

Denver then was like San Francisco in the days of Forty Nine, and its downtown streets were as crowded as Fifth Avenue in New York is at noon. The streets were brilliantly illuminated by gas and every shop was open and selling things to customers. Miners and cowboys in rough

By 1879 Denver was an important city not just in Colorado but in the United States. This scene is looking northward on Larimer Street in the year Saunders arrived in Colorado.

From Frank Fossett's *Colorado.*

garb jostled gentlemen and ladies in evening dress on the way to restaurant or to theaters. Spirited women with escorts and hunting for escorts, whom they found speedily, gave one delightful pictures to look at. One could not be on the street without becoming exhilarated; and falling into the smiling spirit of the crowd. I was carried away with the pleasure of the scene, and the feeling that I was a part of this wonderful country where everybody seemed to have plenty of money.

Then I began to wonder how I should begin to introduce my charming idea of colored pictures, with the five dollars I had left. Suddenly I felt as if I had been plunged into a cold shower bath. In the window of a one story photographer's studio I saw some colored pictures exactly like mine. I looked at them closely. They were really better than mine. I went in and asked the photographer, "What do you charge for making those?"

"Oh, those things?" he answered. "We don't make them anymore. They went well when they first came out a year ago but nobody wants them now, and I was going to take them out of the window tomorrow."

I went out in the street again downcast, and then I saw big posters on the walls, lighted brightly—

"HOW TO GO EAST"

That sent me into a panic. I've been thinking that everybody was going West, and here people are going back East. I was sick at the stomach with chagrin.

I wandered about the streets for a while, and then went into a brilliantly lighted Keno room, desperate and rather hoping for a sign for some luck.

Keno was then the popular gambling game in Denver—it could not be crooked, and it was a much more genial game than the cold and avaricious faro, roulette and poker. Moreover, it was cheap and the returns were quick to both the house and the players.[19]

In these Denver Keno Halls, the dealer stood on a raised platform and spun a clicking wheel, with numbers around it. When the wheel stopped spinning, a pointer rested on a number. Oblong cards with 16 numbers, four in a row, were bought by the players for a dollar a piece. The dealer shouted out the number on which the pointer rested, when the wheel stopped and the players whose card had that number on it, covered the number with a wooden counter, many of which lay about

---

[19] Keno was a popular game because it had the highest percentage of winning for the gambler. The house cut was only 1¾ % and in other games it could be as high as 6%.

the tables. When the player had four of these numbers covered, in a row, he shouted "Keno" and there was a loud groan from other players who were within one number of the goal.

A man once described keno —

"The dealer turns a wheel; one fellow yells "keno" and all the other fellows say "Oh, Hell."

When the shout of quote "Keno" came with its variation to the other players, checkers rushed up to the shouter and called off the covered numbers to the dealer, who had written them down on a pad as the wheel chose them —

"Forty three."

"Right."

"Eighteen."

"Right."—and so on.

The winner at once received three quarters of the whole amount paid by all the players for their cards, the housekeeping one-quarter.

Then the cards were sold again.

A big keno house usually made two or three thousand dollars a day, and ran no risk of losing. The gambling houses where faro, roulette and poker were played often made $100,000 a day, but often, too, they went broke, when some player had a good run of luck. The faro dealer was the aristocrat of his profession, and the keno dealer the lowest.

(Keno is an extinct game nowadays, although there is a survival of it called lotto, which I believe is a favorite among societies of ladies wanting to raise money for a charitable purpose.)

I sat a while, watching the crowd; then bought a card for a dollar and lost.

"Try again, partner," advised the man sitting next to me. "Keep it up till you hit it."

"I'm broke," I said. "I'm hunting for something to do. I want to go to Leadville." He took a look at me. I was wearing a blue serge suit, very thin, light shoes and a straw hat.

"My God," he explained. "What in the hell did you come out here for? What can you do?"

"I am a journalist," I said proudly.

He sniffed with contempt. "A reporter. Denver and Leadville are full of them on their uppers. Don't go to Leadville. Men are sleeping in the streets there, and nobody cares whether they live or die. Better go to a mining camp like Ouray, and get a job on some little sheet. Ouray is in the San Juan country and it's booming."

I returned to the hotel in despair but slept the sound sleep of youth. The next morning I sent a telegram to my father in Norfolk, collect.

"*Am without money in Denver. Please send me some quick.*"

I learned afterwards that when my father got this message, he and my mother held a consultation. She wanted to send me money at once. Said my father, "No. Now is the time to see what there is in him. He will not starve out there, but will get along some way. If we send him money, he will always remain dependent."

He sent me no telegram, but wrote me a letter which I did not get for a week, saying that he could send no money. He wrote kindly and affectionately, but told me firmly that since I was twenty years old[20] and had put my hand to the plough, I should not turn back and call on him for help.

He closed his letter, saying,

"*There are some Norfolk men in Ouray now. Ouray is not far from Denver, I suppose. Maybe they will help you find something.*"

Strange that both the gambler and my father should suggest Ouray.

Before I got this letter I had gone away from the hotel, leaving my trunk as security for my bill, and had rented a room for two dollars a week, living on bread only. I did not have sense enough to look for a job even. I spent most of my time in the rooms of the YMCA, but the clerks there, while they were willing to have me come in and read, did not offer to help me to find employment. I seemed to lack initiative, utterly, or I should have gone around to newspaper offices looking for employment, but I did not even do that. I waited for my father's letter, believing he would send me money.

His letter stunned me. I felt that I had been abandoned, but my father really was wise. I developed some initiative after I had got over my first terror at the refusal. I must get to Ouray in some way.

To get to Ouray, which was a little mining camp in the southwestern part of the state, one had to go to Alamosa, which was the end of the railway line; thence by stage to Lake City, another mining camp. From Lake City to Ouray by the buckboard, which went over a rough mountain road, it was a hundred miles[21] and it took two days, but it was only thirty miles across the range, and that could be made in a day by a man with a good horse.

---

[20] This pegs the date of Saunders coming to Colorado as 1878.
[21] Saunders is referring to the mileage of the Mears stage toll road (Barnum/Lake City to the Uncompahgre Agency) for this mileage. The Engineer Road was much shorter but much more difficult.

I had now only two dollars left. I got the name of the passenger agent of the Denver and Rio Grande Railway, which ran to Alamosa, and called at his house on the evening of the day when I got my father's letter. Two children opened the door when I rang the bell, a boy ten years old and a girl of eight.

"They are gone visiting," said the boy. "Won't you come in and wait?"

I went in and sat down, chatting with the children for a while. Then I saw a guitar.

"Who plays it?" I asked.

"That's mother's," said the boy. "Can you play?"

I could play accompaniments to the songs I sang on both the piano and the guitar, and I took the guitar and sang for the children. I sang, "I'se Gwine Back to Dixie," and how I did put my heart in it—

> "I'm trablin back to Dixie; my step is low and feeble;
> I prays de Lord to help me, and keep me from all ebil;
> But should my strength forsake me, then kin' frens come
>   and take me;
> My heart turn back to Dixie and I mus' go."

This sentimental song I intended especially for the little girl, but both children seemed to like it. Then I sang a rollicking song I had once heard a medicine seller sing at a Virginia Fair, with the chorus —

> "There's the monkey and the dog, and the goat and the hog,
> The 'skeeter, the wasp and the flea,
> And the pretty little squirrel, with his tail up in a currel—
> Oh, they've all got a wife but me."

The children laughed greatly at this and strange to say, the little girl seemed to prefer this to the darkey song, and I had to sing it over and over again. While I was singing it for the third time, in came the parents. I got up and introduced myself and plunged into my request at once. I have no doubt that the parents were appreciative of my effort to entertain the children, for when I had finished the father said, "meet me at the train for Alamosa tomorrow morning at seven o'clock and I'll give you a pass."

We got to Alamosa toward evening, and I ate a sandwich and drank a cup of coffee. I found that there were two stage lines running to Lake City and they were fighting and so had cut rates. The fare, usually ten dollars, was down to two. I went to one stage, which I saw was not filled. The agent was standing by the driver.

"I want to go to Lake City and I have only a dollar and a half. Will you take me?"

"Where's the money?" asked the agent.

I handed it to him. "Get in," he said.

When I got in there were six passengers, one of them the wife of a mining man in Lake City. Four horses were in the traces and the driver was a bearded old fellow with his mouth full of tobacco. The road ran through the mountains, and much of the distance along precipices. The driver started the horses with the whip and kept it busy all the way. The horses very seldom walked; they usually went at a fast trot and sometimes galloped. The four horses were changed at every station, twenty-five miles apart.

At daybreak the stage stopped at a station for breakfast. All the passengers and the driver got out and ate, except me. I had no money and I was too miserable and dispirited to ask the station master to let me have something to eat without money. I walked around the place and then came back and sat in the stage till we started again. Probably nobody noticed that I was not eating.

At noon we stopped again for dinner and again I did not go into the dining room. This time the driver asked, "Going into dinner?"

"I'm not hungry," I answered.

He gave me a sharp glance but said nothing.

We got to Lake City at dark and the stage stopped at the only hotel in the place with a shout from the driver. The passengers climbed out and went into the hotel for supper, and the stage rolled away for the post office to throw off the mail.

This time I entered the dining room with the other passengers. I was faint from hunger and desperate. I had eaten only bread those last few days in Denver and only a sandwich in Alamosa. I ate for a week past and a week to come and I am sure that the waiter was amused at my appetite. As I ate my spirits revived and when I went out into the lobby I felt that fate could not harm me.

I ask for the landlord and he was pointed out to me by the clerk - a

(Editor's note: Unfortunately one page from here to the end of the chapter is missing from the original manuscript we received)

CHAPTER 7

A Gold Mining Camp Fifty Years Ago

Prospectors and their burros outfit for the mountains in Ouray... gold seventeen dollars an ounce, silver one dollar and everybody rich... paying for Saturday night's whoopee in gold dust... mining camp journalism... snowed in for the winter... vigilantes lynch a woman... Murderous snow slides on the trails.

OURAY, which had been named after Chief Ouray of the Ute Indians, whose reservation was twenty-five miles away, was then one of the liveliest mining towns in Colorado. Gold was seventeen dollars an ounce and silver a dollar an ounce. In the mines or mountains surrounding the camp there was plenty of both gold and silver. Everybody in the town had money. The camp had been started only a short time and there were only 300 people living in it, men, women and children, but on Saturday nights and Sundays when the miners came down from their work to have a good time there were a thousand or more. Many of these miners used to bring down on these holiday Saturdays little bags of grain gold, from their mines on Mount Sneffels or the other mountains around the town. This was not the gold dust that comes from placer washing. It was free gold, found in quartz. The miner would crush the quartz in a pestle, wash it and carefully pick out the gold from the rock. He got seventeen dollars an ounce for it in Ouray wherever he spent his money.

The mountains came close up to the town and there were four trails leading down from the mines connecting on the ridges with the other trails going over to Silverton, Durango and Lake City, the other mining camps nearby—that is within a distance of forty miles or so. The houses were all of wood, some of them log cabins. The camp was like a frying pan, the mountains the rim and the road the handle.

Ouray had no telegraph office but it had a telephone to Silverton, and we had to telephone our telegrams to there to be relayed to Lake City. If we had important messages to telegraph we had to ride thirty miles over the trail to the telegraph office in Lake City.

The road leading out of Ouray which eventually reached Alamosa was very bad always, and in winter when the snow drifted across it from the foothills, it was impassable. I once saw, as I was riding by in a light buckboard, seventeen wagons stalled in snow drifts, loaded with supplies for Ouray. The teamsters, finding it impossible to get through the drifts, had cut loose their horses and had ridden and driven them to the stage station.

This road had developed from an old Ute trail. It went from Ouray to Los Piños Indian agency, and thence wandered through canyons and mountains to Lake City, a hundred miles distant, across the Ute reservation. From Lake City to Alamosa, the nearest railway point, the road became a little better, but was still mountainous and rugged. Buggies and light wagons were unknown and they would not have stood that road for a day. Only buckboards, the frontier vehicle, built with springy hickory flats for the floor instead of the usual wagon bed, and the sturdiest freight wagons dared the road from Ouray to Lake City. From there on, the stages, luxurious by contrast with the buckboards, went on to Alamosa, the end of the railway.

This is one of the earliest photos (about 1878) of the Town of Ouray when the town's streets were still full of stumps. There are no brick buildings yet and the town has an unsteady and uncertain look.

P. David Smith Collection.

7 | A Gold Mining Camp Fifty Years Ago

Ouray was supplied with the things needed by its people through wagon trains, which came from Alamosa, and since these trains came only once a month during the summer and not at all in the winter, the stores always had very large stocks of goods on hand. The mines bought their supplies from Denver, but in the winter they had to depend on the Ouray stores for emergencies. The road, when it entered the camp, became its principal street, and running straight through stopped at the foot of a mountain. On both sides of this street were the shops, the saloons, the gambling houses, and the livery stables and the post-office. There were two hotels, one on the main street, and the other on a side street. Separated entirely from the town and 200 yards from the shops was the red light district. The courthouse and the dwellings were some distance from the main street in the foothills.

There were two papers in the camp, the *Times* and the *Solid Muldoon*, both weekly, of course. The *Muldoon* was owned by Dave Day, who had brought me over the mountains from Lake City.[22] He was a veteran of the Civil War, who had fought with the Confederate forces in Missouri and he had a great scar of a saber slash on one cheek. He got out a paper that was enormously popular, because it was full of humor and wit, much of it very coarse, but funny always. His paragraphs reminded me of the broad humor of Sut Lovingood or of George D. Prentice, of the *Louisville Courier-Journal*.

Dave Day was a personal editor. He attacked people and things without fear and was a leader in the politics of the town. To this day his name is remembered with liking by the old-timers of Ouray and of Durango where he lived in the last days of his life.

The *Times* was printed by two brothers named Ripley. They set the type and did the job work. I wrote the paper[23], addressed the wrappers for its subscribers, who numbered about 350, put up the papers after they were printed and took them up to the post office. I helped the Ripleys to run the papers off the press also.

The *Muldoon* had a larger circulation than the *Times*, because of Dave Day's humor, but the *Times* had more news. I was the outside man

---

[22] Apparently the missing page of this manuscript that is noted two pages earlier referenced Saunders's trip over today's Engineer Pass jeep road from Lake City to Ouray. Saunders evidently traveled from Lake City to Ouray with the latter town's famous editor, Dave Day of *Solid Muldoon* newspaper fame.

[23] This is probably one of the few times in his manuscript that Saunders exaggerated a little. Saunders may have been allowed to help lay out the paper or to write an article, but it would never be possible for a newcomer like Saunders to write the entire paper. The Ripleys were more printers than newspaper men, so it is possible Saunders basically wrote the paper after he had been in Ouray a while.

Henry Ripley, Ouray Times *newspaper editor was evidently out prospecting in 1878 or 1880. He is the man in the middle with his hand on the black burro. Henry's newspaper office is just behind him.*

P. David Smith Collection.

and spent much time with the miners as they came to town, getting reports of their work and the gossip generally.

The price of each of these papers was two dollars a year, and anything was taken in payment of subscription, money, gold dust, vegetables from the ranches in the valley below the town or promises. The circulation of the *Times* was small and so were the paper and ink bills. The job printing and advertising sustained the papers.

The advertising was paid for partly in trade, not often in money. I boarded at one of the two hotels in town and the hotel took advertising in exchange.

I got thirty dollars a month and my board, and made the advertising pay me thirty dollars. These were the days when typesetting was done by hand, but no tramp printers ever appeared in that faraway camp.

Most of the store-keepers grub-staked prospectors and usually made money by it, for there were always visitors from the east looking for good prospects. Any kind of a hole in the ground, whose owner could show an assayer's certificate that the ore ran well in silver or gold could be sold. Some of these prospects were worked by the companies that bought them and turned out well, and some were never touched after they were sold.

7 | A Gold Mining Camp Fifty Years Ago

The Uncompahgre River ran through the town, and was the water supply. In the Spring, every grocery store in the camp was crowded from morning to night with prospectors outfitting for their trips into the mountains and ten or twenty burros in front waited patiently for their loads.

Two prospectors usually went together. Food for three months could be bought for about one hundred dollars; coffee, beans, bacon, flour and some canned stuff like tomatoes, corn and peaches. Of course, the men had their mining tools, and cooking utensils, but no prospector ever packed a tent. Most of them had cabins in the mountains, and if they were going to some new place, they built a cabin as soon as they got there.

The prospector had small respect for the geologist, because his experience taught him that gold and silver and other minerals as well are where one finds them and not where a geologist says they ought to be. Leadville is a good example of that. Geologists went all over those fields, and solemnly declared that there could not possibly be silver in that kind of a formation. And yet, when a silver strike was made there by a prospector who didn't know that the geologists had shooed everybody away from there, and the real mining began, Leadville came to the front as one of the richest silver producers the world had ever known.

Once, in Ouray, word came to us that there were good silver indications up on Red Mountain, about seven miles away by the trail, and Billy Stoddard, the county treasurer, sent to Pueblo for a geologist to examine the field. I went with that party. We stayed up on Red Mountain all day, and the geologist made a most painstaking examination of the formation in the outcroppings. So did we. We all agreed with the geologist that there was nothing there. Stoddard paid the geologist and dismissed Red Mountain from his mind.

Three years later, the Yankee Girl, the Guston and other rich mines were found in the very places we had walked over and decided to be worthless ground. Fifty million dollars was taken out of the ground—fifty million we might have had if we had been wiser.

From the first of December on until late in the Spring, the heavy snows cut Ouray off from the outside world. The buckboards became sleds, and the mail carrier, who came over the mountains from Silverton plodded through the heavy drifts on web snowshoes. The miners who came down to town from the mines above, used these, too.

Early in the winter the prospectors and miners who had come into the camp to stay until Spring all had money and the faro games and the bars did a good business. But as the weeks wore on, the money passed into fewer hands and the gambling took the form of careful games of poker. Church socials and volunteer concerts managed by the twenty or thirty women in the place sprang up and even the men went to them. The arrival of the weekly mail was an exciting event that drew nearly all the people of town to the post office and newspapers from Denver were torn into pieces and passed around.

Now and then there were unusual incidents that relieved the monotony of the life, such as the coming of the geologists and development of Leadville mining possibilities after it had been damned by them.

I spent parts of two winters in Ouray. The first was in 1879, and I shall tell about that later, when I describe the outbreak of the Ute Indians. The second was in 1883. There lived then in the valley below Ouray, about seven miles down, a couple who raised potatoes and beans for the Ouray market. They were both strong and tall and thick-bodied, of low intelligence and disposed to be surly when accosted. They came to town, sold their wagon load and went back, after buying what they needed, without talking to anybody except their customers. The man's name was Cuddigan. Passers-by on the road noticed one day that they had a girl of about fifteen years working for them outside. The couple said, when asked about the little girl, that she was their niece and had come from Alamosa a short time before, upon the death of her mother, a widow. Two sympathetic women of Ouray went down to the ranch in a sled one day to ask the farmers if the little girl might not come to Sunday School, and were rudely rebuffed. But they saw the girl and described her as emaciated and frightened, afraid even to talk to the callers. Then the girl disappeared and was seen no more about the ranch and the couple, when asked, when they came to town next, where she was, said that she was dead. "What did she die of?"

"We don't know. Just suddenly died one night."

No doctor had been summoned from Ouray, and the word spread about that the girl had been killed by cruelty.

One morning the Sheriff dropped in at my office, where I was writing, and said, "We want to see about that little girl down yonder, we may want to dig her up. Will you go along with the posse?"

There were seven in the posse and I went with them. We found the sullen couple sitting by the fireplace in the only room of the cabin. The Sheriff came to the point without ceremony.

"John," he said to the man, "what was the matter with the girl?"

"I don't know."

"Well, we've brought along picks and shovels and we'll just have a look."

7 | A Gold Mining Camp Fifty Years Ago

Two men were left in the room to guard the couple, and the rest of us went out.

"Where is she buried?"

"We buried her at night, and maybe I can't find the place."

"Can't you? Well it will be pretty bad for you if you don't. You better think a little and show us. Come along."

The man came reluctantly. One of the posse was left to guard the woman. The man gave us no help, but following deep tracks in the crusted snow, we found a grave, about a hundred yards from the cabin. The ground was frozen hard but the picks went to work and in half an hour the body was exposed. The girl had been buried in the frock she wore when she died, just one garment. The body was frozen and hard as a rock. The Sheriff lifted it out of the shallow grave and laid it on the snow and then gently took off the dirty and bloody frock. The site was a horrible one. The face was bruised and the nose broken in on the body. From the neck down to the ankles were wide and deep cuts, as if they were made by a sharp-edged plank. One glance was all that we needed. The Sheriff replaced the frock and took the body back to the cabin, where it was wrapped in a blanket.

"We'll take you to Ouray. Get ready," he said.

The couple was lodged in jail[24] and the body of the girl was placed in an undertaker's shop. That night, the posse men and a few others met, without the Sheriff, and at midnight, they went to his house and knocked. None of them were masked. That would have been child's play, since the Sheriff knew all their voices. The Sheriff came to the door and opened it.

"Throw up your hands," said the leader of the party, "and don't give us any trouble. Give us the keys to the jail. We want that man and woman and we'll bring back the keys to you and put them on the doorsteps."

The sheriff handed the keys to the speaker and the party entered the jail and opened the cell where the couple was huddled together on the floor.

"You know what we've come for," said the leader. "If you got any messages, let's have 'em."

The man said nothing. The woman began to whimper and moan. "Oh my God," she begged, "don't kill me. I'm going to have a baby in three months. You wouldn't hang a woman carrying a baby."

---

[24] Ouray had no actual jail at the time of the hanging. Other sources say the couple was kept locked in a room in the Delmonico Hotel. The hanging occurred on January 18, 1884, so if Saunders was there and invited to see the body it was during his second time living in Ouray.

The men hesitated. "Go get a lantern, somebody quick," ordered the leader. One of the lynchers ran off and was gone fifteen minutes, coming back with the clear lantern. The party crowded into the cell. "Let's see now," said the leader. The woman showed her body. It was true. She was big with child.

"Why didn't that baby make you kinder to that other child?" demanded one of the posse.

"Well, men," said the leader, "what about it? Do we hang the man and let the woman go? She's a fiend and the baby's not alive yet. She made that girl's life a hell. Hang 'em both?"

All the others agreed. There was no opposing voice. And so the couple was taken down to the edge of the camp and there hanged to one tree.

The bodies were taken down and buried the next morning. In Ouray there was no censure of the lynchers, but when the news got to Denver and was printed in the papers there, there was an outcry among the people of the state, in protest against the barbarity of lynching a woman about to become a mother. The Ouray people winced under the criticism, which continued for days, and after two weeks of it, a fund was raised in Ouray; the body of the wretched little creature was again exhumed and in charge of John Kelly, manager of the *Solid Muldoon*, was sent to Denver and put on exhibition in an undertaker's place there. It was intended to show, by the wounds on the body of the girl, the justification for the lynching.

Gus Begole, a bearded Missourian, who had fought with General Elijah Gates for the Confederates, during the Civil War, came to the Ouray mountains prospecting, and stumbled on the most marvelous outcropping of rich ore that was ever known in Colorado, about three miles above the town. He put up his location stakes and took other men with him, enough to claim about twenty acres of ore. The ore assayed high in silver, nothing else, some of it running, when sent to Denver for a mill run, as much as $150 a ton. The average outcropping was about three feet high, but I have seen some of the ledges that were ten feet high.

The strike was known as the Mineral Farm of Ouray and became known all over the state. Begole and his companions tried to find the motherlode, but they had not enough money to sink the shafts and tunnels that seemed to be necessary, and went broke.

So they put the discovery on the market. I don't know how its fame has spread to that remote part of the country, but the investors of Norfolk and Richmond, rich Virginians all of them bought the Farm.

Begole was canny enough to demand the price of the Farm in cash. He would not take even drafts or certified checks, and so one day, in a lawyer's office the Virginians paid him $75,000 in real money, and with his share of that he started a grocery store in Ouray and made money.

The Virginia company built a smelter and a stamp mill down near Ouray and began exploring the property in a systematic way with diamond drills, sinking shafts and tunneling.

The surface ore was good and some income came to the company from its sale. But the mother lode was never found. The company spent altogether nearly half a million dollars on the property and then gave up in despair and sold the Farm and all the machinery for a song. It is now owned, I think, by a man in St Louis.

One cold afternoon, in January, I was sitting in the office of one of the hotels when a man, so exhausted that he could hardly stand, threw open the door and collapsed on the floor by the stove in the centre of the room.

"Give him some whiskey, quick," said one of the men to the clerk.

We lifted up his head and poured the whiskey down his throat slowly. He began to gasp out words at once.

Up at one of the mines on Mount Sneffels, seven miles by the trail, there had been a snowslide the night before that had buried the house where the miners slept as well as the cook house. Fifteen men had been killed. Twenty had escaped death, as they slept in one end of the house that had not been covered by the slide. The survivors had got to work at once to dig out the buried men and had brought them out all dead, either crushed or suffocated. Rough sleds had been built hurriedly and ten of the miners had started down to Ouray, with the bodies on the sleds.

Another gigantic slide had come down and overwhelmed the funeral train, sweeping into the canyon the sleds with the bodies and the men pulling the sleds, and burying them under tons of snow.

"I don't know why the slide didn't get me," said the man on the floor, as he drank whiskey and ate some soup that had been brought. "I was the first man in the line on the rope."

Within an hour a rescue party started up the canyon with ropes, pickaxes and sleds, all on snowshoes, of course. They were courageous men and hardy, and they stayed on the trail all that night, returning to Ouray during the early morning. They had found it impossible to recover any of the bodies, and they had to stay covered by the snow until it melted in the Spring.[25]

There were twenty-four men killed by these two snow slides in twenty-four hours.

---

[25] Saunders is probably mixing up two events. The Liberty Bell Mine avalanche slide occurred across St. Sophia Ridge from the Virginius Mine. The Virginius was in Ouray County and the Liberty Bell in San Miguel County. The Liberty Bell did have an avalanche that killed a total of twenty-four men (twelve miners and twelve rescuers) that were killed in a series of four slides. The Billy Mayer slide occurred at the Virginius several years earlier. Billy was warming dynamite on a stove when it blew up and injured him severely. Four men from the Virginius Mine responded to take him to the doctor in Ouray. Billy died on the way down and the four rescuers died in an avalanche and their bodies were not found until spring.

CHAPTER 8

A Hunt with Chief Ouray and Chipeta

Chief Ouray and the Utes and his wife Chipeta, a spirited Apache girl... Chipeta's marksmanship and graceful riding... Chipeta gets a mountain lion... by invitation of Chief Ouray we attend an important council of Ute chiefs at his home... the atmosphere is ominous.

IT WAS SEPTEMBER in the mining camp of Ouray and the prospectors were coming down from the mountains with their burros to hole up for the winter. Some of the luckiest ones had brought with them small bags of gold which they got by crushing quartz that contained free gold. All of them had specimens of ore from the richest parts of the vein they had been working.

The town was livelier than it had been all the year; the saloons had put on extra barkeepers and the gambling houses had relief dealers for the faro and the roulette tables.

Ouray was twenty-five miles from the Ute Indian reservation, which included twelve million acres of the wildest land in Colorado. It was heavily wooded with evergreen trees, spruce, cedar, and fir, and with pine and cottonwood. Two large rivers ran through virgin forest that had never been trodden by man, the Grand and the Gunnison Rivers, and these were fed by many smaller streams. The waters were full of fish, and game abounded, bear, lynxes, mountain lions, deer, while wild turkeys, grouse, and quail were so thick that they could have been knocked down by stones flung by a skillful hand.

I was sitting one Saturday in the *Times* office, talking with the two Ripleys, when the door opened, letting in a light flurry of snow, and a slender young man, wearing a sombrero in corduroys.

"Well, have you been helping the honest miner to unload his prospects on the unsuspecting tenderfoot?" he greeted us, with a most engaging smile.

He was John H. Lacey, the doctor at the Los Piños Ute Agency. He and I knew each other quite well. I had met him shortly after I came to Ouray, and we had liked each other at once. Naturally. He was from Raleigh, North Carolina, and I from Virginia, and each rejoiced to find another man out there in the west who slurred his "Rs" and said "You all." I had been to the agency many times and the doctor had taken me on several of his trips visiting Indians who were ill. He was very earnest and enthusiastic in his work; the ailments of the Utes were as a rule very simple and yielded quickly to intelligent medical treatment, so in the two years he had been at the agency he had gained the confidence of the Indians and they sent for him when they were sick, in preference to their own medicine men, who sulked, of course, but gave no outward sign of their feeling.

I had been introduced through Lacey to all the Ute chiefs in a friendly way, and I always made his office my headquarters when I visited the agency. So was my office in Ouray, his. He was warming up thoroughly at our fire.

"Come down with me and stay until you have to come back Monday," he urged me, "Chief Ouray and Chipeta are coming in to see me Sunday, and they're both interesting."

I went, and the next day the Chief and Chipeta came to Dr. Lacey's office. I saw at first sight why Ouray had been made chief of all the Utes. He was about fifty years old, six foot tall[26], with a pleasant countenance, but courage and determination marking his features. He walked slowly and with great dignity. He knew only a few words of English, but he spoke Spanish well, that bastard, border Spanish in use among the Mexicans of Colorado and New Mexico. He was not wearing civilized clothes but had on buckskin trousers, moccasins, and buckskin jacket. His hair he wore in braids hanging down on each side of his face, and he wore no hat.

Chipeta, his wife, followed him shyly into the doctor's office and sat down. She had been there often before, but the presence of a stranger embarrassed her. She was twenty years[27] old, a straight, slender figure, dressed in buckskin jacket, fringe leggings and moccasins. In the two braids with black hair hanging at the side of her head were laced many little nuggets of yellow gold. A light girdle of small hammered silver links, polished till they shone, with pendants of light in dark blue turquoise, circled the loose jacket.

Her skin was the color of deep Amber, and she did not have the flat face of the Ute squaw, but her features were regular and well-defined,

---

[26] Chief Ouray was about fifty years old but only 5' 7" tall – about average for a Ute. He was bigger than life in his conduct and perhaps he "grew" over the years in Saunders's mind.

[27] Chipeta was closer to thirty-five years old at this time, but she was very attractive, active, and a joy to be around. Saunders was probably just guessing at her age.

8 | A Hunt with Chief Ouray and Chipeta

The post office and agent's office at Los Piños II, also called the Uncompahgre Agency. Joseph B. Abbott, the agent at the time the photo was taken is sixth from right and Moreno, the interpreter is third from left.

P. David Smith Collection

and her nose with straight and finely modeled. Her eyes were quick and observant, sparkling with intelligence and good humor, and her whole manner highly animated. Her wrists and hands were small as were her feet. Usually moccasins are clumsy looking. Chipeta's were well-shaped. She told me afterwards that she made them herself, although the Utes had a professional moccasin maker. They were entirely plain, without the least ornament. She wore no rings on her fingers and not in her ears, for a very good reason, for her ears were in perfect harmony with the rest of her beautifully shaped features, and earrings would have disfigured them.

Nor was she the servile thing the other Ute women were. She treated Chief Ouray and all of us like her equals. Indeed she was so different from the other Ute women I had seen in camp and about the agency that I sat looking at her intently and wondering from what race this spirited creature had sprung.

Chipeta got used to my presence very soon, and gave free rein to her natural vivacity, talking in Spanish, mostly about the two pets she had, a mountain lion and a deer, which she had trained to consort with each other on most friendly terms. Her voice was low and clear and melodious and she talked with a fascinating play of feature and gestures.

Chief Ouray listened with a smile to the cheerful conversation of Chipeta and Doctor Lacey, but he plainly was thinking about something else. Presently he showed us what it was. He thought that he had found out that agency supplies, bought by the government for the Indians, were being sold to merchants up in Ouray. The Utes did not receive the food, blankets and clothing, although the things were being charged to them on the agency books. He asked us how he could get this complaint direct to Washington, without going to the agent. He spoke with strong feeling, and his voice was heavy and harsh, his dark eyes glowing as he told of his discovery.

Lacey and I undertook to write a letter for him to the Secretary of the Interior, and we did. I never followed this thing through, but the agent at Los Piños was removed by Secretary Carl Schurtz some weeks later.

When we had finished with this matter, Chipeta turned to the Chief and they exchanged a few words, and then, smiling she spoke to Doctor Lacey.

Five of the key players in the 1880 negotiations after the Meeker Massacre are shown in this Matthew Brady photograph. Ouray and Chipeta are shown to the right front with Charles Adams, who headed the rescue of the captive, standing behind them. Next to Ouray is Charles Schurz, of the Department of the Interior which included the Department of Indian Affairs. Ignacio, Chief of the Southern Utes is at the left front.

P. David Smith Collection.

8 | A Hunt with Chief Ouray and Chipeta

"Muy bien," I heard him say, and then he explained to me,

"Ouray and Chipeta want us to go down to Ouray's house tonight and then spend two or three days hunting and camping with them. Can't you get off? We'll get a messenger off Ouray town this afternoon and get your leave from the paper."

Could I get off? You bet I would. Here was an opportunity for a twenty year old youth to go camping and hunting with the head Chief of all the Utes and his wife. I would have thrown up my job with the *Times* for this trip.

But that was not necessary. The messenger came back from Ouray before the sun went down with the word that Ripley, of the *Times*, said that it was alright for Saunders to go with Ouray, and late that evening, we started for Ouray's house by moonlight, the Chief riding in his carriage driven by a Mexican, and Chipeta, Doctor Lacey and I riding on horseback.

Lacey was a good doctor and I thought I was a good newspaperman but we certainly cut sorry figures as horsemen, by the side of Chipeta. She rode like an Amazon and she and the horse might have been one, so perfectly did her body meet the movements of his. Her horse was a sorrel, a pony she told me she had raised herself, and he was that unusual horse, a natural single footer.

The home of Chief Ouray was a very grand affair for an Indian reservation. It was the only house on the reservation. It was an adobe house, with six rooms, all on the ground floor. Ouray slept in one room, with a Mexican and Indian guard lying just outside his door. Chipeta had another room, and Lacey and I shared a third. There was a dining room, where Chief Ouray met his sub-chiefs. The kitchen was in an outhouse, and there was a Mexican cook.

All the rooms were comfortably and even expensively furnished. The beds were of iron and there were rocking chairs and sofas. But the council room had only one chair and a table. That was where the chiefs sat. The sub-chief sat on the floor around him, and they preferred that. They would not have known how to sit in chairs.

We had a very good dinner of venison and vegetables fresh from Ouray's farm, and then we went into the sitting room, and made ourselves comfortable. Dr. Lacey and I smoked; neither Ouray nor Chipeta did. We sat in silence for a while and then the Chief spoke to Chipeta in Ute, evidently making a request. She demurred, and Ouray then appealed to Doctor Lacey in Spanish.

"Ouray wants her to sing," said Lacey to me, smiling.

"Oh, please do," I said to her.

She hesitated, and then went out and brought in a guitar. She played and sang for an hour the Ute songs, love songs, and war songs. Her full, round, sustained soprano tones were astonishing and moving, and I wondered at the perfection of her notes. Feeling and fire were in her voice.

"Lacey, where in the world did she learn to sing?"

"I understand English," replied Chipeta quickly, "I like to sing, and our Utes will do what I want when I sing to them. I sing in the woods when I am riding."

Chipeta was the only Indian I've ever known who played the guitar. She told me that she had been taught to play it by one of the Mexican servants. She played it well, not only accompaniments to her songs, but also the Ute dances and Mexican fandangoes. The Utes usually accompany their songs and dances with small drums and an instrument like a flageolet, a reed pierced with holes for the fingers and blown from the end.

"Chipeta is a Kiowa Apache," said Lacey. "Her mother and father were killed in a raid made on the camp of their tribe, and she was left behind by the Apaches to starve. A hunting party of the Utes found her crawling around the deserted Apache camp and brought her down to the Ute reservation, where she was adopted. That explains her aquiline

This is one of the earliest known photos of Chief Ouray's house. It was made of adobe and was really quite nice. It was located about a half mile west of the present day Montrose Ute Museum.

Steven G. Baker Collection.

8 | A Hunt with Chief Ouray and Chipeta

features and her slenderness. The Ute face is round and the women are all stout, you know."

We were up before daybreak the next morning. This time we all rode horseback and Chief Ouray showed us that he was a very good rider. He threw off all his dignity and became just a keen hunter. We had two pack mules, carrying one tent and supplies, in charge of two Mexican camp men.

"Do you like fishing?" Lacey asked me.

"I'd rather fish than hunt," I said.

"I rather thought so, because of your eyes. Well, we have a complete lot of tackle and you can fish while we hunt. It is not too late for trout down in this valley."

"What will the rest of you do?"

"Hunt bear and deer and quail, and maybe we can get a mountain lion or two. They are fair game because they kill the deer and the colts."

"Chipeta?"

"Why man, Chipeta can out shoot all of us. You'll see her presently."

We could not gallop or even lope over the rough trail but the ponies walked fast and in two hours we were at our camping place, on the rocky banks of the Gunnison River. The Mexicans unsaddled the horses and put up the tent, and we all examined our hunting and fishing equipment. Or rather, I examined mine. The others had got everything they wanted in good shape the night before.

"Chipeta," said Lacey, "Saunders wants to see you shoot. He believes you can."

Do you remember the old Winchester repeating rifle? That was the kind all of our party had. The hunter today would scoff at this weapon, and yet fifty years ago, frontiersmen did very accurate shooting with it, at 200 yards. It had a magazine, carrying fourteen cartridges, with one in the barrel, ready to shoot. With every shot, one had to throw forward a lever under the stock, which ejected the shell, and then throw the lever back again, which forced another cartridge into the barrel. The lever could be worked by an expert without taking the rifle from the shoulder, but a novice had to take the gun down to work it.

Chipeta took her rifle from the tree against which it leaned; looked it over with care, and then holding it in front of her, looked at me and laughed.

"Throw your hat," she said, with a mischievous gleam in her eyes.

I started to do it, but Chief Ouray interfered, pointing to a hawk, flying high above us.

Chipeta fired and the hawk fell. She fired again, and the hawk jerked as the second bullet hit it before it struck the ground. Nothing for an expert marksman to brag about, but mighty good shooting for an old Winchester rifle.

They left me in camp picking out my flies, while they went off separately for their hunting.

At that time, deer were hunted generally with the stand system. In deer country, it was well known where the deer ran when fleeing from human or animal hunters, and the hunters took their stands in the places where the creatures would pass when the dogs began to chase them. In this way, there was little chance of escape unless, as often happens, the hunter got "buck fever" when he saw the animal and could not fire in time.

In Colorado, deer hunters most often watched at their drinking places on streams, going on guard early in the morning, and shooting them when they came to the water.

But this party of ours was real hunters and the woods were full of deer. They would walk through the woods until they saw one and either shout so as to make it run, or fire a shot that startled it into flight.

They never shot a deer standing.

Chief Ouray had taken a Mexican with him and he came back with haunches of venison wrapped in gunny sacking for our dinner. He had shot four deer. Chipeta brought in fifteen quail, with which she girdled herself, and said that she had killed and hung up in the woods three deer. Doctor Lacey killed two.

I contributed five trout, one three pounder and the rest smaller, all caught with a coachmen and a gray hackle.[28]

What an evening of pleasure that was, after dinner. We lay on our beds, which the Mexicans had made up with spruce boughs, and talked, and as he looked at the stars Chief Ouray unbosomed himself of his thoughts about the Utes and the United States government. The things he said sounded stilted, when put into English, but they were said very sincerely, and, spoken as he expressed himself, partly in Spanish, a bit

---

[28] The trout that Saunders caught were surely cutthroat trout, as brown trout and rainbow trout were not stocked in Colorado until the 1880s.

in Ute, and now and then a few words in English, they were convincing to Lacey and me.

> "I have resigned myself to submission to the United States government," he said, "and I have persuaded many of my chiefs to think as I do. We see that you white men submit yourselves to your government, too. But we want to be left alone in the possession of our lands and this free life we are leading. It is very hard for me to keep the young men of the tribe quiet now. They are restless and I know that they have fights with the hunters and the prospectors who come on the reservation without right. Some day some of these troublesome Utes may do something that may bring the troops down on us, and we will be destroyed. We are only 10,000 and there are ten times that many troops. If the government would guarantee to let us alone we would not even want the agency rations because we have on this reservation game that we can trade for flour and bacon and sugar and coffee, and we have besides much gold that we can tell no one about. We know where it is—no one else does. I trust you and Lacey. You will not tell."

Lacey and I reassured Ouray as to the future of the Utes. "The government will not move the Utes from this reservation," said he, "so long as they do not make trouble with the settlers around here. But you must not let anyone know there is gold in these streams or these mountains."

We were out hunting three days, and the deer that were shot or hung by the Mexicans in trees and afterward given by Ouray to the Indians— some of it sent to the agency.

After the first day I abandoned my fishing and went hunting with Chipeta. It was much more fun watching her as she made her way noiselessly through the forest, and seeing her accuracy with the rifle. She had the hunter's instinct that was positively magical to me.

Once, as we stood on the crest of a hill I saw something move down below, in the thick bushes.

"Deer," I said, and threw up my gun to be ready. She put her hand on the barrel.

"No," she warned me, "Man."

We watched, and presently out of the coppice came Chief Ouray. Chipeta slapped me on the cheek with her fingers, lightly and laughed.

"Very bad hunter," she said.

I thought that Ouray was childless, but on the second day of our hunt we were sitting by the campfire when he suddenly began telling us about his son. His first wife had died, after giving birth to a boy. This child had been stolen by the Apaches when he was four years old, and that was twelve years before, so the boy was now sixteen years old. Ouray had led a war party after the Apache thieves but they had escaped into Mexico.

The boy had then been sold by the Apache to the Arapahoe, and young as he was he had so distinguished himself in hunting exploits that they had made him a sub-chief.

Ouray had sent messengers to the Arapahoe and had asked the boy to return to the Utes. He did not remember his father nor his tribe, and word came back to Ouray from him that he refused, that he was now an Arapahoe. Ouray was deeply hurt, and harassed by doubt, for he could not even know that the boy had really got the message and really sent that answer to his father.

"Washington could make the Arapahoes give me back my son," he said to us, "but they say that they do not want to make the Arapahoes mad. That is not right to me and I will not forgive that."

Lacey and I were deeply impressed by Ouray's recital of this story, and offered our aid with the government.

"No," said Ouray, "Wait, I'm going to try again with Washington after a while."

Chipeta, who of course knew all about this lost son, got up once, when Ouray was talking and going to him, laid her hand on his shoulder. Then she came back to her place by the fire and sat silent and melancholy.

Lacey rallied her on her mood and she threw it off smiling.

"I am too sad," she said. "The woods always make me sad. Now I am going to sing you one of our serenades."

She sang without accompaniment, for we had not brought the guitar. Compared to our serenades the melody seemed broken and unexpected, but Chipeta's voice was mellifluous and she felt the words of the entreating lover. At one point, she rose from the ground, stretched out her arms, and acted.

"Now, we will do some dancing," she announced, and seizing Lacey for her partner, she made him go through the Bear and the Sun dances with her. As she danced, she threw off, one by one, the encumbering hunting garments, even the leggings, until she wore nothing but her jacket, short buckskin skirt and sandals. She wore no stockings, and her legs were beautifully symmetrical.

Presently she stopped dancing and came and sat by me. "We have got deer and quail and fish but no bear or lions," she said, "And we must

8 | A Hunt with Chief Ouray and Chipeta

not go back without one. We must all be up early tomorrow and hunt for lions." She spoke to Ouray in Ute.

"Bueno," he answered in Spanish.

"Isn't this very dangerous for Chipeta?" I asked Lacey.

"Why no," he said, "She had hunted lions before and besides, mountain lions are not so very fierce. They have the reputation among hunting novices of being formidable, but really they are cowards, and they will not attack a human being unless they are driven into a corner. They like to climb out on an overhanging limb and leap on a small and weak animal passing beneath the tree. If a hunter approaches they stay quiet on the limb and try to efface themselves. Our job is to see them in the dark just before daybreak. That is the best time to get them."

Chipeta came up to us. "You go with me," she addressed me, "And Lacey go with Ouray."

About five minutes later, it seemed to me, Chipeta waked me with her hand on my shoulder. The Mexicans had got a hasty breakfast and long before light appeared, we were on our way. Chipeta led me into a virgin forest and presently we came to a deer trail, down which the deer went to the river.

"Lions in the trees along here," she said. "Come after me. Can you see me? Make no noise. Don't shoot. Whistle to me if you see one. Lions won't run."

She crept along, like a wraith, making not the slightest sound. I strained my eyes, but saw nothing. After a while, I lost sight of Chipeta, and then she whistled low and long. I hastened and came to her, with rifle ready. She pushed my gun back and pointed up in a tree. I could make out indistinctly the form of the lion, and it seemed to me as large as a grizzly bear.

"Get off the trail," ordered the huntress, and I did. She fired. The lion leaped straight at her, and I shot at him and missed. She caught him with a second shot in the air, and stepped aside at the same instant. The beast fell where she had stood; kicked and then lay still.

Chipeta put both her hands to her mouth and gave a call, on a high note that must have carried a mile. "That will bring Pietro," she said. "He is back there. We will sit down and talk."

Pietro came with the other Mexican and took the lion away to skin it. It measured six feet and two inches from the nose to the tip of the tail.

When we returned to Ouray's house from the hunt, the chief asked us to stay one more day, as he was going to have a council of his chiefs and he wanted both of us to meet them.

Fifteen of the sub chiefs came to the council. Ouray gave us all dinner in his dining room and after dinner they sat around the room on the floor and talked in Ute for two or three hours.

Ignacio, chief of the Southern Utes, whose headquarters and agency were at Pagosa Springs, was there, a short squat Ute, who said little and deferred to the Great Chief Ouray, always. He seemed to me rather negligible. Then there were Johnson, Douglas, Jack, and Pursune, sub chiefs of the White River Utes, with independent and free manner and talkative. Johnson and Douglas were middle-aged Indians and both of fierce aspect. Jack and Persune were young warriors and I noticed that they looked much at Chipeta, who sat in the council, on the floor too, but said nothing.

Shavano, Sapavanero, and Colorao were the sub chiefs of the Uncompahgre Utes who were there. Both Shavano and Sapavanero were tall, stalwart Utes, of force and influence. When they threw off their blankets as they did in the council their muscular and straight bodies were pleasant to look at. All of the chiefs had brought rifles to the council which were stacked in a corner of the room, and all of them wore knives in their belts. Both Sapavanero and Shavano were my friends and I had learned many Ute

Saunders found Shavano to be helpful and easy to get along with. Shavano is seen here wearing a peace medal he was given while at treaty talks.
P. David Smith Collection.

words from them. I often took them into the agency store and bought them candy, of which, like all those Indians, they were very fond. They especially like gumdrops.

Shavano was called the war chief of the Utes because in all the wars these Indians had had with other Indians, he had led them to victory — the raid of the Utes on the Apache several years before when they tried to rescue the stolen son of Chief Ouray, being a conspicuous instance. Shavano's face and body were covered with old knife scars, which he had got in battle with the Apaches and with the Cheyenne, and he walked with a limp, relic of a deep stab in the thigh. He told me once that he had eleven hand-to-hand fights with knives and had killed every one of his foes. I accepted this as true, since he was treated with deep respect by the other Utes.

Shavano also was said to have been the best archer among the youths in the days when the Utes, like the other Indians, used bows for weapons, before they began to use rifles. I never saw a shotgun in the hands of a Ute. They were permitted to have rifles since they were needed in hunting game.

I had never liked Colorao. That was the way his name was pronounced, although the agency records it was spelled "Colorado." The name means "red," and he was so named because of a very light red tint in his hair. He was a stout ugly Ute, with a large following among the younger Indians, and his manner was always disagreeable toward the whites. Colorao was the only one of the Uncompahgre Utes who made trouble for Ouray, and very often he joined Chiefs Johnson, Douglas, Persune, and Jack of the White River Utes, in violently opposing Ouray's policies during the councils. These rebellious resented the higher authority of Shapavanero and were unwilling the he should succeed to the leadership of the tribe upon the death of Ouray, which had been agreed upon by all the other Utes.

Moreover, Colorao felt bitterly that he could never hope to be chief of the tribe as long as Shavano lived. Shavano hated him, believing him to be a coward. So, he contented himself for the time with plotting to frustrate the plans of Ouray.

Both Doctor Lacey and I had met the Uncompahgre chiefs before, casually, in their teepees, when Lacey went to make his sick visits, and at the agency, but we had not met Ignacio, chief of the Southern Utes, nor any of the White River chiefs.

Such a general counsel of all these chiefs was most unusual, and Lacey and I talked about it that night, as we got ready for bed.

"What are those fellows up to?" I asked Lacey, "Getting ready for a big hunt?"

"I don't know," answered Lacey. "Something worse, maybe. I'm not borrowing trouble, but this Council looks ominous to me. Watching the faces of those fellows I've rather got the idea that those White River Utes are brewing something and that Ouray has got wind of it and is trying to head it off. He wanted us there to show the chiefs he was standing in with the whites."

Ouray and Chipeta told us good bye the next morning, as we mounted our horses, Chipeta smiling radiantly, with her pet mountain lion rubbing against her legs, and Ouray in the white man's way, with a shake of the hand. I looked back and Chipeta was waving her hand, while Ouray was walking back to the house, not erect as usual, but with head bent in thought.

"I'm going to keep my eyes peeled," said Lacey, "And will send you word if anything turns up. I feel uncomfortable and so does Ouray, you can see. Don't print a word about the Council. Ouray wouldn't want it known, and it would only make people uneasy. And we may be all wrong, too. Well, hasta luego!"

The Utes have a very complex language, and the University of Colorado, at Boulder, in late years, has made a study of it. But all the time I was with these Indians, I learned only a few words of Ute. I spoke English with Chipeta, and with Chief Ouray, with the other Utes I got along with some English and some very bad Spanish. How bad that was I did not know until I lived in the City of Mexico years afterwards.

Utes often spoke Spanish to us—never among themselves, of course—and I wondered where they learned it until Ouray told me.

He said that they had learned Spanish first from the Apaches, and the Apaches had learned it from the Yaqui Indians of Mexico. The Utes found Spanish much easier to speak than English and they preferred it.

CHAPTER 9

White River Massacre and Rescue of the Women Captives

The Utes go on the war path, defeat the United States troops, murder the whites at the Agency and carry the women into captivity… we guard the town of Ouray against Indian attack… the ride up into the mountains to rescue the captives… Chipeta uses her influence to make me one of the party…Shawsheen, the sister of Chief Ouray, cows the War Bonnets and makes them surrender the captives to us.

ONE SATURDAY, at the beginning of October 1879, a commotion arose along the streets of Ouray and the word was passed from mouth to mouth:

"Meeting at the court house. The Utes are on the warpath!"

In thirty minutes after the first alarm the courthouse was filled, and Charles Munn, a merchant of the town, mounted the judge's bench and read a telegram from Governor Frederick W. Pitkin. It told us that the White River Utes were on the warpath; had attacked and whipped United States troops near the reservation; had massacred the Indian agent, Father Meeker, as he was called, and ten white men employed at the agency, and had captured the white women and the children.

The Governor advised the people of Ouray to organize militia at once and protect Ouray, in case the Uncompahgre Utes started trouble. Nearly 200 men joined the militia within an hour, were served with Springfield rifles and cartridges, and told to guard the one road leading into Ouray, and the trails.

I went in, of course, and with twenty others watched the road. A deep snow lay on the ground. Day and night, the guard lay on the bank of the river, concealed in the underbrush, eyes on the road a few steps away. But there was no attack. After three days of this, I went to the captain and said, "We get no word from Los Piños about this. Will you let me ride down there and find out what's going on?"

"Those Indians may have scalped everybody at the agency, as they did at White River, and you are taking your life into your hands," he said.

"But this is foolish," I said. "Here we are, scared to death and knowing nothing. I'd like to go."

"Go ahead," he gave me permission.

I rode down to Los Piños that afternoon, armed with a revolver only. To my amazement, the agency was quiet and the men there going about their customary work.

I went to Doctor Lacey's office. His face showed anxiety but he offered me tobacco and papers for a cigarette and I sat down.

"Why haven't some of you been up to Ouray?" I asked. "Up there, we've been frightened and don't know what the danger is or where it is coming from. Tell me what's going on."

"Here it is," said Lacey. "All the settlers along the reservation are in danger. We've sent nobody to Ouray because we couldn't spare a man from here and we knew you were guarding the town.

"The news we get comes from Chief Ouray and is brought to him by Indian runners. All we know is that the Utes over White River way have gone on the war path; have fought and whipped the cavalry and infantry sent against them; have killed a lot of soldiers; have burned the White River agency, killed all the white men at the agency, and carried off the women and children there into captivity. Of course, they've raped the women, poor things.

"Chief Ignacio, of the Southern Utes, has sent word to Chief Ouray that he is holding his Utes and that they will not join the White River

The women at the Meeker Massacre tried to escape but were easily captured. All the male employees were killed.
        Harper's Monthly, "The Ute Massacre." P. David Smith Collection.

9 | White River Massacre and Rescue of the Women Captives

Utes on the war path, and Ouray says he is sure he can keep the Uncompahgre Utes here quiet. I don't know whether they can control these Utes or not, and we've got to keep on guard till the troops get the upper hand of the hostiles and put the 'Fear of God' into them."

"In the meantime, what about those captives?"

"God knows," answered Lacey. "We can do nothing for them until we get better control of the situation than we have now. You had better go back and tell your people in Ouray to keep up their guard. I'll get word to you if anything happens that is important."

This was broadly the situation, but right here I had better tell the real story of the outbreak and its causes.

Nathaniel C. Meeker, the agent at White River, whom the Utes had killed, was a deeply religious New Englander, a man of ideals, who felt strongly called to work for the welfare of the Indians of the United States. Horace Greeley thought highly of him and got him the post of agent at White River. Meeker took with him his wife, and his daughter, Josephine, a robust, highly spirited, girl twenty-five years old, ambitious for a missionary career, who became the teacher at the agency and went at her work with enthusiasm.

However, from the time he entered on his work, Meeker showed an utter lack of understanding of the Indian temperament. He tried to force the Indians to his own standards. He wanted them to learn to be farmers and to work with agricultural tools instead of with the rifle. He may have had the right idea, but he demanded that they cultivate their land, and sometimes went so far as to cut down the rations of those who obstinately refused to work, a thing he had no right to do.

Before he had been there a year, he was hated by all the Indians, and his influence with them was so little that he himself saw it and began writing letters to his friends saying that he had lost hope of doing anything to better the habits of the Utes. He should have resigned then, but he did not. He stayed at the agency and the feeling toward him among the Indians became more bitter.

Finally, he had a quarrel with Chief Johnson and they fought each other with their fists on the agency grounds. Then Agent Meeker sent for troops, wiring that he had feared the Utes were on the verge of an outbreak. They were not. They merely wanted to get rid of Meeker.

Major T. T. Thornburg was sent to the agency with four companies of the Fourth Infantry, 160 men, and twenty-seven wagons of supplies. Of course, the minute the troops entered the reservation, the Utes knew that Meeker had sent for them, and they were furious, fearing that they would be attacked by the soldiers, or at least, severely disciplined.

Forty miles from the agency, the two chiefs, Colorao and Jack, rode out of the woods where they had been waiting, in front of the soldiers. Major Thornburg was riding ahead, and as he saw the two Utes he threw up his hand and halted his column. He sat silent, grim, and watchful, as a Ute came up. Several of the soldiers heard the colloquy that followed:

"Hao," said the Utes.

"Hao," the Major answered.

"Why soldiers on our land?" asked Jack.

"We're going to the agency, to see that you fellows don't make trouble," answered the Major. As he spoke he fingered a rifle that lay on his saddle before him.

"Utes no make trouble," said Jack.

"All right," said Major Thornburg curtly, and he started his column again.

Chiefs Jack and Colorao rode into the woods.

Fifteen miles nearer the agency, the soldiers approached a canyon, wooded, rugged, an excellent place for an ambush. I have never understood why Thornburg did not throw out flankers on the sides of this canyon before leading his men into such a trap, and I have thought that he had such a contempt for the Utes that he was foolhardy.

At any rate, into the canyon the soldiers marched, the supply wagons following. The troops had gone about half a mile when the Utes opened fire on them from both sides of the canyon, and bad marksmen as they were they dropped nine of the soldiers at the first volley. Thornburg ordered the troops to halt, seek cover, and fire at will, while he himself with a score of his men, charged the hidden Utes. He was killed and so were his followers.

The survivors hastily threw up a rocky enclosure and fought from within that, but since they could not see the Indians, they could not tell what harm their firing was doing. Of course, the natural thought was that the Utes would sack the provision wagons, and they did, looting them of half of their contents before the party of soldiers sent back to the wagons got there. Getting back there, understand, meant crouching and crawling over rocks and between them, trying to keep hidden from the fire of the Indians on the side of the canyon. But the soldiers did finally get to the wagons and although many of the mules drawing them had been killed they managed to get the wagons into a sort of semicircular corral, within which all the soldiers were protected.

It was plain that the Utes had surrounded the soldiers, and were now in the canyon as well as on the sides. A hat placed on a rifle and lifted above the rocks drew fire instantly. A spring was found within the corral and in the wagons was plenty of food. Captain Payne, who took

9 | White River Massacre and Rescue of the Women Captives

"Thornburgh's Last Charge" as depicted in Harper's Weekly, *November 1, 1879 was drawn by H. Viele, who grossly exaggerated the ruggedness of the surrounding mountains.*

Harper's Weekly, *November 1, 1879*

command of the troops after the death of Major Thornburg, felt that he could hold out indefinitely, but certainly word must be got to Rawlins, the nearest military post, that he needed reinforcements. Forty of his men, besides Major Thornburg, we're dead already, and the Utes outnumbered the soldiers four to one. So he gathered several of his most experienced men around him, behind the rocks, and consulted. It had to be assumed that the Utes were going to keep up the siege and make frequent attacks with the hope of wearing down the soldiers.

The scout, Joe Rankin, a man of about forty, small, wiry, grizzled, spoke up.

"If you'll let me go, Captain, I'll get through to Rawlins," he volunteered, "the sun's nearly down now. It will be dark in an hour. I'll slip out of this damned canyon and lead my buckskin till I get a mile away. I know two ranches between here and Rawlins where I can get fresh horses."

"Go ahead, Joe," assented Captain Payne, "we'll hold 'em here."

That was a heroic ride of Joe Rankin, a ride that saved the lives of the besieged soldiers. He cut his blanket into strips and tied the strips around the hooves of the horse, so that they would not clatter on the stones of the canyon as he went out, and by the greatest luck he was not seen by any of the Utes as he passed out of the canyon.

The pony riders of the West used to make fifteen and sometimes more miles an hour, carrying the mail, but they change horses every ten or fifteen miles and they traveled over roads usually well known to them. Felix X. Aubrey, who made that famous ride from the old Fonda in Santa Fe, to Independence, Missouri, 800 miles, in six days, 133 miles a day, had arranged for relays of horses all along the way, and he rode one and led two or three fresh horses, so that he could change from a tired horse to one that had not been carrying his weight.

This forgotten scout, Joe Rankin, with only two changes of horses, rode the 160 miles from the canyon where the soldiers were besieged, to Rawlins, in twenty-nine hours, a greater riding feat than Aubrey's, since he had to ride over much rougher country, most of it unfamiliar to him, and with only one change of mount. But Aubrey rode only to win a bet, and Rankin was riding to save the lives of his comrades.

He slipped out of the canyon at dark Monday night, and at three o'clock Wednesday morning, rode into Rawlins and waked everybody within the sound of his voice. In an hour, General Merritt was on his way to the rescue, with 200 men of the Fifth Cavalry, traveling light.

In the meantime, back in the canyon the fighting had been kept up. Scouts sent out came back reporting that the Utes still held their points of advantage on both sides of the canyon. The stench of the dead men and the horses was beginning to be felt. There was no doctor and only rough first aid could be given to the wounded. Three more died.

Early Wednesday morning, the third day of the siege, about the time Scout Joe Rankin was galloping into Rawlings, there came to the ears of the besieged soldiers in the canyon a cautious hail.

"Hello, Thornburg outfit?"

"Yes," called Captain Payne, "Who is it?"

"There's a company of soldiers here," called the low voice from the rocks.

"Don't believe him Captain," one of the troopers behind Captain Payne warned him, that's a damned Indian trick."

"For God's sake, don't shoot," called the voice, "I'm John Gordon, the mail carrier, and Sandy Mullen is with me. Captain Dodge, with a company of the ninth, is right behind me."

Captain Paine knew that Sandy Mullen was a ranchman on the border of the Indian reservation. He hesitated and there was a pause. Then another voice hailed,

"Payne, are you there?"

"Yes," answered the Captain.

9 | White River Massacre and Rescue of the Women Captives

"This is Dodge, with one company."

"By God, we're glad to see you," called Captain Payne.

Captain Dodge and his men came into the corral.

"How did you get through the Utes?" asked Payne.

"Damned if I know. We didn't see any."

"Think they are gone?"

"Try some shots."

Several shots were fired at the hiding places of the Utes, and the fire was returned by many Indians.

"Still there," said Captain Payne, "We'll have to stay here till Merritt comes. We've sent for him."

The Negro soldiers of the Ninth Cavalry relieved the tired men of Captain Payne in standing guard, and men slept who had not slept for forty-eight hours.

Why the Utes allowed Captain Dodge, with his handful of Negro soldiers to pass into the canyon without a fight, we never knew. The Indians could have wiped out the small party of rescuers with one volley. We always thought that they believed that Captain Dodge was leading the vanguard of a much larger force, and they did not want to invite a heavy attack.

Two more days of anxiety went by. The soldiers were now all fighting as skirmishers, spread out as they like, and firing when they saw a chance for a good shot. Twelve more of the troops were killed, Negroes and whites, by the Utes. Nobody of the whites ever knew how many Indians were killed. Their bodies were carried off by the survivors.

And then came General Merritt, with his 200 men of the Fifth Cavalry. He avoided the mistake that Major Thornburg had made, threw flankers out on the sides of the canyon and entered to raise the siege without a shot. The Utes withdrew as his men advanced.

It was while Thornburg's men, for whom Agent Meeker had sent in hope of protection, were in prison in the canyon, that a body of Utes attacked the agency: killed Agent Meeker and his twelve clerks and workmen, and carried off Mrs. Meeker, Mrs. Price and Josephine Meeker, with the two young children of Mrs. Price.

General Merritt's troops, marching out of the canyon, went on to the White River agency, and found it burned, with the mangled bodies of Agent Meeker and his twelve men lying about. They buried them, as they had the bodies of their own dead, reported to Washington, and got orders to pursue those Utes and clean them up. The War Department also ordered all the troops in Colorado and New Mexico that could be spared from their posts to chase the Utes and attack them wherever they could be found.

This sketch depicts the scene at the Meeker Agency when the soldiers arrived a few days after the massacre. The bodies were evidently buried where they were found. At the center rear is the smokehouse where the women and children stayed during the massacre.
Frank Leslie's Illustrated Newspaper, December 6, 1879.

So, this was the situation when Doctor Lacey and I were talking that day at Los Piños. Of course, at that time I knew only what Lacey had told me. That was enough to show us that we were on the verge of a serious Indian war. Our fear was that the Utes and Apaches, already on the war path in New Mexico, would join in warring on the whites, and we knew that if this happened we would be in for a long and bloody conflict.

Back I went to Ouray and reported, and we kept up the guard of the road and the trails until everybody was sick of it. "I'd rather go down to the reservation and clean out those Utes than do this sort of stuff," said one of our company one night as we trudged down the road to go on watch.

Then one day, October 18th 1879 it was, I got a message from Doctor Lacey, sent by a man on horseback:

"Come to the agency at once, ready to ride a long distance. We're going to try to rescue the Meeker captives, and you can go if you get here in time."

In half an hour I was on a horse, galloping to Los Piños.

THE RESCUE PARTY

I got to the agency at Los Piños in the early afternoon, and went directly to the office of the agent. In the office sat agent William H. Stanley, a pleasant, weak-faced, politician from Illinois, who that early in the day had drunk so much whiskey that he was nervous and uncertain of his movements, talking with a stout spectacled man who had an air of authority. With these two was a young man, small and dapper, with a nicely trimmed mustache and beard and a foreign air about him.

"Come in, Saunders," the agent greeted me. "We're going to get those captives and General Adams here represents the government in treating with the hostile Utes. This gentleman is Count Doenhoff, of the Austrian Embassy, who is going with General Adams." He tried to fill his pipe with tobacco and spilled the tobacco as his hands shook.

"Have a cigar, Stanley," said General Adams. "You're nervous."

"Haven't had enough sleep for nights," said the agent, taking the cigar. "When do you want to start?"

"As soon as it is light tomorrow morning."

"I should like to go with you, General," I said.

Adams turned, and bored into me with his eyes, through his thick lens glasses.

"Who are you?" he asked.

"Saunders, editor of the *Ouray Times*."

A young and anxious correspondent of a little mining camp sheet. How did I look to General Adams?

"I want no newspaper men with me," he said, and turned his back to speak to Count Doenhoff.

The curt rebuff filled me with anger, but I said nothing, and going outside I stood for a minute on the wooden steps, wrestling with my disappointment. I looked around. Affairs at the agency seemed to be going on as usual. It was issue day, and hundreds of Utes were on the grounds, men, women and children. Many of the men were armed with Winchester or Remington rifles. Some of the squaws were in the warehouse loading themselves and the boys with the week's supplies which the two clerks were distributing. These were the substantial things: flour, coffee and bacon, and clothing for the women and the men. Other squaws were going in and out of the agency store, where the trader sold luxuries not given to the Indians by the government—sweet things, canned stuff, and candy.

In the great corral of the agency, twenty-five steers had been driven from the agency herd for the week's supply of meat. The blanketed Utes would climb on the fence of the corral and shoot down the cattle. They were mostly poor marksmen,[29] sometimes it took ten or fifteen shots to kill a steer. When one fell the squaws rushed to the animal and leaning over, cut it up with their knives. As they did so, the little pappooses [sic] in the boards hanging on the backs of the squaws would be thrown forward so that they almost stood on their heads, but there was never a whimper from one of them.

Several agency laborers were working on a new stable, smoking and going at the job most leisurely.

Regarding this scene, it was hard to realize that we were at the very center of an Indian war. None of the agency men were armed. The Utes could have made short work of them, as they had a few days before the arrival of men at the White River agency.

The whole situation puzzled me.

I walk down to Doctor Lacey's office and found him there, with Chief Ouray and Chipeta. Ouray was writing his autograph on some cards for Lacey, laboriously forming the letters, thrusting his tongue out of the corner of his mouth as he pushed the pen, and all three were smiling at his efforts.

I shook hands with them. "Como te va?" I saluted the Chief and Chipeta and then I exclaimed to the Doctor:

"My God Lacey, we're all afraid to sleep at night up at Ouray, and here you are taking it easy and having fun. Good news?"

"No, worse and worse, but if we let ourselves get excited, my boy, we all break in two. We saw you go in the agency. You're going with Adams? Ouray is going to send an escort with you to see that those White River Utes don't get your hair, and to show you the trail to the camp of Persune, where the women and children are. That's pretty white of Ouray, too. He's just learned from a runner that the soldiers killed his uncle and his nephew while they were out hunting. Ouray says they had nothing to do with the massacre or the attack on the troops."

I did not answer Lacey, but sat down disconsolately near Chipeta. She saw that something had gone wrong with me.

"Que es malo?" she asked.

I told them that General Adams had refused to let me go with him.

Chipeta spoke to Chief Ouray in Ute.

"You want to go?" he asked me.

---

[29] The Utes were actually generally known as superior marksmen.

9 | White River Massacre and Rescue of the Women Captives

"You bet I do," I said.

"Bien," he said, "You go."

He got up and walked out to General Adams, who was still arranging with Agent Stanley about the preparations for the journey. He told the General that he must take me along.

The General looked me over again.

"Can you drive a team?" he asked.

"Of course I can."

"All right, come along and take the wagon. When we leave you can either stay with it or come along with us on the trail, ride one horse and lead the other."

Now, I had never driven a team of horses hitched to a wagon. I had sometimes driven my father's buggy, when he took me with him on Sunday to one of the country churches where he preached. But I had made up my mind that I must be with that rescue party, and I was trusting to luck to see me through.

We gathered in front of the agency at daybreak the next morning and a shiver ran through me when I saw the team I was to drive. Instead of two docile horses, there was one big Missouri mule with a bad eye which he threw to the rear now and then as if on the lookout for some mischief, and a very devil of a black horse that the agency teamster told me had been in harness only once before and that time had kicked himself free of the traces and broken the shafts.

"'But it is the only team we have on the agency fit to make that rough trip, and we've got no time to send up to Ouray for another," he said. "That mule is bad by himself, but the two will hold each other. You know how to harness them up?"

"No, I don't."

He laughed uproariously. "Well, you'll certainly have a hell of a time. But I'll tell you. When you stop at noon for dinner, don't unharness the devils. At night, hobble them front and side and let the Indians find them for you the next morning."

Chief Ouray came up from his house in his carriage with a Mexican driver, to see us off. The fifteen Utes who were to escort and guide us to the camp of the hostile Utes and guard us on the way, gathered around him, and he gave them directions in Ute, in words that sounded like a mastiff growling. They all listened attentively and grunted understandingly.

Shavano, who was to have charge of the Ute escort, stood close to Chief Ouray as he talked. By him was Sapavanero, and the other Utes clustered back of these two. Colorao was among them. He had insisted with Ouray on being sent with the party, I think hoping that he would find some way of thwarting Ouray's plans and getting the whites killed.

General Adams, of course, was in charge of the whole rescue party. The other whites were Count Doenhoff, of the neat mustache and beard, Captain Cline, an old time Colorado scout, who had been with Chivington in his famous massacre of the Cheyenne[30], George Sherman, the clerk of the agency, and myself.

None of the Utes carried rifles and no knives were in sight, but we all knew that they had them in their belts. None of the whites were armed. I asked General Adams, "Are we going to take any weapons?"

"We are not," he answered curtly, "we are on a peace mission." He grasped the bridle and the mane of his horse, mounted with astonishing activity for a man so heavy, and from the saddle threw over his shoulder:

"What good would guns do us if the hostiles want to get ugly?"

All of the party was mounted on tough and sure-footed little Indian ponies.

Lacey came to me just then, with a scribbled message on a bit of paper. It was from the *Denver Tribune*, by telegraph and telephone over the mountains, asking me to wire the paper an account of the matter.

"The whole state is aflame and we want every word you can send. Will pay well for your story."

"Lacey," I said, "Please wire the *Tribune* that I will send them a full account of the thing as soon as we get back."

"Why don't you get offers from some other papers?"

I knew only the *New York Herald* and the *Chicago Tribune*, and I asked Lacey to wire to them and ask how much they would pay for an account of the trip. Then before I climbed into the wagon and took the reins from the waiting teamster, I took Shavano aside and told him of my inexperience with the team and asked him to help me. He nodded, and that was enough for me. I said to the teamster, "I can drive this team if the harness is sound and will hold."

"It will," he assured me. "It's all new and the wagon is new. When you start, give 'em the whip and hold 'em. The whip's new too. You'll strike the foothills in five miles and then the sons of bitches won't be so gay. That wagon is loaded heavy."

We didn't have portable cameras in those days. What a pity. That start would have made a wonderful picture. The Indians raced ahead and were out of sight in a few minutes. General Adams, the scout, Captain Cline, Count Doenhoff, and Sherman, followed at an easy trot, and then I came with my team, biting at each other and kicking. I plied the

---

[30] A combination of Arapahoe and Cheyenne were at Sand Creek under Chief Black Kettle.

9 | White River Massacre and Rescue of the Women Captives

heavy black snake whip on both of their backs, and when they began going too fast, I put on the brakes and made them pull against the brake. That took the turbulence out of them, and they had settled down into a steady trot before we got into the foothills.

We followed a disused wagon road, made by Johnson's army marching into Utah in 1859, grass grown and rocky, but still plain enough to show the old ruts. Our way led through a dense growth of spruce, fir and balsam, with now and then groves of heavier and taller trees, pine and cottonwood. The sun was shining, and fortunately for us, there was only a light snow on the ground this early in the year, the first heavy snow having gone.

At noon, General Adams turned on his horse as he rode ahead of me and threw up his hand. I pulled up the team beside the stream.

"We'll stop an hour here for something to eat," he said.

Captain Cline made a fire and put on a big coffee pot. The Indians apparently dropped out of the sky.

"Tell them to help themselves out of the wagon," ordered the General to Shavano. We have no time to cook."

All of us raided the wagon which was filled with prepared food, done by the agency cooks, and drank scalding hot coffee. In less than an hour we were on our way again, and began to climb to a low wooded plateau, where the road was little more than a trail. Six more hours of that, and then, just as the sun was going down, when we had gone forty miles, we came to the Gunnison River, and General Adams called a halt for the night. There were no tents. Everyone got his blankets out of the wagon, and picked his sleeping place. It had been an exhausting ride of thirteen hours. I undid every buckle I could find on the harness of the horse and the mule, and turned them over to an Indian whom Shavano brought to me. He hobbled them and let them loose. Captain Cline had built a big fire and made coffee, and after we had satisfied our ravenous hunger, we sat about the fire and smoke pipes while General Adams unbosomed himself to all of us. The Indian sat with us and understood a little of the General's talk.

"Ouray tells me that there are only two hundred of those hostile Utes in the camp where they are holding the women," said the General. "They are in command of Douglas, Johnson, Jack and Persune. We ought to get there day after tomorrow. I want to have a council as soon as we reach the camp, and demand that the captives be surrendered to me. Shavano here bears orders from Ouray to Douglas to give them up. If he does not want to do it, I'll threaten him with the troops. The rest will depend on the way Douglas talks. If there are too many young bucks they may want to wipe us all out and go on the warpath for keeps."

"Well," said Captain Cline, taking off his big hat and rubbing his smooth, bald head, "General Adams and I don't offer these devils much temptation, but the rest of you have some pretty good-looking scalps."

Count Doenhoff took off his new, big, Stetson he had bought in Denver and pulled at his blonde hair with a comic expression of terror. I laughed.

"You can't scare us Captain," I said. "Anyway, Ouray told me the other day that the Utes stop taking scalps after their last fight with the Apaches."

"That's so," said the scout, "They don't take scalps now, but some son of a bitch did scalp Major Thornburg in the canyon, though they didn't scalp any of the other soldiers they killed nor the agency people."

The word "scalp" was among frontiersmen a symbol of Indian ferocity. We sat that night talking about scalp taking. Captain Cline knew most about it practically, for he had seen Indians take scalps, expecting his own would be the next, but both General Adams and Count Doenhoff had vicarious information which they had got, General Adams from Indians while he was agent in Los Piños, and the Count from books. I had always believed that the custom was a common one among all the Indians. Up in Ouray we used to say jocularly to a prospectors who was thinking of entering into the forbidden land of the Indian reservation, "Better look out. You'll get your hair lifted."

The conversation was rather ghastly, but still it was a diversion from our anxious minds, a counter irritant. At one point, General Adams called on Chief Shavano to verify something he said, and the chief drew his knife and gave us a demonstration of the best and quickest way to take a scalp. He caught the hair in the center of my head; twisted it around his fingers; pulled it up tightly; ran the knife in a circle about as big as a saucer around the lock and then jerk the hair up. Then he pretended to shake the lock to free it from the dripping blood, and pulled it through his belt.

"The American Indians did not invent scalping," said Count Doenhoff. "Scalps of nemies were regarded as trophies long back, in the days before Christ, among the barbarians. The Scythians took scalps and so did some of the Norsemen."

"The American Indians that the first colonists fought did not take scalps," said General Adams, "But the Indians allied with the whites in the wars of the English and Americans against the French when the country was new, did take them. It's said that the whites paid the Indians bounties for those scalps."

9 | White River Massacre and Rescue of the Women Captives

"Now, who started the custom in this land?"

"Ouray tells me," I said, "that the Indians used to hang scalps on their bridles when they were going into a fight, to terrify the other Indians."

"They do," said the General. "But usually they pulled them through their girdles, like Shavano here, so they can have them to look at and stroke."

"I understand that you were with Colonel Chivington when he attacked the Cheyenne camp and killed all those Indians," said Count Doenhoff to Captain Cline. "Did the "Cheyenne take scalps?"

"They did," answered the scout, "and we found white scalps in some of the teepees after the fight. Chivington was blamed by the Indian lovers for telling his men to kill the squaws and the pappooses [sic] with the bucks, but I think he did right."

"Tell us how that happened, Cline," said the Count.

"Well, that was fifteen years ago, and I was a good deal younger and more of an Indian hater than I am now. The Cheyenne were on the warpath, and had been raiding ranches and killing men, women, and children. The whole country was unsafe. The war was going on back east, and the government wasn't paying much attention to us out here in the wild and woolly West. I've heard it said that our government was treating with the Cheyenne for peace and that we Colorado people ought to have waited for the result of those peace powwows, but that was too much to expect from us when those Cheyenne were raising hell every day and killing people. So Chivington just organized the militia and went after them. There were several bands. We found out where one band was in camp on Sand Creek, and forty of us surrounded the camp one night. Colonel Chivington ordered us to lie on our bellies all night around the camp and told us that at daybreak he would fire a shot and then we must turn loose on the camp and kill everything in sight. I was standing by the Colonel when one of the men asked him, "What about the squaws?"

"Kill them," ordered the Colonel. "Kill the pappooses too. Nits make lice."

"When we heard the Colonel's shot, at daybreak, we began to fire at the Indians and they ran out of the teepees, and in fifteen minutes there wasn't an Indian left alive. I didn't count them, but Chivington did, and he said that there were 115 dead Indians altogether, bucks, squaws and pappooses [sic]. Of course the other bands of Cheyenne fought to a finish after that, and it took the United States troops to whip them. But they were whipped and there's never been a whimper out of them since that time."

"Wasn't Chivington a preacher?" I asked.

"He had been. Anyway, he was deeply religious, and he always carried a little Bible with him. But he really thought these Indians had no souls and you didn't think of them like human beings."

We were all silent for some time, thinking of these dreadful atrocities, massacre and retaliation. Finally, Captain Cline got up from the ground and kicked the logs of the fire together.

"Well, he said, "we may find out pretty soon whether the Utes have gone back to scalping or not. Anyway, I think we all had better turn in if we want to get off early."

Captain Cline woke us all long before daybreak. The Utes brought up my team and after a hastily snatched breakfast of boiled ham, bread and coffee, I tried to harness the animals but found the harness in an inextricable mess. I called to Shavano and he got an Indian, and we all three struggled with the tangled harness.

Everybody was ready to go but me. General Adams came up.

"What the hell's the matter?" he demanded.

"We can't harness them," I answered.

"My God, I thought you said you were a teamster," and he sighed and swore and grunted all at once, as he climbed heavily from his horse.

That man should have been driving eight mules to a freight wagon, instead of wasting himself at a desk in Washington. In five minutes he had the tangled harness buckled and off we went again. It was really funny to me to see how the Utes surrounded my wagon. Warriors and hunters they were, but they liked good eating too, and they had got the idea that their food supply depended on this wagon and that it had to be watched and guarded.

About two o'clock we came to a pretty little stream, Whitewater Creek, and General Adams ordered a halt for dinner and rest.

"I'm going to have Sapavanero send runners ahead of us to the Ute camp, so they will be ready to talk turkey when we get there," he said to me, riding along by my wagon, and I want to give them plenty of time. Don't unharness, but feed the team."

We lay by the fire and slept. As the sun was going down over the spruce trees, General Adams called me.

"Let's start. We'll go to the Grand River and camp for the night, and if we move at daybreak tomorrow, we can make the camp at morning."

The sun went down. The moon came up and gave us light enough. We traveled till near midnight, and then got to the Grand River. The banks there were low and flat, and the river was shallow. Fifty feet from shore there was a little island, with a jungle of fir and cedar growing on it.

9 | White River Massacre and Rescue of the Women Captives

"We'll cache the wagon in those trees," said the General.

I drove into the river, to the island, and then, as far as I could force the team, into the trees and bushes.

There was no conversation that night and we did not even build a fire. We ate very little, getting what we wanted from the wagon, and jostling our Utes as we fumbled in the dark for the prepared food. Then we rolled in our blankets and slept.

A shout from Captain Cline woke me. It was still dark. He had made a fire and had coffee boiling.

"Everybody eat what they want quick and fill their pockets with food," ordered General Adams. "We're going to ride fast now."

We bolted whatever we could lay our hands on, and filled our pockets with food. I didn't notice what the others took; I stuffed my pockets with crackers, ham and tea, which I chewed.

Then we started on the last lap of our journey. I got a saddle out of the wagon, put it on the mule, and led the horse. It was the most fatiguing six hours ride I ever made. The Ute escort took pains to remain in sight as guides. The trail was an Indian trail and seldom-used; it went through thick evergreen forests and along the edge of streams and precipices, and recent light snows had made it very slippery. The horse I was leading became nervous and balky and the effort to manage him made every muscle of my body ache.

Shavano suddenly appeared by my side, on his wiry little pony.

"Kill him," he suggested, pointing at the balky horse and drawing a huge knife from his belt.

"No," I answered, "we'll need him later."

The trail had been rising from the start, and now ran along the Grand River cliffs. On one side the cliffs dropped 400 feet to the Grand River rushing along with the roar. The trail was only three feet wide. On our other side the cliffs rose towering above us.

Count Doenhoff rode ahead of me, and he had just rounded a turn in the trail when I heard him call, "Saunders, help, quick."

I kicked my mule and got around. The horse of Count Doenhoff was standing, sweating with terror, on the very edge of the trail, not an inch between him and the fall to the river. The saddle had slipped and turned to that side, and the Count had thrown himself to the other side, as he felt the saddle going. He was clutching a projecting bit of the cliff, the only thing holding him from the fall to the river. It was still dark, but the streaks of the coming daylight in the east were just enough to let me see his dangerous situation.

I got down and crawled under his horse, and stooping, righted his saddle and cinched it tightly. The count slid back into the saddle and Drew a long breath.

"My God," he exclaimed, "what a narrow escape, and what a country. Adams told me this would be a little pleasure trip."

"Wait till we get to the Ute camp," I said, "and don't lose your nerve. We may catch hell there."

About ten o'clock, the cliffs left far behind, we suddenly rode out of a thick forest into a beautiful glade, where eleven teepees had been set up, scattered over the place. A canyon cut one side of this meadow. Not an Indian was in sight and there were no dogs, a sure sign that a war party occupied the teepees. Smoke was coming from only one teepee, that a very large one, plainly used for councils.[31]

As I rode slowly behind the rest of the party, a girl appeared at the slit in one of the first teepees. A white girl of about twenty-five, slim and black-haired, with big brown eyes and a straight nose. She wore an Indian blanket and moccasins.

I stopped as she saw me, and suddenly ran to me and clung to my saddle. Then I saw her shocking state, that miserable, filthy, state of the despised captive. Under the covering blanket her clothes were in rags, but her eyes were bright now with a feverish excitement.

"Oh, have you come to save us?" she cried, "I'm Josephine Meeker."

"Have they hurt you?"

"You ought to know what those Utes will do. They threatened to torture me. They've nearly killed me."

"Where are the rest?"

"They've hid them somewhere, but they're here."

"We'll be back to get you presently. Do you want anything?"

"Only some tea, but I suppose you haven't any of that."

What luck, that I should have filled my pockets with tea that morning. I emptied them into her hands and then rode on to the big tent, where I saw all of our party, including the Utes, except Shavano.

"Where is Shavano?" I asked, as I approached.

"In there, with the head devils," answered Captain Cline, "laying down the law to them."

"What are we supposed to do?"

"Damned if I know. Just sit till they tell us. They're waiting for Chief Johnson, and he'll be here soon." He was at his camp, nearer the troops.

---

[31] As best as the editors can determine, the Ute site was about where the town of De Beque is presently located.

9 | White River Massacre and Rescue of the Women Captives

We were all weak from hunger. We took the saddles off the horses and let them graze on the thick grass around the camp, and we lay down. I fell into a sort of stupor, but I was aroused in half an hour by the scout, who pinched me and muttered, "Here comes Johnson."

I sat up. Coming out of the woods surrounding the camp, were five Utes. Riding in front were Chief Johnson, wearing a war bonnet, his face painted, and a resolute looking young Ute woman, who took in the whole scene with one flashing glance. Three Indians rode behind.

"Who's the woman?" I asked.

"That's Shawsheen, Johnson's squaw and Ouray's sister. We call her Susan," said the scout. "She's one of the Ute bosses, too, and mostly what she says goes. A white man saved her life once, when she was a child and got lost off the reservation, in a canyon. I don't know, but they say she's a friend of the whites."

Those Utes dismounted, and with not a sign to us, went into the council tent. Loud voices were coming from it, in Ute speech. Silence followed the entrance of Chief Johnson and Shawsheen, and then there was low talk.

Presently Shavano came out and beckoned to us. We stooped in and found the tent filled with Utes, some standing and some squatting on the ground. All of them wore war paint streaking their faces, and Chiefs Douglas, Jack, and Persune, as well as Chief Johnson, had on war bonnets, besides the feathered back piece reaching to their knees. A space had

Shawsheen (Susan) was Chief Ouray's sister and lived with her husband Johnson at the Meeker Agency. She was very instrumental in keeping the white women alive, but they still suffered indignities.

P. David Smith Collection

been cleared for us to sit on the ground and we took it, but General Adams at first stood.

Then followed a four hour conference. General Adams spoke in English; Captain Cline interpreted into Spanish; and Shavano translated the Spanish into Ute. Then the reply had to come back through this tedious channel of translation. We were all faint with hunger. Outside there was an enormous pot where a venison stew simmered, and the smell of that stew aggravated the keenness of our craving for food.

Once I whispered to Captain Cline, "What are they saying?"

"Persune, Douglas and Jack want to kill us all, with the captives, and escape with the White River Utes and join the Apaches down in New Mexico. They've heard some big stories about the way the Apaches are cleaning up the whites down there."

"Well, if they'll only give us something to eat, they can scalp us and welcome."

The question was still in doubt. Our fate, and much besides, hung in the balance, when Shawsheen rose to her feet. She walked slowly around the circle of Utes, looking at each one narrowly, and then she stopped and spoke, with wide and passionate gestures.

"You know that Ouray wants you to let these women go. He is not here, but I am the sister of Ouray and I am here, and I tell you to let these women go."

And then she pointed her hand at Douglas.

"You, Quignant," she denounced him using his Ute name, "Try to persuade us to keep the women, and kill these white men. You say it is for the sake of the Utes. It is not. You want the women for yourself. Did I not take the young squaw from you and give her to Persune because you were beating her. Now you want this other woman for yourself, not for the Utes."

Chief Johnson was the conservative of the hostiles. He was older than the other two and besides he had fought with Shavano and Sapavanero and respected the good sense of those scarred old warriors. He arose from the ground while Shawsheen was still speaking, and when she had finished he pushed her back and said shortly, "We will let the women go with the white men."

Quignant yielded. First, he spoke, defending himself against the charge of Shawsheen that he was merely lustful and not considering the Utes. Finally he said, "We will let you take the women and children if Adams will go to the soldiers and tell them not to attack us here. We do not want to fight any more. All of us, with the white men, will wait here till he comes back. The soldiers are here —"

9 | White River Massacre and Rescue of the Women Captives

And kneeling down, with the feathers of his war bonnet falling over his face, "Quignant," as Shawsheen had called him, drew in the earth floor of the teepee a diagram of the White River country, showing that the cavalry men were about sixty miles away.

"I'll promise you to stop the soldiers if you will give us the captives right now," replied General Adams. "Captain Cline will take the women and children to the Los Piños agency, while you and I will go to the soldiers."

"I will not go with you, but I will agree to that," said Chief Douglas, "and now you go outside and eat, and I will talk to my warriors."

All of our party, including our friendly Utes, left the tent, and going outside fell upon the venison stew, eating with our fingers, and wiping them on the grass. While I was eating I looked around the Ute camp. Near the big tent, two forked poles had been driven into the ground; a cross pole laid on them; and on the cross pole was some of the spoil of the fight with the cavalry men. There were seven saddles, army blankets, and overcoats, and bridles. Horses and mules with the U.S. brand were grazing about the camp.

After eating, General Adams and Captain Cline went back to the tent, where Chief Douglas was haranguing his men, and there was another long counsel. This time Chief Shavano, who was sitting by me on the ground, refused to go in when General Adams beckoned him.

"Too much talk," he said sententiously, and went on eating.

It was a long time before Chief Douglas finally got the consent of his Utes to surrender the women. "Kill the white men and keep the women" was the temper of the hot-blooded young bucks. But finally Douglas came out of the tent, and calling two of his men gave them orders.

General Adams joined us in high good humor, as we still sat around the pot of venison stew. He was unused to the saddle, and the trip had told on him. Usually rubicund, the responsibility and the anxiety of the mission had paled his face and worn deep lines in it, and he had ridden on the trail grimly, but the result of the conference had restored his cheerfulness.

"Saunders," he called to me, "don't you want to send some telegrams to your papers? I'm going to wire Washington, and a runner will start over the mountains with my dispatches as soon as I can write them."

I set a saddle across my knees and wrote to Lacey at the agency, through which the runner would pass, asking him to hold the runner till he could write telegrams to the *Denver Tribune* and to the *New York Herald*, saying that we had the captives and were bringing them back to safety. So those two papers were the first to print the news of the rescue.

By the time we had finished our dispatches and the runner had started with them, the Utes sent by Chief Douglas appeared, climbing out of the canyon, leading Mrs. Meeker, Mrs. Price, and the two children of Mrs. Price.

Mrs. Meeker was nearly seventy years old, and showed the strain of the hardships she had undergone since the massacre at the White River agency.

"I thank God! You men have been sent by God," she said as she saw us. "I have prayed every minute for deliverance from this awful thing."

Mrs. Price was a comely woman of thirty years, but now haggard and demoralized like Josephine Meeker. She was followed by a squaw carrying the little fatherless Price baby in a blanket, and coaxing the other child by the hand.

"I hope you are going to punish these fiends," said Mrs. Price.

Josephine with Mrs. Price and her children after their rescue.
Harpers Monthly, "The Ute Massacre." P. David Smith Collection.

9 | White River Massacre and Rescue of the Women Captives

"That must come later, Madam," answered General Adams. "We are not safe yet."

"Safe! I should say not," said Captain Cline, "General, all our Ute guides have disappeared, and Douglas says he wants us to stay here till he finds them."

"Can you find the way back to the wagon on the Grand? All our blankets are there, and the rest of the food."

"No, I can't," answered Captain Cline.

"Well, those Indians are around. We'll put up a bluff and tell them you don't need them. And besides, I'm going to threaten them with the wrath of Chief Ouray if they don't turn up before we start."

It was midnight then, but the moon was up, and we were all so excited that no one was sleepy.

I touched Shavano on the arm, and he got up and came with me to the teepee where I had seen Josephine Meeker. She was alone. Her captor, Persune, was in the council tent still.

"Come along with us," I said. We're going to take you all away. Bring everything you have."

"I have nothing, except what I have on," she answered, and came with us. I sat down with Josephine and Mrs. Price and got the story of the fight with the troops and the tragedy at the agency for the first time. Poor Mrs. Meeker sat a little apart from us. Somehow, she had saved from the fire at the agency, a huge *Pilgrim's Progress* with brass clasps such as the old-fashioned family Bibles have, and she rocked this in her lap, as she hummed snatches of hymns.

"She has lost her mind," said Mrs. Price, "She saw Father Meeker, with his head mashed in, and just went crazy."

None of us slept much that night, but when we arose at daybreak the next morning we found that the squaws had heated the remnants of the venison stew and we made a hearty breakfast on that. Captain Cline came up to me with a twitch of his face which he meant for a smile.

"Our bluff worked." he said. "Our guides are on the job. Savano and Sapavanero are going with General Adams to meet the advancing troops and we will start for Los Piños as soon as we can get saddled up."

We had horses for each of the women, and Mrs. Price and Captain Cline were to carry the children. It was so dark that we had to light matches to pick out our saddles and bridles from the pile where they had been thrown the day before.

When the horses had all been saddled, and those who were to ride them were standing by them waiting for Captain Cline to order the start, Shawsheen suddenly appeared from one of the teepees and came to us, followed by Persune. Shawsheen went straight to feeble Mrs. Meeker and stroked her face with pity, and then examined carefully the saddle of the horse she was to ride. It was split in places and there was one break on the side that certainly would have chafed the leg of the rider.

Shawsheen threw up the flap of the saddle; uncinched it; flung it to the ground; and gave an order to Persune. He went off and got another saddle from a pile of accoutrements that had been taken from the soldiers. He brought it back to Shawsheen who put it on Mrs. Meeker's horse and with great care cinched it. Then she patted Mrs. Meeker's cheek, and taking her in her strong arms lifted her to the saddle and placed the bridal in her hand.

While Persune was gone after the saddle, Mrs. Meeker beseeched me to take the gigantic *Pilgrim's Progress* she had been fondling. "It is the only thing I have saved," she said. "Please carry it for me."

I lifted it from her hands and carried it on my saddle all the way back. It weighed about thirty pounds, and certainly was a strain on my muscles. More than once, as we rode along that trail, above the Grand River, the evil temptation came to me to drop the burden into the torrent below, but of course I didn't.

Arvilla Meeker was with the women at the Meeker Agency and also suffered many indignities. Being elderly, she suffered severe psychological trauma from which she never fully recovered.

P. David Smith Collection.

That feeble old woman had clung to that heavy book for secure refuge when she was carried on horseback from the agency to this mountain fastness of the Utes, and had persuaded her captors to let her keep it when they wanted to throw it away. Certainly it ought to be kept in the Meeker family as an heirloom and I assume that it was.

We got to the wagon on the Grand River that

9 | White River Massacre and Rescue of the Women Captives

night. It was a cruel ride for the women, but we wanted to secure the blankets and the food, and indeed that was necessary, for we found the Utes of our escort rifling the wagon of the canned goods when we came inside. We spread our beds all around the wagon to guard it, and after we had had supper, Captain Cline, who was now in charge of the party, spoke very frankly:

"I want to tell you the truth. We are still in danger. Those Utes may change their minds, now that they've got General Adams out of the way, and they may come after us. I shan't feel easy till we are in Ouray's house. Now you women must stand some hard riding. It'll take us a day and a half to get there."

"We will stand anything to get away from these Indians," answered Mrs. Price.

So we rode the next day as fast as we could, stopping for an hour at noon and again at sundown for a little supper, and camp at ten o'clock, beyond the Gunnison, leaving only twenty miles to go the following day.

Breakfast, the morning of the third day, was a mere gesture, because there was little food left, but we had coffee and tea and flour, with which Josephine Meeker made pancakes. We reached the house of Chief Ouray about noon, and informed by runners who had gone before us, the chief, with Chipeta and several Mexican farmhands, were waiting outside for us.

When we stopped in front of the house, Chipeta, followed by the Mexicans, came to the horses. The Mexicans lifted down the women and the children. Chipeta patted the shoulders of Mrs. Meeker and Mrs. Price; then went to Josephine Meeker, threw her arms around her, drew her close, look into her eyes, and began crying. She knew all this poor girl had gone through. And then Josephine, who up to this time had shown no sign of emotion, began weeping, with great sobs that racked her and sent chills through me. Chipeta shielded Josephine from the eyes of the others with her arms and guided her into the house.

I waved my whip to the party and drove on the ten miles to the agency.

As I sent the team along at a fast trot with the empty wagon, I remembered that it was Saturday and that up in Ouray, my paper, the *Times* would be put to press that evening. I wondered if they had got any news of the rescue in the town, and I made up my mind to get there in time to get an account of the affair in the *Times* if I had to kill a horse.

As I drove on, I reviewed the incidents of the trip and composed the story I would write, and the only really funny thing that occurred on the way I forgot to write.

We harnessed up the mule and a horse again to the wagon on the island in the Grand River—and, by the way, those two animals had got such a dose of hard traveling that they were as docile as sheep—the ugly and ferocious Chief Colorao came up to me and asked if he might ride with me and let one of the other youths lead his horse. Colorao had failed in his effort to defeat the plan of Chief Ouray to secure the release of the captives and was greatly chagrined, fearing that he would lose his status among his warlike followers. Indeed, a few years afterward, he incited and led another revolt among the Utes.

However, just now he was very humble, as he made his request to me. I told him he might ride with me, and he sat by my side on the high seat.

As the team struggled up a hard hill, I put the long black snake whip to them, and as I whirled it around my head, the lash curled around the big hat Colorao wore, and snapped it off his head and onto the ground, among the bushes. I stopped the team, and laughed, boy like, at the murderous look he gave me. He looked for a Ute whom he might order to get his hat, but there were none inside, and then he looked at me, but I shook my head. I had to hold my team.

He was very heavy, and sore from riding horseback, and he groaned as he climbed down from the wagon and retrieved his hat.

When he had mounted to my side again, I put my hand on his shoulder and said,

"Sorry, old fellow, I didn't mean to do it," and although he did not understand, my tone and look mollified him and he smiled.

I was more careful with my whip after that, but upon my word, I did exactly the same thing the next day!

There were Utes around the wagon this time, since it was getting along for dinner time, and when Colorao looked around he saw some of them grinning. If you have heard that Indians do not laugh, just take my word for it—they do. Not a Ute volunteer to rescue the hat, and the savage old Chief had to dismount again and get it himself.

This time, when he got back on the seat, he did not look at me. He kept his hat between his knees and brooded darkly all the rest of the way.

I got a hasty lunch at the Los Piños agency, giving a story of the trip to Dr. Lacey and Agent Stanley, who sat by me as I ate, and in half an hour I was in the saddle again and loping to Ouray. It was cold weather and the horse was a good one. I made the twenty-five miles in three hours; left the horse at a stable and ran to the *Times* office. The last side of the paper was being run off by the two Ripley brothers. They stopped working and I told them the story in a few words.

9 | White River Massacre and Rescue of the Women Captives

"Henry," said William Ripley, "we've got to get that in the paper. We'll scoop everything in the state."

They took the paper off the press and, since we did not have enough type to set up my article, those two men distributed into the type boxes the whole first page, while I sat and wrote steadily. We went to a short supper, and I stopped to talk to nobody. We came back and the two Ripleys then set up my story and got the paper to press again. It was midnight when I took the wrapped edition of the *Times*, 350 copies, in my arms, and waked up the postmaster. When I told him what we had in the paper he was glad to go to the post office with me and put the papers in the mail bags for the buckboard which left Ouray with the mail early in the morning.

At Los Piños agency, Doctor Lacey had given me two telegraphs and I read them as I sat in the post office. One was from the *Chicago Tribune*, naming the price the paper would pay for an account of the rescue by wire to be followed by a longer one by letter. The other was this:

> "Send full particulars and then come to New York." —
> James Gordon Bennett.

I did not know who James Gordon Bennett was, and since he named no price and the *Chicago Tribune* did, I decided to ignore his telegram and to accept the Chicago offer. I was very tired. The riding and the nerve-wracking strain for more than a week had exhausted me, and I had not even had time to boil my clothes, which were full of lice. Coming back from the Ute camp, we had done up all the blankets together each morning, after sleeping in our clothes, and the lice that came from the clothes of the women and the children had got into ours. The poor captives were, of course, unspeakably unclean, after the days and the nights of intimate association with the dirty war party of Indians.

I went from the post office to the livery stable and slept in a chair there until six o'clock the next morning, when I got a hasty breakfast at the hotel before anybody was up except the cook and the sleepy night clerk, and started over the trail to ride the thirty miles to Lake City, the nearest telegraph office. I stopped to talk to no one in Ouray, except livery the man, and to him I said, as I mounted:

> "We got all the Meeker women and the children and they're down at Ouray's house. I don't know whether the Utes are going to stop fighting or not. You fellows had better lookout. I'll be back tomorrow."

Thirty miles over a rough mountain trail is a hard ride at the best. I had a good horse and I drove him. I didn't stop to eat, and as I rode I composed the story I was going to write for the *Chicago* and the *Denver Tribune*. I knew that the world had only the barest word that the women had been rescued, and that the details would be read with avidity. I felt elated as I thought that I would be the first bearer of the news. As I reached the top of the mountain, up above timberline and even above the quaking aspen, there was a bare place and the ashes of a fire, where some man, disgusted with the loneliness of the country or possibly frightened by the Ute outbreak, had stopped for a midday camp on his way out to civilization. He had taken the time to put up a sign, made out of the side of a wooden box, and had scrawled on it with a big, black, carpenter's pencil:

"*This way to Lake City and the United States.*"

The sign to me was pregnant with the disillusionment of the man who had put it up. I have often wished that I could meet him and learn what had happened to him. Here I was, just beginning to love this wild San Juan country, as it was called by the natives, and he was going out, hating it.

I got to Lake City in the afternoon; put my horse in a livery stable, and left him eating while I went to a little restaurant and ate my dinner. Then I went straight to the telegraph office; told the operator who I was, and persuaded him to let me come inside and to give me a table to write on. I first wrote my telegrams to the *Chicago Tribune* and to the *Denver Tribune*, duplicated, and handed the sheets, as I finished each one, to the operator.

After I had finished the telegrams, I began, without resting, to write my letter to the *Chicago Tribune*. When I closed that, it was nine o'clock at night. I took the letter to the post office myself and then walked to the hotel.

I did not even reply to the somewhat peremptory telegram from James Gordon Bennett, of the *New York Herald*. I have often since then, laughed at my ignorance. I got all together from the *Chicago Tribune* for my letter and telegram twenty-four dollars and six dollars from the *Denver Tribune*, and neither paper paid my expenses for the trip to Lake City. When I counted up, I found that I had made no money on the adventure. Had I accepted the offer of Bennett; sent him an account of the rescue and then gone on to New York I would have had another story to tell.

In the office of the hotel I found waiting for me, my friend, the owner, who had so cordially helped me to get to Ouray, when I had

9 | White River Massacre and Rescue of the Women Captives

come to Lake City, months before, broke and hungry. He held out his hand and slapped me on the back.

"The dining room's full of people who want to hear the news," he said, "come in and eat your supper and tell us all about it. We won't let you alone till you get through your work."

I had never in my life seen such a gathering as there was in this hotel dining room. The place was full of men, mostly miners and workmen in the smelter, everyone armed with rifles and pistols. Some in the room were militiamen, of the company that had been organized in Lake City when Governor Pitkin first wired to the town that the Utes were on the warpath. There were a few women. Not one in the room was smiling or even at ease. Every face there was set into an expression of restrained anger. I was afterward to feel that atmosphere of quiet fury when I was in a gathering of men who were, under strong provocation, planning a lynching.

The hotel owner was the chairman of the meeting. He hammered on a table with a glass, introduced me, and then said, "Go ahead now, Saunders. Eat, drink and talk."

I did all of these things. The people of Lake City were in communication with the outside world by telegraph, and they knew more about the fight of the soldiers and the Utes than I did, but they had heard little of the massacre of the whites at the White River agency and nothing at all of the treatment of the women by the Utes. So I told them these things, between mouthfuls. I was often interrupted by questions and by loud threats against the Utes, and now and then a woman sobbed as I told of the way in which the Utes had maltreated the captives.

We sat beyond midnight, and I left the meeting and went to bed, unable to hold my head up longer.

The next morning, while I was having breakfast, the hotel keeper came and sat by me.

"You folks at Ouray are nearer the Utes than we are," he said, "and you have more reason to be on your toes. But the ranchmen all around the reservation and the miners up in the hills are scared and are coming into the towns with their families, and that's going to last till we get rid of those Utes."

Then he added savagely, slapping a big hand down on the table and making the dishes jump. "If the government would let us get at 'em, we'd clean them up in a month and make good Indians of every one of them, like Chivington did with the Cheyenne. And I'm not so sure that Chivington wasn't right when he told his men to kill the squaws and the children that time when he surrounded the Cheyenne camp on Sand Creek and laid the whole outfit out cold."

I asked the hotelkeeper what news he had from Denver about the feeling in Colorado on the trouble.

"The whole country is boiling mad," he replied, "the soldiers want to get at the Utes and the government won't let them, and is holding 'em. The settlers want to go after the Utes but neither the government nor the military want that. You know how the military feel toward the civilians. They think we can't fight Indians, and we know they can't. Would you ever have seen a lot of frontier Indian fighters march into a canyon the way Thornburgh took his men? That was just plain suicide."

"General Adams left us after we got the captives and started over the mountains to stop the troops from advancing," I said, "Do you know if he did it?"

"No, I don't. We get all sorts of rumors about fights between the soldiers and the Utes and we know that there are several parties of troops on the reservation, but we don't know what they are doing and I don't believe the war department in Washington does either."

And that was quite true. There was many a little fight between the Utes and the soldiers in the mountains on the reservation that was not thought worthy of a report to the war department in Washington, and both Utes and soldiers were killed in these skirmishes.

When I got back to Ouray, I found the feeling among the townspeople, who had by this time learned from the account I had written all about the massacre at the White River agency and the maltreatment of the captives, one of deep resentment against the government because orders had not been given to the military to exterminate the Utes and because the settlers were forbidden to go into the reservation and attack them.

The feeling of the people in Ouray was a feeling of the citizens of the whole state.

Action was demanded, not the peace desired by Washington.

CHAPTER 10

The Knife Vote for Peace or War

General Hatch demands that the Utes give up the ringleaders in the agency murders and promises pardon for the Indians who fought the troops... the knife-flung vote for peace or war... Ouray outwits the government agents... Governor Pitkin's unfair testimony... Ouray's death... Chipeta becomes Chief of the Utes and sends me a gift... the aura of Josephine Meeker — a psychic experience.

THE COLORADO WINTER CAME ON, with its severe weather, its heavy snows, and its blizzards, and the cold did more than all the threats and persuasions of Chief Ouray. The Utes went into winter quarters in the canyons and the woods of the reservation, the troops were withdrawn from the reservation and sent back to the Colorado and New Mexico forts, and to fighting the Apaches down in New Mexico.

But the cry of the Colorado people did not cease for the removal of the Utes from the state, and the demand of Governor Pitkin was insistent that the leaders of the Meeker massacre should be punished.

At last, in December of 1879, General Edward Hatch[32] was ordered to come to Los Piños agency and make a formal investigation of the tragedy. He was authorized to tell Chief Ouray that the leaders in the attack on the agency should be given up to the government or there would be reprisals.

Chief Ouray replied that he would summon all the Ute witnesses General Hatch wanted and let him examine them.

General Hatch came to the agency with General Adams, representing the Interior Department, and just fifteen soldiers of the 15th Infantry. He was a man of the most remarkable courage. He had served in the Civil War with General Sherman, and he was carrying on the Apache campaign in New Mexico with great success. The secret of that success, he told me, was that he kept scouting parties of cavalry men out day and

---

[32] Edward Hatch served as a brigadier general and then a brevet major general under Ulysses S. Grant during the Civil War. After the War, he became involved in Indian campaigns in the west. He died at Ft. Robinson, Nebraska in 1889.

night, all over southern New Mexico, on the plains between Roswell, Deming, Fort Cummings, and Silver City, and the Apaches never felt that they were safe in planning a raid on the settlers' ranches.

General Hatch looked around the agency and chose a newly-built and unoccupied log stable for the sessions of the military commission. It was a large building. At one end was a long table and chairs, and that was all the furniture. At the table set the two generals, and the interpreter, John Townsend, who had come up from Santa Fe with the General, also Lieutenant Valois and Lieutenant Gildersleeve, of the Ninth Cavalry. The fifteen soldiers were camped outside, near the stable.

General Edward Hatch was commander of all the federal troops in the military District of New Mexico which included some of the Ute homeland territory in today's Colorado.
Photo Courtesy of Wikipedia

Beginning with the first morning of the session of the Commission, the thirteenth of November 1879, the Utes rode into the agency grounds on their ponies and lounged around all day. There were never fewer than 500, and sometimes there were more. Most of them were as well armed as the soldiers. They had Winchester rifles and Colt revolvers, with knives that were hidden under their blankets.

General Hatch had asked Chief Ouray to bring to the Los Piños agency fifteen of the White River Utes, whom he named. He wanted to see what they knew about the massacre in the fight with the soldiers. These Utes came, accompanied, naturally, by a good many other White River Utes. The White River Utes were usually supplied with food at the White River agency, but since it was burned, they had now no source of supplies, and when they came into the Los Piños agency, some of them at the request of General Hatch and of Chief Ouray, they had reason to believe that they would receive food, as the Uncompahgre Utes did, from Los Piños.

10 | The Knife Vote for Peace or War

The first day of the Commission sessions, the agent at Los Piños fed all the Utes, and then so many came that he became fearful that his supplies would not be enough and so he telegraphed to the Secretary of the Interior, Carl Schurz, asking if he should feed the White River Utes who had come in to the agency.

Now, Carl Schurz was a very wise man in some respects, but his answer to Agent Stanley showed his absolute lack of understanding of the Indians and his ignorance of the dangerous situation.

"Give the White River Utes nothing to eat," was his telegram, in substance, "They stole hundreds of cattle from the White River agency. Let them eat those."

Agent Stanley showed us that wire from Secretary Schurz and we were amazed at the Secretary's pettiness, and his folly. No matter what these Utes had done, they were hungry and bad-tempered and must be fed. And they were fed, too. We all advised agent Stanley to do it. How the books of the agency were manipulated to cover that we never knew or inquired.

Chief Ouray sometimes sat at the commission table with General Hatch and sometimes he sat on the floor, with the other sub-chiefs and more influential Utes. The Indians on the floor made a semicircle, surrounding the table.

In the semicircle of Utes were not only our friends, Shavano and Sapavanero, but Colorao, the wicked old rascal who had ridden with me in the backboard, Johnson, who we knew had killed Colonel Thornburg, Douglas, Persune, and Jack.

General Hatch would choose one of these and begin to question him about the attack on the agency. He spoke in English. The interpreter, Townsend, would translate into Spanish, and Ouray would put that into Ute. Then came back the answer in this roundabout way, just as we had talked with the Utes when we rescued the women.

Chief Ouray insisted that the Ute witnesses, as they were put on the stand, should be allowed to take the Ute oath, and General Hatch consented. So each Indian, as Ouray called out his name and he got up from the floor and came forward to the table at which the members of the commission sat, held up his hand, looked up, and chanted:

> "There is One Great Spirit governing the Heaven and the earth. He looks down upon me and sees upon earth as well as in Heaven. Therefore I can speak nothing but the truth."

And then, after taking this solemn oath, every Ute put on the stand perjured himself calmly, just as the white man does in our courts. To believe those Utes we should have been obliged to think that they knew nothing whatever about the attack on the soldiers in the canyon or the massacre at the White River agency.

Officially I was barred from the sessions of the commission, but both General Hatch and General Adams, as well as Chief Ouray and the rest of the Utes knew that I was standing at the open door of the stable, listening.

I was astonished at the patience of General Hatch, a soldier of action, but I knew that he was getting telegrams everyday telling him about the Apache campaign in New Mexico, which he was directing, and that he was satisfied with the way things were going down there, so his mind was not disturbed. During all the long sessions he never relaxed his vigilance, but paid close attention to every word that came from the Indians.

Sometimes a session lasted only an hour; sometimes the court did not open until the afternoon. General Hatch and General Adams were always ready, but the sessions had to depend on the presence of the Utes, who were indifferent and insolent in their treatment of the tribunal. We believed that Colorao was instigating rebellion.

This went on for twenty-seven days.

On this twenty-seventh day, Thursday, December 7th, the snow lay thick on the level ground around the agency, but the sun shone; there was no wind and the cold was endurable. The Utes poured into the agency, more than 500 of them. Many of them were armed with the usual rifle; some of them seem to be unarmed, but of course we knew that they had knives under their blankets. They filled the agency office and the store, and lounged about the grounds. The room of the Commission was filled with them, sitting on the floor and standing. I stood at the open door and watched. The fifteen soldiers whom General Hatch had brought with him were scattered about the agency.

General Hatch rose and read to Ouray a list of the Utes whom the government wanted delivered to it by the tribe. This list included Douglas, Johnson, Persune, and nine others.

"Why do you think that these Indians were the ringleaders?" asked Chief Ouray.

"We have got the names from people who saw them with guns at the agency."

"You have got them from the women, and the women gave you the names of every Ute they could think of, without knowing whether or not they were leaders," said Ouray shrewdly.

"We are perfectly satisfied to accept the evidence of the women," said General Hatch sternly. "If we accept the word of the Utes, we must believe that not one of the tribe was present at the agency massacre."

General Adams stood up. "The Interior Department has been your friend," he said to Chief Ouray, "and we have wanted you to save the innocent Utes from punishment by giving up the guilty. Now your future treatment, good or bad, rests with you."

And then General Adams washed his hands of the whole business by walking out of the room.

The Utes were troubled by his words and by his leaving. Sapavanero pulled out a long pipe and passed it to Colorao who filled it, lit it, took a few puffs, and passed it along. Each Ute drew his knife and laid it on the floor in front of him.

That meant the vote for war or peace. Chief Ouray sat at the table, watching — there was dead silence for five minutes, and then General Hatch rose to his feet and shouted, as if in a cavalry charge, pointing his finger directly at Colorao.

"Tell those Utes, Townsend, that I am tired of all this nonsense, and I will stand no more of it. Will you or will you not give up the men whose names are on this paper. I came here to help you and what have you done? You have come here day after day with lies. Now what will you do? I want no more lies. Washington holds no anger against the Utes who fought the soldiers, and does not intend to punish them. That was a fair fight. We want only the Indians who killed Meeker and the agency people and who maltreated the women."

Townsend translated faithfully the forcible words.

For an instant there was no answer. Then Colorao, rising to his feet, threw his knife into the floor between him and General Hatch so that it stuck there and quivered. The other Utes took their knives from the floor and place them on their knees.

"My God!" said a soldier who was looking over my shoulder at the door, "we're in for it."

And he left for his tent on a run to warn the other soldiers.

But no knife joined the knife of Colorao. It quivered and was still, and solitary. And suddenly Ouray spoke, quickly, almost carelessly, just a few words to the Utes, and two of them left the room, and mounting their horses, rode away.

"I am willing," then said Chief Ouray, with an air at once arrogant and resolved, "to give up these men to the government on condition that they are tried in Washington and not in Colorado or in New Mexico. If you will agree to that I will send for them, and give them to you."

"How long will it take?" asked General Hatch.

"Five days."

"You have our word that they will be tried in Washington."

Then Chief Ouray spoke to General Hatch and General Adams, bitterly.

"You are our enemies and we can expect no justice from you. Adams is a Colorado man and the Colorado people are all our enemies. You — pointing to General Hatch and Townsend, "are New Mexico men and are also our enemies. "You — pointing to Lieutenant Valois, "are a diabolo Francois[33], and hate us all. I want none of your states to try my people."

Lacey and I rode down to Chief Ouray's house that night and had a long talk with him. We did not tell either General Hatch or General Adams that we were going. They would have forbidden us. Neither one would have understood our intimate relations with Ouray. Said the Chief to us—and of course I'm remembering only the sense of his confidences, expressed partly in English and partly in Spanish:

> "The Utes are not to blame in this. I told you when we were out hunting that I was having trouble in restraining my young men. White prospectors and hunters came on the reservation and shot the Utes when they saw them. You know yourselves that this happened. My uncle and my nephew were killed by the soldiers a few days ago, while they were hunting. The soldiers said that they had no right to have rifles. They have when they hunt.
>
> "Meeker made the Utes work for his own glory and refuse to feed them when they did not work as he wanted them to work. He had no right to do that. The government in our treaty said nothing about work, but agreed to give us these lands and to give us supplies, blankets and food. They have violated that treaty and my men were angry. They heard that Meeker had sent for the soldiers to punish them for not working and coming to church, they always remember what Chivington did to the Cheyenne, and they tried to prevent the soldiers from getting to the agency by killing them. Then they went crazy and killed Meeker and the other white men, and took the women and children. They should not have done that."

"Will you give General Hatch the men he wants?" asked Lacey.

"They think they will be shot or hanged if they go to Washington. I will try. I don't know."

---

[33] This translates as "French devil."

10 | The Knife Vote for Peace or War

I had never seen Ouray so moved. He was sitting when he began to talk, but as he spoke he got up and strode about and went to a chair which supported several rifles, which he took up and handled. Once, as he spoke of the shooting of his kinsfolk by the soldiers, he drew a knife from his girdle and gestured with it. Chipeta, who was in the kitchen giving the Mexicans some directions, came in and sat down listening, but said nothing.

"These women," went on the Chief, "have told Hatch and Adams tales about the way they were treated by the Utes. I do not believe them. Most of these Utes had their own squaws with them in camp and it would have been impossible for such things to have happened as that girl says."

Chipeta looked at us, shook her head, in disagreement with the Chief.

"Persune, Douglas, Jack, very bad Utes," she said.

Dr. Lacey and I sympathized with Ouray in much that he said, but we were young and rooted in the conquering race. We felt that his racial feeling was carrying him too far into defending the Indians, as was natural. Especially we knew that the women had been outraged. On the ride back from the camp of the hostiles, all the women had told me this. Their privations had broken down their reserve and they had no motive for concealment.

But we told no one of Ouray's confidences and we rode back to the agency that night in silence.

I was curious to know if Ouray's angry speech had any effect on General Hatch, and asked him about it the next day.

"Oh, no," he said, "The Chief was entitled to that outburst and I felt sorry for him. He will get those Utes if his authority is strong enough."

A few days later, General Hatch went back to New Mexico, to resume his direction of the campaign against the Apaches who were on the warpath down there. I went in his military ambulance as far as Alamosa, the nearest railway station, and with us went General Adams, Chief Ouray and Chipeta, Sapavanero, Shavano, Jack and seven other Utes who rode in wagons and buckboards, escorted by the cavalrymen and the infantrymen who had been on guard at the agency. I accompanied the party to Denver and there parted company with them, going to a desk in the city room of the *Denver Tribune*.

General Adams took the Utes to Washington, where a Senate Committee questioned Chief Ouray, Chipeta, Jack and Josephine Meeker, about the outbreak and its causes. The ringleaders in the agency massacre and the Utes who had raped the women were not surrendered by Ouray, to the great chagrin of General Adams, who had especially wanted Chief Douglas and Persune. Jack, who had directed the attack on the troops in the canyon, came because he trusted the promise of General Hatch that the Utes who had fought the soldiers would not be punished.

The behavior of these Utes on the witness stand in Washington, when the Senate Committee was questioning them, was admirable. They were not nervous and were not disconcerted by the most searching questions. Chief Ouray and Chipeta especially were calm and gave the committee no information that helped.

Jack, secure in the promise of General Hatch, told the story of the fight with the troops in the canyon, but he insisted that the soldiers had fired on the Utes first and he did not know who had killed Major Thornburg nor who had scalped him.

Governor Pitkin did not appear to advantage on the stand. He was a politician and was plainly bent on representing strongly the wish of the people of Colorado to be rid of the Utes, without the least thought of justice or of the obligation of the United States to these Indians under the treaty that had been made with them.

Governor Pitkin tried to prove that not only the White River Utes, but all of the tribe, including the Uncompahgre Utes, had been engaged in the fight with the troops. The Governor was anxious to show that the Utes were so dangerous to the people of Colorado that they were retarding the development of the State and that their removal was necessary.[34]

In his effort to prove that the Uncompahgre Utes were in the attack on the soldiers, Governor Pitkin testified that I had told him that the uncle and nephew of Ouray had been killed by the soldiers. So I had, but I had told Governor Pitkin that when I met him in Denver, adding that these two Utes were out hunting when they were shot by the soldiers, were not at all hostile to the whites, and that their killing was one of the provoking causes of the outbreak. The Governor told the committee only part of what I said; was not candid, and created a false impression.

I was in New Mexico when the Governor appeared before the Senate Committee, and did not know of his testimony until long after the Utes had been removed from Colorado, or I should have got the facts before the Senate.

---

[34] Governor Frederick W. Pitkin was heavily invested in Colorado mining and an avowed "Indian hater." After the Meeker Massacre he took the opportunity to try to get the Utes totally removed from Colorado, even removed from the United States if possible. He sent messages around the state after the massacre that the Utes were ready to strike many Colorado towns (they were not), and that Utes could be shot on sight. Obviously Saunders recognized his bias.

My last sight of Chief Ouray and Chipeta was in Denver, where all the Indians stayed overnight on their way to Washington. I went to the station with him in the morning and shook hands with the chief, who was very grave and thoughtful. Chipeta put her hands on my shoulders, and said, "I come back soon."

I did not stay long in Denver, only until I could write the complete story of the Ute outbreak unhurriedly, to be used by the paper in some way, and then I went down to Santa Fe, where General Hatch had asked me to come, promising that he would get me the editorship of the Santa Fe *New Mexican*, which was then a weekly paper, printed half in English and half in Spanish.

"The owner of the paper, Billy Manderfield, is a close friend of mine," said the General," and I know he wants a real newspaper man to run the paper. He's sick and tired of doing it himself, and he's got enough money to retire."

In the spring[35] of the following year, 1880, Doctor Lacey walked into my Santa Fe office, in the uniform of a cavalryman, yellow stripes down his legs.

"Well, I'll be damned, Lacey," I said, as I got up and shook hands with him. "What on earth does this mean?"

He laughed. "Don't I look well in this uniform?" he asked. "Well, it seems that I got tired of that monotonous life at the agency, and with the help of General Hatch, I got a transfer to the army as a contract surgeon, and I am assigned to the Ninth Cavalry. I'm going on down to Fort Cummings tomorrow and will be in the thick of the Apache fighting."

"Give me the news about Ouray and Chipeta," I said.

"Ouray is dead," said Lacey soberly. While he was at Pagosa Springs, he got a strangulated hernia,[36] somehow. He sent a runner for me, who waked me up at midnight. I saddled up and went over that trail to Pagosa Springs in the pitch-black. That trail is the damnedest thing in Colorado, and it's a wonder I didn't break my neck. I trotted and loped the whole way and that Ute kept up with me, on foot. But when I got there Ouray was dead, and they were already making preparations for the funeral. I wanted to see him buried, but Chipeta came to me with tears in her eyes and said that the Utes had a law against any strangers

---

[35] Chief Ouray died on August 24, 1880, so it must have been Fall instead of Spring of 1880 when Lacey brought Saunders news of Ouray's death.
[36] Ouray is usually reported to have died of Bright's Disease, however a strangulated hernia could have been the immediate cause of death. Certainly Lacey knew more of his health condition(s) than any other doctor in the West.

seeing their burials. So I waited, and all I know is that they took him on a horse up a canyon and didn't come back for hours."

"I tell you, Saunders," went on Lacey, "It's a damn shame the way we have treated those Utes. I'm in the government service, and I can't open my mouth, but you are a newspaper man and you ought to do something about it. The government has taken that whole reservation away from the Utes and scattered them around Utah and New Mexico, making another treaty with them and giving them $75,000 for the reservation. Think of that. Why that land is worth millions.

"Ouray came to his death riding to Pagosa Springs to meet the Commissioners who had been sent out by the Secretary of the Interior to persuade the Utes to make another treaty and give up the reservation. He got a hernia on that trip and was so anxious about the situation that he wouldn't take the time to attend to it, until he saw it was serious and sent for me, too late. Ouray tried to temporize with the Commissioners first by demanding that they make the Arapahoe give him back his son, and then by making Ignacio refuse to sign the treaty. He didn't want to oppose the treaty till he got back his son. If anybody thinks that Ouray wasn't smart he is missing his guess. If Ouray had lived that treaty would never have been signed. He died while the negotiations were going on, and then Ignacio weakened and came into the commissioners and signed."

"Who is Chief now of the Utes?"

"Chipeta herself—but it doesn't amount to much now, I guess.[37] Shavano and Sapavanero wanted her to be Chief and the others consented to it, Uncompahgre Utes, White River Utes, and Southern Utes. There were too many jealousies among the sub chiefs and they were all willing to accept Chipeta. The first time a woman has ever been Chief of the tribe, and she not a born Ute. But she has good sense and will make a fine Chief."

CHIPETA REMEMBERS AN OLD FRIEND

Chipeta was then only twenty years old.[38] Forty years after that, I was on a hurried mission, passing through Colorado on a train, when

---

[37] No matter how much Chipeta was loved and respected, she would not have been seriously considered to become the overall chief of the Utes after Ouray's death. Perhaps she was simply telling the Tabeguache band what Ouray would have wanted if he had lived.

[38] Chipeta was born about 1843. The exact date is unknown as she was found by Utes abandoned in a deserted Kiowa camp and was estimated to be about two years old at that time. She was about 35 years old when Ouray died.

in the club car I met a Colorado man, an old settler, who naturally took great interest in the history of his state. I told him of my life in Ouray and of the intimacy I had had with Chief Ouray and Chipeta.

"I live in Montrose," he said, "and we are going to have a fair there next week. Chipeta is coming over from Utah, with some of her Utes, as our guest. Can't you come?"

If I only could, but I simply could not. I wrote a note to Chipeta:

"Saunders send you his love and wished he could see you," and put my address on it.

"Will you see that she gets this, surely," I asked the Montrose man.

"She'll have it in three days."

About a month after, I got by registered mail, a pair of the most beautiful fully beaded moccasins, made by Chipeta, and her photograph, taken in Montrose for me. Ah, me, I almost wish that she had not sent it. She was old and wrinkled and no longer slender, yet her face retained the beautiful spirit and the kindness and the sunny look that I remembered. I hung it in my study. The moccasins were too flatteringly small for me, and my young daughter, who loved the story of Chipeta, begged me to give them to her, and I did. She kept them carefully and wore them proudly, and says she is keeping them still for me.

I wrote to Chipeta a letter wishing her well, and asking her to give my warmest regards to Shavano and Shapavanero, if they still lived.

Chipeta died not long after this, though she was not an old woman.[39] Sapavaneo and Shavano are dead too. The people of the town of Montrose, which includes the land where the house of Chief Ouray once stood, have set up a monument to Ouray and Chipeta, but there is no memorial to Shawsheen, except a forgotten poem written by a Colorado woman.

Josephine Meeker was a vigorous, athletic girl at the time of the massacre, and was looking forward to a missionary and teaching life among the Indians. Her treatment by the Indians which was unusually brutal, because of her physical comeliness, broke her health, and she died two years after, while a Clerk in the Interior Department in Washington.

Twenty years after her death, I was in Washington, and, calling on the Secretary of the Interior, I sat down at a desk in the department, while I waited to be summoned. My mind was on my business with the secretary, which concerned the Indian Warehouse in St Louis, and certainly I was not thinking of the Ute war, but suddenly there rose before my eyes the thought of Josephine Meeker, as she stood before the teepee

---

[39] Chipeta died at about age eighty in 1922, but except for very bad cataracts, she was in pretty good health until her death.

that day and asked me for tea; and since I had heard nothing of her since then, I was wondering what had become of her when I was called into the secretary's office.

Coming out, I stopped to chat with the clerk who had ushered me in, and remarked on the old furniture of the department.

"Well, it is old," he said, "that desk there," pointing to the desk at which I had just been sitting, "is the desk that was used by Josephine Meeker twenty years ago. Josephine Meeker, who was captured by the Utes. You've heard of her. She was working here when she died."

By the way, our popular drinking salutation, "Here's how!" comes, greatly corrupted, from the Utes. The greeting of a Ute Indian for a friendly white man was an explosive and long-drawn-out grunt, sounding like "Ough!" "Ough-u!" Almost two syllables, flowing in to one.

The frontiersman and the army officers who fraternized with or fought with the Ute adopted the salutation and corrupted it into "Hough!" Then came the "How" and when the army man came East he introduced the "How," before drinking, and it was taken into the saloon vocabulary.

The "Here's How," was an eastern adaptation, and one will never hear an old-time drinker use it.

CHAPTER 11

My Duel on the Santa Fe Plaza

Russell Kistler, famous frontier editor of the Las Vegas Optic… a murder and a lynching caused by a St. Louis drummer who wanted soft boiled eggs… Ad. F. Bandelier among the Zunis… the old Fonda in Santa Fe where the manager wore two guns and sent bills once a year… A crooked gambler tries to kill the reporter who exposed his game to credulous soldiers… the funny sequel of a serious gun fight.

GOING TO SANTA FE FROM DENVER, my ticket carried me to Cañoncito on the construction train, twenty miles from Santa Fe. That was as far as the rails had been laid. The train stopped at Las Vegas about breakfast time and I thought I would get off there, stay a day and look at the town, and then go on to Santa Fe, through Cañoncito. I had only a little roll of clothing with me and I was husbanding my money. The new town of Las Vegas, now the principal part of Las Vegas, was just starting, frame houses going up, but an omnibus took the passengers over to the old town, where on one side of the plaza was the only hotel in the place.

The dining room was crowded but I found a seat next to a table where sat a drummer from St Louis, named Morehead, who had evidently been out the night before and was in a very bad humor. He was being waited on by a man who looked like a tramp; certainly he was not a good waiter. He had been drinking that morning and was in a belligerent mood. Moorehead, the St. Louis man, ordered soft boiled eggs.

"Now, you get 'em right, do you hear?" he said, in a bullying tone, to the waiter.

"You go to hell," answered the waiter, "I'll bring you what the cook gives me."

Those at the table were startled.

"I'll report you for that," grumbled Moorhead, as the waiter went off.

The rest of us went on eating. In a few minutes the waiter came back with Morehead's eggs. He looked at them and broke one.

"There, they're hard, by God," he said, "I'll have you fired," and he started to get up from the table.

"The hell you will" sore the waiter. He pulled a pistol from the side pocket of his trousers and shot Morehead through the head, killing him instantly. The dining room was in an uproar at once. The waiter ran, but someone tripped him before he got out of the room, and as he fell, several men jumped on him and disarmed him. He was held while word was sent to the Marshall, but he was in the new town and there was no telephone.

"Hang the son of a bitch," a man in the crowd shouted. "That fellow didn't have a gun."

A rope was brought from a hardware shop on the plaza, and in five minutes the waiter was hanging to a limb of a tree there. From the time he had shot Morehead he had not opened his mouth, and no one ever knew who he was.

Las Vegas, as the name implies, meaning "The Meadows," was built on a plain, surrounded by mountains, and it had always been the headquarters of ranchmen and cattlemen, a great outfitting point, with stores carrying immense stocks of goods. It had never been a wild town. The miners, with their money, went to Santa Fe, over the mountains fifty miles away.

Now, Las Vegas, as the Santa Fe Railway built shops and employed many men, found itself growing rougher. The old peaceable settlers were being shoved aside.

Young Russell Kistler came to the town from Kansas, hearing of its boom, and he started a paper, the Las Vegas *Optic*, that became famous all through the southwest. I have seen only one paper that was its equal and that was the *Solid Muldoon*, in Ouray. It was full of local news and gossip, most of it written by the alert Kistler, and he never suppressed anything, either from fear or favor. Naturally he was always in fights and often went about his work with a disfigured face, but he was such a popular favorite that none of his enemies dared to shoot him.

Kistler deserved a better fate than he met. He died from too much conviviality,[40] but he had set the pace for honest newspapers in New Mexico, and his influence did not die with him.

---

[40] "Conviality" means eating, drinking, and socializing.

11 | My Duel on the Santa Fe Plaza

The construction train took nearly the whole day to crawl from Las Vegas to Cañoncito, (which was just a little Mexican settlement, without even a station, nothing but adobe houses and those of the poorest kind, the homes of laborers. Several wagons awaited the train there and we climbed in, hungry, and rode the twenty miles to Santa Fe, over the roughest kind of a road, often a bare trail.

All of the wagons pulled up in front of the old Fonda, the only decent hotel in the town. It was owned by a woman and managed by Harry Simpson, a man well known to all frontiersmen. I went into the dining room and had supper, and then coming out I told Simpson who I was and why I was in Santa Fe. I told him, too, that I had very little money.

"That's all right," said Harry. "You live here, if you are a friend of General Hatch and maybe in six months or so I'll send you a bill." The Fonda was sometimes called the Exchange Hotel. The word "fonda" means simply "hotel" in Spanish.

I lived there for a year, and never got a bill. The hotel made its money from the bar and from the gambling rooms attached, and cared very little for the money that came from guests.

The La Fonda was the best hotel in Santa Fe in the late 1800s and was right on the plaza. The name simply means "The Inn" in Spanish.

P. Davd Smith Collection

Ad. F. Bandelier[41] was a frequent visitor in the office of the *New Mexican* when I first took charge of the paper, and afterward, when I was printing the *Albuquerque Review* he came into that office often to see me.

When he came to the office of the *New Mexican*, Henry Brooke and I would drop everything we were doing to hear him talk. He was then carrying on his research among the Zuni Indians. He was delightfully simple and unaffected and full of humor.

Neither Brooke nor I ever heard of him when he first came to New Mexico. One day, Brooke, dropping into the office of the old Fonda saw Bandolier's name on the register.

"Who is that?" he asked Harry Simpson, the manager.

Simpson was the hotel man who had treated me so generously when I first came to Santa Fe. He was a tall, handsome, reckless chap, who always wore two Colt .45s stuck in the waistband of his trousers, and never used them. They were simply decoration. He knew a lot more about poker and faro than about science.

"Why, he's one of those fellows that goes about digging up old things," he answered.

"An archaeologist?" suggested Brooke.

"That's it," said Harry, "an archaeologist."

Brooke came back to the office and wrote a personal item, something like this:

"Ad. F. Bandelier is at the Fonda. His business is not definitely known, but Harry Simpson says that he is an archaeologist, a biologist, a geologist, an ethnologist, philologist, an entomologist and a gynecologist."

Bandelier came around to the office and next day, but instead of being annoyed was much amused at the absurd paragraph, and then he told us what he was really doing.

He asked us to write nothing about the matters he described to us, since he was making reports to his institute, and we didn't. Often he wrote his reports in our office.

---

[41] Adolph "Ad." Bandlier was one of America's foremost archeologists and anthropologists of the late 19th and early 20th centuries, whose most famous book is *The Delight Makers*, a wonderful book about Anasazi life. He also wrote several technical books on the desert Indians like the Zuni, then continued with field studies in Ecuador, Bolivia, and Peru. He died in 1914. Bandolier National Monument, a national park with ancient Pueblo ruins near Los Alamos, New Mexico, is named in his honor.

11 | My Duel on the Santa Fe Plaza

Once he went to a Zuni village and disappeared for weeks, and none of us could find out where he was. I telegraphed the story that he was missing to the *New York Herald*, and in some mysterious way Bandelier learned of the commotion his absence was causing. He turned up in the *Review* office in Albuquerque and asked me to telegraph east that he had merely been out on a difficult exploration.

Bandelier's great grief was that he had to work in a field that he thought was too restricted. He would come into my office sometimes, sit down, put his feet up on a chair, roll a corn husk cigarette, and break out into something like this:

> "I suppose I ought to be satisfied to be known as an authority on the Pueblo Indians and especially the Zunis, which I am; but that is not all I want. I want to be a thorough ethnologist. I want to know what caused the extinction of the cave dwellers, beyond mere theories, and I want to know why the Maya Indians left Guatemala for Yucatan and then vanished from there. If I had life and money I could go into these things."

Once, he asked me, "How did the Ute Indians have babies?"

"Almost like animals," I answered, "I went into a teepee once and there was a woman there, lying on her back, and another squaw was kneading her abdomen with her feet. The mother was perfectly motionless. Presently the baby was born and that was all of it."

"What a pity our civilized women can't have the bodies of these Indians," said Bandelier.

"The Zuni Indians as well as the other Pueblo Indians have midwives, and childbirth is almost painless. I once saw a Navajo woman, in the throes of childbirth, hold onto a projecting limb of a tree above her head, while two other squaws held a blanket to receive the youngster when it came. An Indian woman will be getting around more or less about her work an hour after she has borne a child."

Bandelier would have been entirely at home in any fashionable parlor, because he was a gentleman born and bred, but how bored he would have been by the conversation and the manners. Knowing the Zuni language as he did, he was happiest among these Indians, and he was entirely accustomed to their habits and tribal manners. Once he said to me, "You people here in town are too fastidious. You ought to come out and live with the Zunis and you'll get over that. Now, the other day, I was lying on my blankets in a Zuni home, watching a Zuni girl kneading the dough for the bread of the evening meal. She wore only a loincloth and she should have been using a cloth to wipe off the perspiration, but instead, she was using her hands, wiping them on her flanks, and going right on with her kneading."

"Did you eat the bread?"

"Oh, I don't know. I forgot all about it."

Bandelier afterwards realized his dream of broader ethnological fields, but his life among the wild tribes of South America and Mexico broke his health and he died young. When I knew him he was a sturdy, light mustached blonde man in perfect health, all muscle, quick in movement and with a mind of great eagerness. He made nothing of walking fifty miles in a day. The Indians loved him, because he was truthful and helpful to them, having enough knowledge of medicine to treat many of their maladies successfully.

In the Santa Fe museum, which is in the old Governor's Palace, on the plaza, there is a department devoted to exhibits of the work of Bandelier, and to the discoveries he made both among the Zuni Indians and among the Indians of other countries. He seems to have satisfied his craving for knowledge after he left New Mexico.

The scout of the Apache campaign in New Mexico was Captain Jack Crawford.[42] He was a brave man, a good trailer, knew the habits of the Indians, and was valuable to the troops in the field. He was one of the most accurate and fastest shots with a Winchester rifle on that part of the frontier, and that, with a Colt 45, were his weapons.

He was known as the Post Scout. His weakness was the writing of sentimental verse, and that, with his long hair, made people who met him for the first time, mistake his character and believe him effeminate. The soldiers, who went on hard and dangerous campaigns with him, knew his manliness.

Captain Jack came to Santa Fe on leave while I was on the *New Mexican* and after a day of monotony in town, announced that at eleven o'clock the next day, he would give an exhibition on the plaza of rapid firing with a Winchester rifle.

---

[42] John Wallace "Captain Jack" Crawford was a popular performer in the mold of Buffalo Bill Cody, who was one of his good friends. Crawford served in the Civil War and later became a journalist and scout during the great Sioux War. In the 1890s, he earned a reputation as the "Poet Scout," speaking on the Frontier West before audiences nationwide. He eventually wrote seven books of poetry, and was a leading advocate of the temperance movement.

11 | My Duel on the Santa Fe Plaza

That morning, just before Jack was to make his appearance with his rifle, I started on my rounds of the shops on the plaza, where I got the gossip of the day, and as I passed the place of John Lucas, who made Mexican filigree jewelry, he ran out and exclaimed, "Did you know Gilbert is hunting for you with a gun? Says he is going to shoot you on sight."

Gilbert was a gambler who dealt a crooked faro game, and I had exposed the game and warned the soldiers not to play at it.

"He's in earnest," went on Lucas. "Have you got a gun?"

"Mine's in my office."

"Come in here," said Lucas, as he went inside. His shop was crowded with customers, men and women. As soon as he was inside he began loudly, so that everyone in the shop could hear him, "No Saunders, I can't lend you a gun. Sorry but I can't lend you a gun." Then he passed behind the counter and handed a Colt 45 across the showcase to me.

I slipped the pistol inside the waistband of my trousers and went out on the plaza, looking from side to side as I got out in the open. I was only twenty years old, and I could not realize that my life was actually in danger. I had been in plenty of fights from school days on, but this was something different. This man was out to "get me." It seems incredible to me, somehow. I thought I had better go back to the office, and had started in that direction when I met Gilbert, face to face.

He was a tall, burly man, with unsteady blue eyes, and the blotched and swollen face of a hard drinker. Both of us were startled. He was not a professional killer or he would have been ready. We stopped as we saw each other. Neither of us tried to draw a gun.

"Are you telling people you are going to shoot me on sight?" I demanded.

"No, I'm not. That's a damn lie," he answered, "but you ought not to have written me up."

I turned my back on him and walked away, and that's where I made a mistake. I had taken three or four steps when he shot at me from behind, and the bullet missed me. I turned, and he was aiming at me again. I was frightened and my legs wanted to run, but my pride forbade, so my legs and my pride compromised. I jumped from the sidewalk into the street, and as I did so he fired twice more. Then I got into action and got two shots at him while he fired once again. He missed me all together—whiskey had made his nerves unsteady—and I shot him in the shoulder. He ran.

Hearing the shots, the people thought that Jack Crawford had begun his exhibition and poured into the plaza from the shops along it. Jack thought somebody was stealing his thunder and came rushing out into the plaza.

The police came and arrested Gilbert and me, and then Jack got to work with his show.

I was fined, and Gilbert was ordered to leave town on the next train.

Five years afterwards I was a reporter on the St. Louis *Republican*, and was sitting at my desk one night writing, when a man came into the office and stood behind my chair.

"Saunders," said a voice, and it sounded familiar.

I turned, and there was Gilbert.

"Well, he's got me now," I thought.

"Saunders, I'm broke, and I want something to eat, and then I'm going to Kansas City with a brakeman I know. Will you lend me a dollar?"

Would I? I never in my life lent a man money with so much pleasure.

CHAPTER 12

Lew Wallace, Ben Hur, and Billy the Kid

General Hatch introduces me to the author of Ben Hur, *the General tells how he could stop the raids of Chief Victoria and his Apache if the Government would give him a free hand… the last drop of whiskey on a scout… the desperado, Billy the Kid appeals to Governor Wallace through me… Billy's talk with me… His escape by killing his two guards… Pat Garrett, Sheriff of Lincoln County, gets him*

LEW WALLACE WAS THE GOVERNOR of New Mexico when I came to Santa Fe in 1880.[43] He was writing the last part of *Ben Hur*, and reading the proof of the first part.

He had written *The Fair God*, a tale of the conquest of Mexico, long before this, and the book had only fair sales, greatly to his disappointment. He was by no means sure of the success of *Ben-Hur*, and he sometimes expressed his feeling of uncertainty to me, when I would drop into his office and find him correcting proof.

I had read *The Fair God* and had found it fascinating—at that time, all I knew about Mexico had been got from Prescott—but long after, when I was living in Mexico I read it again and thought it very dull and quite untrue to the history and character of the country.

However, back there in Santa Fe, young and adventure-thrilled, I wondered why Governor Wallace had not written another book about Mexico instead of *Ben-Hur*, and he told me that the idea of this book

---

[43] Lewis "Lew" Wallace rose to prominence during the Civil War, serving under U. S. Grant. His maneuvers during the Battle of Shiloh put him at odds with Grant, and this controversy dogged him the remainder of his life. He was appointed territorial Governor of New Mexico by President Hayes in 1878. Wallace was a prolific writer; his novel *Ben Hur—A Tale of the Christ* was published in 1880 and became the best-selling novel of the nineteenth century.

Lewis "Lew" Wallace was governor of New Mexico but best known as the author of Ben Hur, *the best-selling book of his time.*
Photo Courtesy of Wikipedia.

had been suggested to him by Mrs. Wallace. Some of the book, he told me, had been pure drudgery to him, and I got the impression that Mrs. Wallace had had much more to do with the writing than mere criticism. But the chariot race and the galley scene I know were all his. He read those aloud to me and revised much as he read. I never ventured to suggest, and indeed I was rather indifferent as the whole story seemed to me uninteresting.

Years afterward, I read *Ben Hur* and appreciated it very highly, wondering at my youthful lack of understanding of its beauty.

There was little ceremony in Santa Fe at this time, and when I first came General Hatch had left his commandant's office in Fort Marcy and had taken me himself on a round of introductions, first to the owner of the *New Mexican*, William Manderfield, who had told me to start work the next day on the paper, and then to the Governor's office, where he presented me to Wallace.

This was a very interesting visit.

Both these men were Civil War veterans and had fought bravely. They respected each other. They discussed their problems in my presence without the least restraint and I was delighted by the confidence reposed in me.

They were very different in appearance. General Hatch was tall and straight, wearing a mustache but no beard, the ideal cavalry man. Governor Wallace was shorter and a little stouter than General Hatch, bearded, his face reflective. Both men were gray and their faces worn into deep lines, but the eyes of both were youthful and in conversation lit up with great spirit.

General Hatch spoke of the trouble he was having in stopping the raids of Chief Victoria, whose Apaches were burning ranches, killing and torturing settlers, capturing stagecoaches, and making travel unsafe in Southern New Mexico.

12 | Lew Wallace, *Ben Hur*, and Billy the Kid

"The reservation is the breeding place of these devils," said the General. "The troops press them hard but they sneak back to the reservations and swear they've never been off it. If the government would allow us to follow them on the reservation, we could go into their teepees and prove that they were with the band we had been chasing, but the government won't let us do it."

Governor Wallace told us that he was planning to offer Billy the Kid a free pardon if that young devil would promise to leave New Mexico forever.

"But," said the governor, "I am at a loss for a trustworthy emissary. I can't write a formal letter to the rascal, and I haven't a messenger I can trust to keep his mouth shut until I am ready to announce the agreement. And nobody seems to know just now where Billy is."

"I made this offer to him several months ago," added the Governor, "I went down to Lincoln expressly to see him, and when he got word that I was there, waiting for him, he came into town and rode down the main street, with bridle in one hand and a Winchester rifle in the other, while lying on the saddle in front of him was his belt stuck full of pistols. He rode right past three of his bitterest enemies, sitting on the porch of a house, eyed them defiantly as he went by and dismounted at the house where he knew I was."

"We had a long talk and all the time Billy kept his hand on his rifle and had his ears open for sounds from the street, as I could see from his alertness.

"Billy refused my offer. I'm going to live and die in New Mexico," he said, "it's all the country I know and I would starve anywhere else. Besides all my friends are here. I'll get killed sooner or later," he went on, "but before they get me, I'll get a good many of them."

"But then he said something from which I gathered a hope that after all, we might be rid of him."

"Maybe I'll change my mind, I'm getting damned tired of this hiding out all the time, and I'm going to get some of my people together and raid some of these sons of bitches that have murdered my friends and have been trying to shoot me in the back. And then, if they don't get me in that fight, I'm going to light out for Mexico. They tell me that the President down there wants Americans for his rurales."[44]

"Now," continued the Governor, "I think Billy really may have changed his mind about leaving the country. The chase has been getting hotter and he has been finding out that he hasn't as many friends as

---

[44] "Rurales" is Spanish for "Armed Forces."

he thought he had. I believe he would accept my offer of a pardon if he leaves the country."

I was on the point of offering myself as his emissary, but I was growing prudent, and held my tongue. I had just undertaken the responsible work of managing the *New Mexican*, and must settle down. Nevertheless, foolish as it was, I nursed this idea of hunting for and finding Billy the Kid and inducing him to leave New Mexico.

General Hatch told us an amusing story, full of the flavor of camp life, which he had just heard from one of his captains, on leaving Santa Fe from Fort Cummings.

This Captain had been on a scout the month before, after Apaches, with twenty cavalrymen, a lieutenant and a cook. They had been out a week and had not sighted the Indians, and the supplies were running low.

One morning the Lieutenant showed the Captain a bottle. "That's all we have left," he said, "just two big drinks."

The Captain looked. "We've got to give Cookie a drink," he said.

"All right," assented the Lieutenant, "we'll make it three."

The two of them downed their last drinks and savored them solemnly. Then they called the cook.

"Here's a drink for you, Cookie," said the Lieutenant, and he poured the last of the whiskey from the jug into the glass.

Cookie wiped his hands on his apron and received the glass while they watched him with covetous eyes. He raised the glass and was about to drink when he saw a bit of cork floating on top. With a large annoyed gesture, and before they could move, he flipped that precious whiskey out on the sand, and then held out the glass to the Lieutenant.

"Hell, there's a fly in that," he said, "Give me another."

"Well," remarked Governor Wallace, "if they had shot him it would have been justifiable homicide."

Governor Wallace was in poor circumstances and had an idea that he might make something in mining. He was always on the lookout for a chance to stake some prospector, and in that way find a fortune as Tabor had done in Leadville.

Once news came to Santa Fe of a rich quartz strike that had been made in the hills near Bernalillo, and the Governor led a party of us to the little village of Las Placitas, in the outskirts of which the strike had been made.

We examined the prospect and found it only of average value. No rush of miners followed. The Governor was greatly disappointed with the outcome of the trip. Coming back, I sat in the seat with him on the train.

"I'll tell you," said he, "I've just about made up my mind to resign this office as Governor. I'm not going to be lucky at mining and I'm just burying myself and getting out of touch with the world."

A few evenings after that, I was sitting at my table in the office of the *New Mexican*, editing telegraphic flimsy[45] for the printers, when the Governor came in and sat down beside me.

"Any news from Washington?" he asked.

Our telegram sent out by the Associated Press, came to us repeated from Topeka, and in the double transmission they were often so mangled that they needed very careful interpretation. Our dispatches from Washington that night were in unusually bad shape. I looked them over and said, "Here are some appointments by the President, and confirmations by the Senate."

"Read those," he asked.

I read, and presently I came to the name, entirely illegible, of someone appointed and confirmed as Minister to Paraguay and Uruguay. That was the way our government did things in those days. Paraguay is an interior country of South America, a thousand miles up the Rio Plata from Uruguay, which is on the coast, and yet Washington thought that one Minister could hold both posts efficiently.

I read that dispatch to Governor Wallace and said, "I can't read the name of the man who's appointed here."

"Never mind," he said, as he rose from his chair. "I know, that means me. Well, damn 'em, I'll show 'em they can't side track me that way. I'm going straight over to the telegraph office and telegraph the President that I don't want the office."

He did, and was appointed Minister to Turkey, a much more dignified post.

The adobe building, running along the side of the plaza, which used to be known as the Governor's Palace, and is still called that, is now used as a museum, and it is a most interesting place to visit.

Fifty years after I had talked with Lew Wallace in his office there, I went through this museum, and the capable woman who was showing me around said,

"This is the room we call the Ben-Hur room, because it was here in the old palace that Lew Wallace wrote the book. We think, but we are not quite sure, that this is the room."

"Oh," I said, eager to show off my old-timers knowledge, "I was here when he was Governor and I often visited him in the room where he worked and I can tell you if this is it."

---

[45] "Flimsy" is continuous sheets coming off the telegraph.

"Really," she exclaimed, "Then you are just the man we've been looking for. Show me."

"Well, I'll go outside and come in the way I used to come."

I walked down the street, to the corner of the plaza, and then turned and came back to the Palace as I had been in the habit of doing in the old days, but as I approached the Palace I saw that there were three entrances instead of one, as I had supposed.

"I am at a loss," I confessed to the lady, who was smiling, "I used to come in at the entrance and then turn to the left and enter the governor's office, where he sat at his desk. Now I don't know which entrance it was, and so I can't tell you what room it was."

Not very long after General Hatch and I had talked with the Governor in his office about Billy the Kid, and the Governor had told us that he was thinking of offering Billy a pardon if he would leave the country, that young scoundrel was captured and brought to Santa Fe by Sheriff Pat Garrett, of Lincoln County, for safekeeping. A great deal of romantic nonsense has been written about this outlaw by sentimental women and newspaper men who wanted to make a good story, including two books; and a popular moving picture has been made in which he appears as a romantic hero, who robs the rich to give to the poor, and is finally helped by an admiring sheriff to elope with the beautiful girl. Frontiersmen who knew Billy sneer at this and with good reason.

As soon as I heard he was in jail, I went to Pat Garrett, and got an order allowing me to see the outlaw privately.

"Don't take any gun or knife in with you," ordered Pat, as he handed me the permit. "That snake will see through your clothes and get the gun."

I took Billy tobacco and cigarette papers, and his face lit up when I pulled the makings out of my pocket, and handed them to him. Everybody rolled his own cigarettes in those days—a made cigarette was unknown. He was not shackled but he was confined in a cell, and was not allowed the run of the corridor as the other prisoners were. The Santa Fe jail was an unusually strong one for that part of the country, built of steel and concrete, and Billy knew it. His first remark to me, when he had begun smoking and talking, was about that.

"This is going to be a hell of a place to get out of. Did anybody ever break out of here?"

Billy was at first inclined to be reticent, and after this first outburst, answered my questions with bad temper and in monosyllables, but when I told him that what he had said to me would be printed not only in the Santa Fe *New Mexican* but also in the Denver newspapers, he became loquacious and bragged of his crimes. Of course, as he talked, I watched him closely.

12 | Lew Wallace, *Ben Hur*, and Billy the Kid

He was then twenty-one years old, about five feet eight inches high, very thin and stooping, with narrow chest. He had a sharp face with retreating forehead and chin. His gaze was furtive. His voice was thin and rasping. When he was not talking or smoking, his mouth fell open, and then, with his greenish gray eyes and his protruding front teeth he was not a pretty person to look at.

He always breathed through his mouth. Certainly he had polypi[46] in his throat, and they had developed from neglected adenoids in his childhood. I am sure that those poisonous growths, polluting his body all the twenty-one years of his life, had been the chief cause of his abnormal development.

So, far from being a creature of romance, the youth was repulsive. Had he appeared on the streets of any large city the police would have arrested him on sight as a pickpocket or sneak thief?

His hands were never still. He was constantly rolling a cigarette or feeling in his pockets for something he didn't find. The reason for this restlessness, I thought, was that he was used to being on horseback and having his rifle in his hands, or hooking his fingers in his cartridge belt when he was on foot. Behind bars, with neither horse, rifle nor cartridge belt, he was uneasy.

I asked Billy to tell me the story of his life. He began with an account of his first killing. That was in Silver City. He told me that he had killed twenty-one men, and he did not even add, "in self-defense," as I have heard other gun men defend themselves. He seemed to think that killing was just a part of life, and a mere common place.

When he killed that first man, he was twelve years old. He was living in Silver City at this time with his family, named Bonney, who had traveled there in a covered wagon from Kansas. He had been to school a short time in Kansas, but he read with great labor, and he had only a few hundred words in his vocabulary.

"I got a horse and gun, and some bread and meat from the house and then I took to the hills," said Billy, "and lived the best way I could. I knew the sheriff wouldn't hunt very far for me."

Then, until he joined the warring cattle factions in the Lincoln County war, he lived by murder and robbery. He would go to ranches when he knew the women were alone; cow[47] them with a gun and take food or money. He had a cabin in the Mogollon Mountains, deserted by a prospector, and it was built on the side of a canyon and hidden by cliffs and trees.

---

[46] Polypi is plural for throat polyps – a fairly common problem in the 19th century.
[47] "Cow" was an old term used for "to frighten into submission."

He did not describe his killings to me, and I was led to doubt that there had been as many as twenty-one. When he spoke of that number once I said, "Somebody told me that you said that you had killed twenty-one men, not counting Indians and Mexicans."

"That's a damn lie," he replied quickly. "I never said that, unless I was drunk, and I don't believe I ever said it."

He told me with great enjoyment the story of a murder that marked him as absolutely abnormal.

He had picked up a companion, who was riding with him, and they met three Navajo Indians, on their way into Silver City. The Indians were riding three good horses, and they had two pack horses, loaded with furs and food. They were peaceful Indians; met the two white men cordially and asked them to ride with them and camp for the night. Billy and his comrade did so; joined them, and at night they ate supper with the Indians and after smoking, lay down in their blankets to sleep.

When the Indians were asleep, the white man shot all three; left their bodies lying about the campfire and took the horses and the furs to Deming, the nearest town, where they sold them.

This he told me as a very clever exploit.

I asked him during the conversation if he had a photograph of himself that I could get.

"I've never had but one picture taken," he said. "That was in Lincoln. It looked pretty rough, too. I was just in from a long ride. I've always wanted to have a good picture—wanted it for a girl in Fort Sumner, but I never could get around to it."

I found a copy of that photograph and I am printing it in this book. It is an excellent likeness of Billy as I saw him, quite different from the idealized pictures of him that have appeared.

I talked with him at length several times in the Santa Fe jail, and printed one interview with him, and I have talked with men of Lincoln county who knew him well from the time he fired his first shot in the Lincoln County cattle war.

He would fight face-to-face when he had to do it, but he had the assassin's instinct, and he would shoot men from behind, when he was afraid of them. A cattle man of Lincoln County, told me that he met Billy near Roswell one day, both on horseback, and the minute he saw Billy's face he got ready to draw—and he would have got out his gun before Billy got his, because Billy was known to be very slow on the draw, strange to say for a killer of so much experience. Probably, that is why, knowing his own weakness, he was willing to take advantage of an opponent and shoot him in the back.

12 | Lew Wallace, *Ben Hur*, and Billy the Kid

During my last talk with Billy he asked me to go to Governor Wallace and say to him that if he was released he would leave New Mexico and promise never to come back. I did not tell him that Governor Wallace had intended to make him that offer before he was taken. I went to Governor Wallace with Billy's message.

"I can't do it now," said the Governor. "I would have done it, gladly, before he was caught, and I should like to do it even now and save the territory much expense, but the people demand that he be punished. He's in the hands of the Lincoln County authorities now and I won't interfere."

I went back to the jail and told Billy what the Governor had said, and he broke into a torrent of invective[48], directed against the Governor and Pat Garrett principally.

According to Billy, this was the only photograph ever taken of him, and the one referred to in Saunder's original manuscript.
Photo Courtesy of Wikipedia

"God damn their souls to hell," he swore, "I haven't a friend on earth. They're all dead or scared to stand by me. Never mind, they've got to prove every one of those killings and they'll have a hell of a time doing it. Where are they going to get their witnesses?"

Billy was taken by Sheriff Garrett to Lincoln County for trial, and the story of his escape from the jail there, after murdering the two guards set over him, is well-known. He rode away and disappeared. Weeks after, when I was surveying, our party passed through Fort Sumner in the afternoon, and camped about five miles out of the town. While we were

---

[48] "Invective" is a violent verbal attack.

eating breakfast the next morning, about six o'clock, the mail buckboard going to Las Vegas, passed along the road, and the driver stopped and came to our fire.

"Give me some coffee and I'll give you some news," he said; "Billy the Kid was killed last night in Fort Sumner by Pat Garrett."

We were all agog for more.

"How did it happen?"

"Pat Garrett knew who Billy's girl was, and he came to her home at dark, and scared her to death by threatening to kill her and all her relations if she let Billy know he was in the house, when he came. Then Pat got under the bed, with his gun ready, and lay there until Billy slipped into the house and got into the bed with the woman. Pat waited till he thought Billy was asleep, and then began to crawl out from under the bed. Billy stirred, rolled over, his hand going to his gun which lay by his side, and asked, "Quien es?" (Who's there?)

"Pat's gun was poking over the bed. His eyes came up, and as soon as he saw Billy he shot him through the head. I've got a telegram here to Governor Wallace from Pat."

"How did you hear this?" someone asked.

"I was hooking up about an hour ago, when the girl came rushing out of the house screaming and calling out that Pat Garrett had shot Billy the Kid. She told how it happened to a crowd of people, but you can just bet that ain't the story Pat's going to tell.

And it was not. Pat Garrett's story was that, knowing Billy had a girl in the house of Pete Maxwell, in Fort Sumner, he went there at night, with two deputies and lay in wait. Billy came and was prowling around the house, looking for something to eat, with his gun in one hand and a butcher knife in the other, preparing to cut some meat, when Pat confronted him and shot him.

The people in Fort Sumner believed that the outlaw was assassinated in bed, and indeed, considering that he was a wild beast, no one would have blamed the Sheriff for killing him so. But the newspapers never printed that story. Pat Garrett was too much feared.

Pat Garrett himself, by the way, was killed on the road to Silver City by a ranchman tenant of his. After he killed the Kid he grew morose and quarrelsome and had made a threatening gesture with a gun towards the man who killed him.

CHAPTER 13

General Ulysses S. Grant Pans Gold With Me

GENERAL GRANT refuses the bait offered him by a Santa Fe mining company which wanted to make him its president... I spend a week with him while he examined the property and show him how to handle a gold pan.

GENERAL GRANT CAME TO SANTA FE to look into a tempting mining proposition when I was editing the Santa Fe *New Mexican,* in 1880.

In those days, Santa Fe was an alluring mining district. The hills between the towns of Albuquerque and Las Vegas, all about the Pecos and the Rio Grande Rivers, were full of prospectors. The camp of Los Cerrillos was only twenty miles away. No big paying mine was ever found there, but there were many small veins of silver uncovered, and on the strength of the rich assays from some of these, prospect holes were being sold daily to men from the East for five and ten thousand dollars, and then used by the buyers as a basis for the organization of companies in Denver, New York and Chicago; and the placing of

Ulysses S. Grant, 18th President of the United States. Photo by Matthew Brady.
Photo Courtesy of the Library of Congress

stock among small investors who were as eager to buy mining stock then as they are now to buy oil stock.

There was an old Spanish turquoise mine, too, fifteen miles from Santa Fe, which had just been sold to a New York company, and we had word that it was going to be worked on a large scale. It was known as Mount Chalchihuitl. Chalchihuitl is the Aztec word for turquoise. This mine was genuine and had proved its value. It had produced the most beautiful green turquoise, shading into blue, during the Spanish occupation of the country, and when the Pueblo Indians rose against their oppressors, whipped them and drove them out of Santa Fe, in hatred of everything these brutal conquistadors had done they threw all the outside machinery of the mine down the shaft and then filled up the shaft, tunnels and drifts, leaving only a dump about fifty yards square.

This dump was full of good turquoise in the matrix, and there were always Indians on it, searching about for turquoise which they sold in Santa Fe.

But the mine was never worked. We understood that when Tiffany heard that it was to be reopened he bought it from its new owners and intended to keep it closed to prevent the market from being flooded by turquoise and the price lowered.

Most of the turquoise, pure or in the matrix, that is sold by the Indians to tourists on the trains and buses passing through New Mexico nowadays comes from this great dump. It is not guarded.

The New Placer Mining, Milling and Smelting Company was the sonorous name of a company organized by a group of eastern speculators who had got an old Spanish land grant near Santa Fe, having on it a mine of gold and copper. A stream ran through this grant and gold dust which it was said had been washed from the gravel in this stream, was brought into Santa Fe in buckskin bags every day or two by the manager of the company. There would have been a mining rush at once to these placers, but the company hired armed men to warn off the prospectors, and since they had the camp of Los Cerrillos so nearby they did not insist on trying out the new diggings. It really seemed that the company had a property worth millions of dollars.

But they now wanted a man for President, whose name would sell the stock. They had put fifty million dollars worth on the market, and the sales were not paying expenses. So they invited Ulysses S. Grant to become the president, and offered him $50,000 a year as salary. General Grant was a poor man. He had left Washington in debt. He had just returned from Japan, and was facing the future with uncertainty. I never understood how he managed to pay even the Japanese valet who

13 | General Ulysses S. Grant Pans Gold With Me

came back with him and went everywhere with him, but the wages of the youth were very small, doubtless.

This salary, very large in those days, was a temptation to him, and he accepted the offer of this New Mexican company to pay his expenses on a trip to examine the property.

When the manager of the company told me that Grant was coming I was really deeply moved. We were drinking together, in a bar on the plaza.

"I want to be with you on that tour," I said.

"All right," he answered, "but you got to promise that you will let nobody out there know that you're a newspaperman."

I was young, full of romance and sentiment, and memories of the Civil War. I had been taken by my father once in Norfolk to see General Robert E. Lee, after the war, and I remembered well his dignity and his noble aspect, as well as his kindness to a young boy. It had been hard to reconcile the tales I had heard during the war, of the barbarity of the Yankees, and especially the cold ferocity of General Grant, with his considerate treatment of General Lee at Appomattox, when he returns the sword handed to him by Lee under that famous apple tree, and asked him to be seated, while they talk over the terms of surrender. Now, I was to see for myself the kind of man this General Grant was.

So I rode in the two seated buck board, with the General and the manager and the promoter of the scheme, when we started for the mine.

It was a four-hour drive from the hotel to the house of the manager where the party was to stay during the week planned for the visit, and if General Grant said one word all the way I didn't hear it. He smoked incessantly and seemed buried in his own reflections. Now and then the manager or the promoter remarked upon the scenery and General Grant would look at the thing pointed out, but silently.

When we got to the manager's house, General Grant climbed down from the buckboard and followed by his valet with his impediments, went to his room where he ate lunch and dinner in the evening by himself.

During the whole week the General ate his meals alone, served by the valet. In the mornings we all got up very early and started on horseback by seven o'clock to examine some part of the company's property. The manager and the promoter usually rode with the General, and the rest of us trailed after them. The valet never went on these trips. One man carried the lunch for the party in a basket and we sat at noon in the shade of some rock or tree to eat it. We always got back to the house by four o'clock and then we all had a nap before dinner.

After dinner we sat on the crude veranda of the house and smoked and talked. General Grant used to come out of his room and sit at one end of the veranda, with the valet behind him. He smoked incessantly, the valet handing him a fresh cigar and taking the stump of the other, very watchful, and sensing the exact time for the change. General Grant took no part in the conversation and none of us intruded on his taciturnity. And not once did he offer any of the party a cigar. We thought that these were probably some made for him just to suit his taste, and that he did not care to risk finding himself without by generosity, or that very likely his life had made him thoughtless of these small courtesies.

One whole morning was devoted to a careful examination of the gold and copper mine. General Grant hammered off bits of the ore with a prospector's hammer and took it himself to the assay office nearby. It was good ore, running very high in both gold and copper content. The general was somewhat familiar with mining terms.

I heard him ask the assayer one morning, "this assay seems high. What would a mill run be on that ore?"

The assayer seemed surprised. He had hardly thought that the General would know enough to think of the difference between an assay and a mill run. An assay shows how much gold or silver or copper or other mineral the piece of ore given to the assayer has in it. A mill run is the result obtained by putting several tons of the ore through the treatment. An assay may show a very rich return because the ore had been chosen from the best part of the mineral bearing vein, while the mill run often, and indeed usually, brings out a much poorer result.

In this case the assayer told General Grant the truth, and he could see for himself looking at the great width of the vein, in fact, that the mill run would nearly equal in richness the assay.

After the inspection of the mine, we spent nearly a whole day on the banks of the stream where placer washing had begun, and here again, General Grant showed his shrewdness. The manager had put up a long canopy, running along a hundred feet or so of the little river, projecting over the bank to protect us from the sun while we washed the sand and gravel in the gold pans. This was placer mining deluxe! But General Grant spoiled this fine plan. As soon as he got out of the buckboard and saw the careful arrangements that had been made for his comfort, he glanced up and down the stream and then said, pointing to a place a hundred yards away,

"Let's try there."

The manager looked at me and grinned cordially, and so did the rest of us. Plainly the General had heard of salting mines and even placers. The canopy was hurriedly placed in the spot chosen by the General and

13 | General Ulysses S. Grant Pans Gold With Me

the four of us washed with the gold pans for an hour. I got a place on the back next to the General, and being a little more skillful than he I proudly showed him the correct twirl of the pan.

I have forgotten what the gold we got in the four pans was worth, but I do remember that the General washed in his pan two dollars and forty cents worth, with one small nugget, which he carefully separated and put into his pocket. We weighed the gold when we got back to the house, and rather plumed ourselves on the result. Undoubtedly, there was a real placer there, and it was rich.

One morning, we were all out riding, and we came to a place where men were building a road. I was riding behind General Grant, who sat on his horse slumped in the saddle, smoking the eternal cigar.

As we came along the workmen drew aside to give us room. One of them glanced at the party, and then, dropping his pickaxe, came forward to Grant's horse and held out his hand.

"General, I was with you at Shiloh," he said.

Grant shook the hand firmly.

"You didn't get wounded?" he asked.

"No, sir."

"You are all right here?"

"Yes, sir."

The General started on again. "I want to vote for you again," the old soldier shouted, as we went on.

We made several trips to the quartz mine, where they were drifting along the vein to discover its thickness, and one more trip to the placers. General Grant never showed enthusiasm but seemed always deeply interested and intent on getting at the real quality of the property. On that last day we spent there, all of the party except the manager and the promoter were asked to take their horses and stay away from the house until the afternoon, and General Grant went into close conference with the two heads.

The manager afterwards told me that he asked many questions about the business of the company, especially being concerned about the method of stock selling, and the kind of people who were buying the stock.

"He says he wants two weeks to decide," said the manager. "We rather hoped he would make up his mind off hand."

It was much nearer a month than two weeks before the company in Santa Fe got their answer from General Grant, and meanwhile all large mining operations were suspended.

Grant was frank and even blunt in his letter, which I saw. He said that he believed the property was good, and that the representations made to him as to its value we're all true, but that after all, the success of the operation was doubtful, and that a great amount of money must be spent before any profits would come to the stockholders. People would buy the stock because of his name. He could not control the literature that would be sent out nor the promises that would be made by the salesmen. The stockholders would grow impatient and blame him for the delay of dividends, and in the possible event of a failure of the enterprise he would have the whole responsibility. So he must decline the offer of the Presidency.

I saw the manager sometime after this letter came. "And he told me he needed the money, too," said this practical man, ruefully.

The company never recovered from this blow. It staggered along for a year or so, selling some stock, and then disappeared.

CHAPTER 14

Surveying on the Plains

A drastic cure for drunkenness... Rattlesnakes, cactus, mesquite and sick nerves... a brush with the Apaches... thirst in the sand hills... the cook and the cowboy... the treasure of "La Gran' Quivera"... a five year game with the demon rum.

SANTA FE, when I began my newspaper there in 1880, was one of the wildest towns in the United States. The Santa Fe railway was just building into the town from Las Vegas, and the town was full of construction men with nothing to do but spend their money and with the ruffian who had collected to prey on them. The Apache campaign was being directed from Fort Marcy, the headquarters of General Hatch not many miles away, and officers and soldiers from the field came to Santa Fe to squander their pay. The red light district was wide open and gambling dens were not only tolerated but encouraged. The Mexican dance halls, called "bailes," with Mexican girls were open all night. Sleep was regarded as a waste of time. It was conventional to drink whiskey, play Faro and Monte from morning till night and then from night until morning again. Killings were common and were never punished if there was any color at all of self-defense. The officers of the law were all venal and it was never difficult to evade punishment for any sort of misdeed.

I was twenty-two years old, fresh from a small southern town, and found a license of this rough life just what I wanted. Working as I did, on the Santa Fe *New Mexican*, writing most of the paper, reading all the proof, sometimes helping the Mexican pressman to run off the paper on a camel country press[49] (when his helper was drunk), often going for forty-eight hours without sleep, drinking

---

[49] "Camel country press" comes from the practice of using a camel engraving to check the quality of the reproduction of a press for illustrations. If it looked more like a horse than a camel it was of poor quality.

constantly to keep myself going, my nerves were shattered in a year and I got so that I had to drink three or four cocktails or bracers of whiskey before I could eat breakfast. As soon as I got up I would hurry to a bar.

I have seen men come into the bar trembling as with the palsy and ask for whiskey. The bottle and the glass were set out. Then the drinker would take his handkerchief, throw it around his neck, clasp one end of it with one hand, with the other hand grip the bottle, pull the bottle up over the glass to steady it, pour the glass full of whiskey and then replacing the bottle on the bar, clutch the glass with the hand that had held the bottle and draw the glass to his mouth. Two drinks of whiskey accomplished in this way would steady his nerves and then the third drink would be taken just for the pleasure of it. After that, breakfast, and the readiness for the day's work.

I never quite reached this stage, but one morning about dawn I waked and saw the room full of animals. I called to Henry Brooke, who was sleeping in another bed in one room of the adobe house where we lived.

"Henry, I'm going to have the jim-jams. Get up and take me to the washstand, I'm afraid."

He got up and led me to the stand and, after drinking a pitcher of water, I went back to bed and lay there shivering until the sun came into the room. This was going too far. I managed to dress in spite of my shaking fingers, then I hastened to the bar and when I had fortified myself with whiskey, I called on the Surveyor General of New Mexico.

"General," I said, "I want to stop drinking."

"Well, why don't you?" he answered.

"Because I haven't the resolution. When I tell a man that I'm going to stop drinking, he says 'that's a great idea! Come on and take a last drink with me.' I do that and then I drink a lot more and then it starts all over again."

"Why don't you taper off?" asked the Surveyor General.

"Well, I can't—that's all. Did you ever see a man taper off?"

"Well, I don't know that I have," said the General.

"I simply can't stop here in Santa Fe, General, and I want to go out on one of your surveying parties where I can't get anything to drink."

"Well," commented the General, that's an idea. You will certainly have a hell of a time for a while, but it may work. There's a party going out in three days, if you want to try it. They will be out nearly ten months and the only town where you can get whiskey during the time will be Puerta De Luna.[50] John Shaw is the compass man and the boss of the party. He doesn't know the taste of liquor and he has no patience with men that drink. I'll get him to take you on as a chain man if you're game."

Then he introduced me to Shaw, who was in the drafting room adjoining, a heavily built man, six feet three inches tall, with a serious square face, clean shaven. Shaw looked at me dubiously.

"All right, if the General says so," he said. "Be in the plaza Sunday morning with your outfit. Get breakfast first."

Shaw was in the plaza, when I got there Sunday morning, a little before six, with my bag, full of clothes. I had had five drinks of whiskey, and a big breakfast. I was resolute and felt I could now stop drinking. A man full of whiskey, always feels that way. There were ten others waiting there, a second compass man for Shaw, seven chain men and mound men, a cowboy on horseback and a cook. All greenhorns but the cowboy, the cook and Shaw.

All of us were stalwart youths, none over twenty-five, except the cook, who was bearded and seemed about fifty. We were cheerful and looking forward with pleasure to fifty dollars a month, with board and the adventure of pioneering in a rough country.

We wore khaki trousers and coat, with blue shirt and heavy underclothing, which kept out both heat and cold, heavy low shoes, hobnail, for climbing over rocky hills and mountains or walking over slippery grass, and boot tops to protect our legs from snakes or the thorns of the mesquite. These boot tops were cut from old boots and we bought them in Santa Fe. They were much better than puttees. They were cut so that the bottom flat spread over the foot and instep, coming well over the shoe. Boots rub the heel of a walker and make blisters. These boot tops were perfect protection against rattlesnakes, and the country where we surveyed was a paradise for these reptiles. Once I saw Jim Ferguson, a compass man leading the party with which I was chaining, step on a coiled rattlesnake, as he was setting his compass for a site on a distant object. He looked down as he felt the snake strike his boots: saw that it was striking the boot top and not reaching as high as the unprotected leg above the knee, and keeping his foot tightly on the snake he finished setting the compass and then stepped off the snake and we killed it with a rock.

---

[50] The Spanish name "Puerta de Luna" is "Port of the Moon" in English and was a sparsely populated area on the Pecos River that was not condensed enough to be called a "town" or even a camp. It was about ten miles south of today's Santa Rosa and was considered at this time to be the end of civilization, or like going to the moon.

We did not wear the usual socks. Instead, we wore the foot covering all plainsmen know as the California sock. It is just a square of cotton cloth, in which the foot is wrapped loosely, folded over the toes. We had to walk sometimes as far as thirty-five miles a day, never less than twenty. The ordinary sock would be worn into holes by a day's walking like that and would rub the foot and make it sore.

With the boot tops and these cotton wrappings for the feet, we never had a man in our party laid up because of sore feet.

Shaw looked at me grimly, as I joined the party, and then at the bag I carried; "Got a bottle of whiskey in there?" he asked.

"I have not. General Atkinson told you about me? All right. I want to go with you and stop drinking."

Shaw grinned amiably. "You're on. You're going to have a good chance to get sober."

Then Shaw examined the whole outfit carefully. There was a covered wagon loaded with supplies, and drawn by six big Missouri mules, in prime condition. Thirty burros were standing packed, each with 100 pounds of food. The usual load for a burro is 150 pounds, but later when we got into dry country, these burros were to be packed with five gallon kegs of water also. There were two horses, one ridden and one led by the cowboy, Bill Martin, whose work was to hobble and graze animals at night and bring them in every morning.

The cook drove the wagon and we the burros.

"Now boys," said John Shaw, "we've got to walk eighty miles to the corner where will start running our lines. I want to make thirty miles today."

We struck out of Santa Fe, going due south, kept to the wide path over the hills called a road and after we passed through Cañoncito we left the road and went straight over the hills and the plains until we had made the thirty miles. Then we camped, too tired to put up tents and after dinner we rolled out our blankets and lay down. Everybody slept except me. I ached from head to foot. My nerves cried out for whiskey, and I could not turn my thoughts away from the craving.

At sunrise, we were up, aroused by the lusty shout of Shaw, "Roll out! Roll out!"

We rolled out of our blankets, rolled them and packed them in the tarpaulin covers, tied them and placed them in the wagon again. The cook had his kitchen set up in an open spot, and around the fire, in a circle, were tin plates and the knives and forks and spoons and coffee cups for each man. One by one, as each threw his bed into the wagon he chose a place, filled his plate and his cup from the center of supplies and squatted on the ground to eat.

14 | Surveying on the Plains

I could eat nothing. My stomach demanded whiskey, my mind was obsessed with the desire. And I knew there was none. I was tempted to desert the party and go back to Santa Fe, where I could satisfy the craving, but I knew I couldn't make the journey. I tried to worry down some coffee, but my stomach would not have it. I looked around furtively. Every man there was eating heartily, it made me sick to look at them. I was trembling all over. The man next to me, John Gannon, a Nebraska farm lad, said to me, sympathetically, "are you sick?"

"I can't eat. I need whiskey," I answered.

"Well, Bill, I'm sorry for you. I know just how you feel. But you can't get any and you better forget it."

Forget it! All that day, as we thrust along the plain, for there was no road, I was thinking of whiskey, and how good it would taste. I ate no lunch, but I did manage this time to get some coffee to stay in my stomach. A stomach that has learned to digest alcohol cannot digest anything else, unless that food is enveloped in alcohol, and when alcohol is withdrawn from that stomach, it is a long time before it regains the healthy tone that enables it to tolerate and assimilate real food.

To make my misery more intense, my nerves, which had been accustomed to the stimulant of alcohol were insisting on it, and resenting its lack they were making me feel their displeasure in every inch of my body. I was twitching and jumpy, and I felt as if insects were crawling over my skin, from head to foot.

In the afternoon of that second day, we were walking along, overland and full of mesquite bushes, some of them five feet high, in clumps, and soap weed, the smaller kind of maguey plant with long broad leaves, each with a spine at the end. Rattlesnakes whirred every now and then, the sunny sand was their favorite sleeping place, and when a rock was thrown at one he would uncoil and vanish into the nearest mesquite bush. Sometimes, as a man near the mesquite bush, the warning rattle would come, and he would stop.

"Say, you fellows, is that a snake or a locust?"

"Locust."

"Rattlesnake."

A stone would be flung into the bush. If a locust flew out, it was safe to push through the bush. If nothing was seen, it was assumed that the sound came from a snake and the walker would go around it. It is impossible to distinguish the rattle of the snake from the sound made by a locust.

I pushed through a great soapweed, too wretched to be on my guard against snakes and I suddenly felt a sharp sting in my leg. Then I remembered, and I leaped with a yell.

"What's the matter?" shouted the man nearest to me.

"I'm struck by a rattlesnake," I said.

I pulled up my trousers, while the others gathered around me. There was one deep puncture, from which blood was flowing. John Shaw came up on the run.

"A rattlesnake got Saunders," the men around me explained.

Shaw looked at the bleeding place, and then grinned. "Hell!" he said, "That's no rattlesnake. A soapweed stuck him. A snake would make two holes."

And so it was, a soapweed. We resumed our march, but from that day on I was known as "Soapweed Saunders," and the nickname clung to me as long as I was in New Mexico.

After we had been traveling for days, I could feel my body regaining its vigor. I was still eating very little and I was weak, but my muscles no longer jerked when I went to bed, and I was sleeping and awaking refreshed. We had walked 125 miles, following John Shaw, who each morning took a sight with his compass and then strode ahead. One afternoon, about four o'clock, he suddenly stopped and halted everybody.

"Here's where we'll begin our work," he said. "We got to find a corner of an old baseline, put here in 1854, when the first survey of New Mexico was made. There ought to be four mounds and in the center either a stake or a rock. We'll be here all week. Now, all hands put up the tents, and get your stuff in them and spread your blankets. Tomorrow morning we'll start looking for that corner."

We pitched camp, and Bill Martin, the horse wrangler, hobbled the mules and the burros and turned them out to graze.

That night I had my first real healthy sleep, and my food at breakfast tasted natural.

Two men, with ten burros, went off towards a line of cottonwood trees that promised water, and the rest of us hunted the lost corner, stooping and examining every foot of ground, and going in gradually widening circles. The winds, of course, had blown away every vestige of earth mounds, but we hoped to find the mark stake or rock. On the second day, we found the rock, so distinctly marked that there was no doubt that it was the corner we sought, half a mile away from the camp. Shaw was greatly pleased.

"We certainly would have been in a hell of a fix if we hadn't found that corner," he said.

"Now, we've got eighty townships to do, and we'll get about eighteen miles a day surveyed at the beginning."

The water party came back, with their ten burros and 150 gallons of water, which they had found in the little creek flowing along by the cottonwood trees, five miles away.

14 | Surveying on the Plains

"Now, I want to give you boys a lesson," said Shaw. "I saw one of you wash his hands a while ago and throw out the water. This water is to drink and cook with, and I'll give the dog water when I think he needs it. You can go over to that creek Sunday and bathe and you can take a wet towel in the mornings and rub the sand out of your eyes, but no wasting water, mind you."

For the whole ten months we were out on this survey we were never in a place where there was plenty of water, except once, when we camped on the Pecos River, muddy but high, so we could get a good bath. So baths were seldom taken and even washing our faces and hands was rare. Most of us were of clean habits, this went hard with us at first, but it is astonishing how men get used to things, after a while we did not even miss the washing.

Since we were in southern New Mexico, where the Apaches were raiding, we had to be prepared to fight off small bands of the Indians that might find us in their search for lonely ranches, so we had a number of Winchester rifles and plenty of cartridges in the wagon, and when we went out surveying the townships, each of the two boroughs we drove along, loaded with kegs of water and stone for the mound building, had two rifles strapped to his pack, one on each side. We ourselves wore belts with cartridges and a Colt .44 revolver in a holster.

We saw Apaches only once. That was one Sunday morning, when we were all in camp, and lying in our tents, Charlie Cornoyer, the cook, came running into Shaw's tent, where I was, shouting, "Here come the Indians."

Shaw leaped out of the tent into the wagon for his rifle. "Get the boys out with their guns," he called as he ran, and in two minutes we were out and armed.

We had shed nearly all our clothing, because of the heat, and one man was stark naked. He certainly made a funny picture, with his rifle and bandolier of cartridges around his middle.

"Lie down behind the wagon and the tents," ordered Shaw. "Spread out. Where's the stock?"

"Bill's got 'em down in the arroyo behind the tents, where the Indians can't see 'em," said Gannon.

"Crawl down and tell Bill to keep 'em there."

Shaw got his field glasses out of the wagon and took a look at the raiding Apaches. "They are a mile away," said Shaw, "and it's likely they are a small party of Victoria's scouts—Eleven in the crowd, and they've all got Winchesters. They're a war party—all painted and feathered. They're trying to make out how big a party we are. Now listen. When I say 'Fire,' all you fellows jump up and let 'em have a shot or two fast and then lie down again quick. Then they can't tell how many we are.

We did that and kept up a lively fire for fifteen or twenty minutes. The Indians returned the fire and galloped around the camp, yelling for an hour. They didn't dare attack us.

We saw no more of them but this little skirmish lost us much time. We didn't dare go out on line for nearly a week, and when we did start to work again, we were always uneasy until we got back to camp fearing that the band might have attacked the few men we had left there, killed them and gone off with our stock. But we found out, after we got back to Santa Fe that General Hatch and his troopers of the Ninth Cavalry had been pursuing the Indians so hotly that most of them had gone back into hiding on the Mescalero Apache reservation, or had fled into the mountains of Chihuahua.

Much of our surveying had to be done in an alkali country, in Lincoln County. None of us, not even Shaw, had lived long enough in that part of the territory to understand exactly the effects of drinking water impregnated with alkali. When the water comes from a spring in the rock it is clear as glass and pleasant to the taste, but it acts like a strong physic, and its continual drinking enfeebles the whole body. During August, we had to spend three weeks in surveying where the only water in the springs was alkaline, and we felt sick and weak all the time, and worked fast, so we might get out of the country.

One morning, while we were in this alkali country, all of us half sick and unable to eat, Shaw called us around him, after we had made an effort to swallow some coffee, bitter as gall, from the alkali water, in the bread and fat bacon the cook had placed before us.

"I'm going to move camp six miles west," he said, "where there is a freshwater lake. If we stay here we'll all be dead. I'll stay with the mules, so that the cook won't get off the line. I want Jim Ferguson to carry the compass, and let John Gannon relieve him. Gannon will chain with Saunders at first and Peters will be mound man. I want you to do eighteen miles on this township, and then, if you are right, and I am right, you'll close within a hundred feet of the new camp. At five miles, you ought to strike a lake of fresh water, so you needn't take much of that alkali water in the keg, and don't drink much of it."

Then he set up the compass and trained its sight on a tall pine tree which stood alone on a mountain peak more than fifty miles away.

"Come here, Jim, and you, John," he said to Ferguson and Gannon, "and take a sight on that tree," he ordered.

Ferguson and Gannon came and sighted the tree. "Now," went on Shaw, "we're going six miles straight towards that tree. You ought to see it anywhere on your line."

14 | Surveying on the Plains

We started off. We were in the sandiest, hottest part of Lincoln County and drinking this alkali water for a week had exhausted us. Shaw evidently planned to make camp near one of the freshwater lakes he knew and replenish the camp supply of water from that. The chaining and the digging of the mounds for the corners was unusually hard work. The sand we threw up was like a furnace and although we started with a supply of flat rocks for the corners we soon had to I seek others and often we had to walk a quarter of a mile for a good one. The walking in the heavy sand exhausted us. Consumed with thirst, we drank the alkali water, trusting that at the freshwater lake we could fill the keg, and even promising ourselves a bath in the lake. We ate as much of the lunch we carried as we could and gave the rest to the burros carrying the stones for the corners.

We ran six miles, one side of the township, and then turned and chained four miles further. There was a deep depression in the plain, about 500 yards square. It had been a lake but now there were only a few gallons of water, muddy and thick as pea soup, in it. We dropped compass and chain and ran to it, but when we scooped it up with our hands, it was liquid mud—entirely undrinkable. It was ten o'clock. The sun above shown on us like a fireball, and heat waves from the sand enveloped us. We sat down and rolled cigarettes. It is a strange thing, but smoking a cigarette seems to relieve thirst in the early stages. The fifteen minutes smoke revived us, at least we were able to respond when compass man Ferguson said, "We've done ten miles and we have only eight more to go before we strike camp. That ought to be easy."

Have you ever felt thirst? No doubt you have been thirsty, as you walked along in a city or road in an automobile or strolled along a country road, but always you have known that you could shake that thirst whenever you please by stopping at a soda fountain or a farmhouse. Sometimes you have even nursed that thirst so that you might enjoy the drink when you got it.

But the thirst that shipwrecked people feel in an open boat, when their water is exhausted—such as we felt on this great expanse of hot sand, under the pitiless sun, is a far different thing. Our hair, our clothes were burning. Our skin was dry and the perspiration no longer exuded, because there was no more moisture in our bodies.

We chained the eight miles in a daze, barely whispering our signals, and throwing up the mounds for the corners in the most sketchy way.

I doubt if anybody ever found those corners we left. We finished the last and threw ourselves on the ground in collapse. Ferguson, staggering himself, aroused us from the coma into which we had sunk.

"Now, listen here, you fellows," he croaked, "just got to find that camp or we're done. It ought to be around here somewhere, over one of those hills."

But it was not. We hunted until dark, and then lay down in a shallow canyon into which we had stumbled, and slept like dead men. The light of the next morning did not wake us, but the sun did, falling across our faces at noon. We sat up and rolled cigarettes, but this time, we could not smoke. Our tongues were thick and it was painful to whisper even.

"We've got to find that camp," said Ferguson, "and you bet they're looking out for us. Let's try over yonder."

We followed him and dragged one leg after another for a time. Then, one by one we lay down strung along over the sand for half a mile. By this time, we were neither hungry nor thirsty, our minds and bodies were without sensation. We lay without moving until sunup the next day and then a shout roused us from our stupor. We looked up. Here came John Shaw, silhouetted against a rise in the plain, with his long shambling stride, his whole six feet of body strung around with canteens.

"This is fresh water, boys," he said. "Got it from a little pool back yonder the cattle hadn't found. Be careful, now. Drink a little at a time, or you'll all be sick as hell."

What a heavenly taste that was—that water, and how it brought back strength into our bodies. I felt as if energy were being pumped into me with every sip.

It was an hour before we could get up and walk, and then Shaw led us to the camp over a rise in the ground, not half a mile away. "You fellows were never a mile from the camp all the time," Shaw said. "There is no water in camp, and I've sent out a party to try for water at a rainwater lake five miles away. They ought to be back now."

But they were not, and when we got to camp, since no tents were up, we lay down in the shade of the covered wagon, still feeble and craving water. All the water Shaw had brought in the canteens had been drunk, but it had not filled our parched tissues. We had in the wagon quantities of canned vegetables and I brought out can after can of tomatoes and handed them around. A delicious drink the juice made.

About nightfall, the party returned bringing to our great joy, ten burros, each bearing fifteen gallons of fresh water. We ate nothing, but lay for hours sipping water with vinegar, and so went to sleep. When we waked the next morning, we were completely restored to strength.

"Why can't we camp by that lake?" I asked Shaw.

"It's too far to walk to our work. We'll send the burros for water every two days, and we'll be out of this hell pretty soon."

I told this incident to an old plainsman once. "Well," he said, "most people would think that forty-eight hours of that water wasn't much of a thing to howl about, but they've never been on the desert of Arizona or New Mexico. If you fellows hadn't been young and strong you couldn't have even crawled back to camp after Shaw found you."

A rough road ran by Pine's Wells, the road the buckboards took carrying the mail. One morning in August as we started out for the day's surveying, and cross the road, a buckboard came by. We all stopped and we begged the man for news. We had heard nothing from the outside world since we had left Santa Fe, four months before.

"Well," said the driver, "I hear that the President, Mr. Garfield, has been shot and killed in Washington."

"My God," exclaimed Ferguson, "Who did it?"

"The Vice President, Arthur. He wanted to be President himself."[51]

That was all the driver knew.

We did not learn the truth of this for weeks later, and spent much time wondering why the Vice President should have killed the President.

We had left Santa Fe early in May, and it was now the last of October. We had surveyed all around Roswell, and had gone down south as far as the celebrated caves of Carlsbad, about which nobody knew anything at that time. The town of Carlsbad had not been settled. Roswell, now a town of schools, colleges, churches and even a military school, was then a settlement only, with a store and post office but nothing more, all the few houses frame. We had been all through that burning Spring and Summer in the hottest part of New Mexico, and had got accustomed to it. Now, it was getting cooler we felt stronger.

"Boys," said John Shaw to us at breakfast one morning, "we're going into Mora County next and work there all winter. There's a lot of land grant lines we've got to run. There are two more townships to run here; then we'll walk over to Puerto de Luna and outfit; we need a lot of things. Then I'll take Saunders and go ahead of you tomorrow and lay out the work, while you stay at Puerto de Luna for three days and rest up."

After breakfast I went to Shaw. "Why do you want me?" I asked.

---

[51] President Garfield was shot by Charles J. Guiteau on July 2, 1881, four months after taking office. Chester Arthur was vice-president at the time and did not shoot Garfield. Guiteau's motive was evidently revenge on an imagined failure to reward him for a political campaign debt. Garfield lived until September 19, 1881 with inefficient medical care and probably died of infection from a bullet in his body that the doctors could not find.

"Well, you're in good shape now, and I want you to help me with my field notes."

I was rejoiced. This was a certificate that I was a man again, not a nervous drunkard. But I had been cured for a long time, and had not realized the change that had come over me.

At Puerto de Luna there was a big outfitting store, in the center of the Mexican town, which was on the mail road to Texas. A train of wagons had just come in from Santa Fe, loaded with all kinds of merchandise. One of the wagons was filled with bottled beer. None of us had tasted beer for five months. Our tissues and flesh were dried out by the heat we had gone through, and when we had camped we made a descent on the store and sitting on boxes, and on the floor, drank beer until the cook called us for dinner in the evening.

One would think that I, of all men, would have abstained but I did not. I drank with the rest. We made our way to the circle around the cook's equipment, where our plates were laid out and began to eat, with appetite already satisfied by the beer. I was falling asleep with my plate in my lap when I was aroused by a yell and looking up I saw Bill Martin, the stock wrangler, with his Colt in his hand menacing the cook, against whom he had cherished a grudge for a long time. They were within the circle, and the frightened cook was backing away from Bill, begging, "Don't kill me, Bill, I ain't done nothing. Don't shoot."

"Dance, damn you," Bill ordered, and Charley danced clumsily, while Bill shot into the ground by his feet. I got up and made Bill put up his gun and we all went off to a Mexican Baile.

The cook made complaint to Shaw, who had not been at dinner, and the next morning, Bill was discharged; got on his horse and rode away.

Of course we were all sorry to lose Bill, but Shaw was right. Next to Shaw himself, the important man in the party was the cook.

He was an expert. He could do anything, if he had plenty of wood and water. It was the job of the camp man to find him wood, very often we were where there was no fuel. There were always mesquite and soap weed. The soap weed had a stick in its middle that burns very well, but too quickly. The root of the mesquite is the best of all firewood, very hard and slow burning, making a very hot fire. When the camp man could not get enough fuel, we would take a burro and go out with an axe and a shovel, to dig up the mesquite roots, and we would come back with a load that would last the cook two days. Sometimes it happened, when we were on the march and did not want to stop to spend the time looking for wood we would hurriedly gather a lot of the round cakes of cattle dung, what the frontiersman calls still buffalo chips. These burn fiercely but quickly, too.

14 | Surveying on the Plains

This little beer spree did not arouse my desire for liquor in me. I had no craving for whiskey when I started for Mora with Shaw. We had five burros, carrying supplies, and instruments, and one horse, which I rode. Shaw scorned a horse, and in fact he could outwalk any horse.

Mora was 200 miles away, and we made it in a week. We passed through the town and camped a mile away. It was cold—snow was on the mountains, and the wind was biting, but we had plenty of wood from the forest nearby, and we got up Shaw's notes in a day, after we began to work. When the main party arrived we were ready for them.

What a change this surveying was from the kind we had been doing. The ground was covered after October with three inches of snow, or more, and often the wind was so strong that we could not put up the tents but had to sleep out in the open. Two men always slept together. We would scrape the snow off the ground where we wanted to lay our blankets, put down one of the tarpaulins in which we wrapped the blankets during the day; spread the blankets, and then lay the second tarpaulin over the top.

We used our shoes and boot tops for pillows, placing them under the blankets. When we lay in the blankets, we would pull the tarpaulin over our heads, and this protected us from the cold and the snow, which at times fell on us during the night. I have often waked in the morning, to find ourselves covered completely with snow which had fallen during the night but had not waked us up.

It was very hard work, though, surveying in the snow. We had gloves, but usually did not wear them. They made compass work and chaining very inaccurate. We had, however, plenty of timber for the corner post, and so this Mora county surveying was more permanent than that done in Lincoln County where the corners were only holes, soon filled up and stones, hard to find after the corners had been obliterated by the drifting sand.

Canyons, large and small, were frequent. The lines we had to survey often led across these canyons, and we had to clamber down their sides, pushing or driving the burros we had to have with us to carry our cornerstones and provisions. These little animals hated the cold and hated worse the climbing with a load. Once we were going up the side of a canyon, and we came to jutting rocks, up which we swung with our chain, but we could not get the burro up.

"What's the matter?" called Shaw, impatient at the delay.

"Can't get the burro up."

Shaw came to the edge of the big rock and looked over. Then he took a firm grip on a tree with his legs; swung himself over till he could reach the saddle of the burro and with both arms lifted the little creature up beside him. That was a straight lift of five hundred pounds.

Another time, we had picked up a wandering sheep herder and had employed him as a burro driver. He was behind the burro climbing the precipitous and wooded side of a canyon behind the chain man, and had nearly reached the top. The burro had been cunningly trying to dodge around him and go down again, but he had been skillfully foiling all these efforts, until he stopped to roll a cigarette, when the burro, seizing the opportunity, with a leap got by him and slid down the side of the canyon. The Mexican, desperately try to intercept him, shouting, "Hodido cabron!" and then, as he saw that the burro had escaped and that he must climb all the way down the canyon and back again, "God dammy son a bitchy!"

And then he sat down on the ground and burst into tears.

One of our men went snow blind and had to be sent into Mora and then into the Santa Fe hospital. He was tied behind the wagon which took him into Mora and walked with that guide.

In this cold of the Mora plateau our wise cook changed our diet, and we lived on beans, beef, which we had now to buy, coffee and clear side bacon. Clear side bacon is bacon without a particle of lean in it, almost pure lard. We were very fond of it. A meal of that, with bread and coffee would send a warm glow through a shivering body.

I don't know how the government surveying elsewhere was done, but that done in New Mexico, certainly, in the eighties, was very bad work. Contracts for the surveying of so many townships were given to surveyors by the Surveyor General. It was paid for by the mile, and for the wooded country and the mountainous parts the surveyor got about one-third more than for the level and plain land. There was no check on the surveyors and often they reported township after township as wooded or mountainous when in fact they were level lands.

Then, too, the surveyor was supposed to survey the four sides of a township, six miles to a side, and then to run the township lines inside, laying off the township into sections and putting in corners every half a mile, marking each corner with a stake or a stone. In fact, the surveyors did nothing of the kind, but intent on making money, they ran the outside lines of the township and then ran into the township, angling about, putting in a corner here and there. We used to do a township in three days—to put in all the corners the law required would have taken at least seven days.

14 | Surveying on the Plains

The profits of government surveying were very large and every surveyor made money. I do not know how in the world the ranch men who afterwards took up the land we surveyed found their "numbers," as the section locations were called. They must have guessed at it or they must have started at a township line, and done a lot of work that should not have been necessary.

We got back to Santa Fe in January. I never felt more fit. I was able bodied and clear-headed. While I had been gone, the *New Mexican* have been bought by the Santa Fe Railroad Company, whose officials had sent an editor from Kansas to manage it, and he employed me at once to edit the telegraph matter and help him with the writing of the editorial page. Henry Brooke, who had been my associate on the paper when I left Santa Fe, had entire charge of the news. I did not return to drinking while I was doing this work, but my open-air life had spoiled me for office work and I chafed at the desk.

Then two Santa Fe men started the *Albuquerque Review*, an afternoon paper and asked me to run it for them. I jumped at the opening, and went at once to Albuquerque. And then I began sliding into that same pit of alcoholism from which I had with such agony extricated myself. I drank whiskey to stimulate myself for my work and for enjoyment. I made an effort to get rid of the appetite and went prospecting with two men who seldom drank. We had a good prospect in Hell Canyon, near Albuquerque, and I kept at the drilling with my companions for two months, but the whiskey craving had me and I left them one morning and walked the thirty miles back to Albuquerque and went to bed that night in drunken satisfaction.

Surveying was not especially accurate in New Mexico at the time Saunders was there. He admitted that his and other crews simply did not do their jobs well, as they were paid a lump sum for the territory they were covering.

Courtesy of educational Technology Clearinghouse, http:lletc.usc.edu

I deliberately surrendered my management of the *Review*, because it entailed too much responsibility, and got a reporter's job on the *Albuquerque Democrat*, so I could be out among the gambling houses and saloons, where there was usually more news than anywhere else. I lost my ambition and cared only to be comfortably drunk all the time.

Then, in alcoholic aberration one day, I abandoned the newspaper business in Albuquerque, and wandered down to Silver City, beating my way in boxcars. From there I went to Camp Fleming, a new silver strike, where I got work as a shoveler for a while, drinking whenever I could get whiskey. One day, the thought struck me that I would like to get back to Ouray. I dropped my shovel and started.

It was six hundred miles. It is hard to remember now how I got there, but I did. I tramped the ties, road and boxcars with unfriendly brakeman, to one of whom I sold my coat; I sat on the driver's seat with friendly buckboard drivers who wanted companionship. I got nothing to drink between Camp Fleming and Ouray, but as much as I wanted among my old friends at Ouray. I stayed in Ouray that winter and towards spring went to Denver, where I wrote for the *Times* and for the *Republican*. I made money and I was never sober.

Then I went to St Louis and got work on the *Chronicle*.

I settled down to serious newspaper writing, but found that the appetite for alcohol was as strong as ever. Next to the office of the *Chronicle* was a "barrelhouse." One went in there, found near the door a barrel of first-rate whiskey, drank as much as he pleased and left a dime in a box. I never went out on an assignment for news without stopping in that place and taking a big drink. I was then twenty-six years old, very healthy and heartily enjoyed the liquor, and while I did not drink as much as I had drunk Santa Fe I was always more or less under its influence. At last I took counsel with myself and resolved to stop it. I felt that the whiskey was no longer stimulating me but was blurring my mind.

"The way to stop," I said to myself, "is to drink no more whiskey, but only wine."

There was a wine house on Walnut Street, where the wine was good and cheap. I did stop drinking whiskey and began to drink wine, when I felt the need of a stimulant. None of my drinking companions cared for that kind of stimulant, I found, so I had to drink alone. I kept to the wine for a month or more, and then I found that the wine made me as drunk as the whiskey had done. I was not satisfied to drink a little wine, slowly in sips, but I craved the effect and drank it till I got the exhilaration.

"Well," I thought, "that experiment is a failure. How is it that my German newspaper friends drink beer all the time and seemingly never get drunk. I'm going to try beer.

So I cultivated my associates of the German press, went to their saloons with them and drank only beer. But I was not satisfied with the small amount of beer that they drank and I drank more. I never left the saloon where we played games for the drinks without having the elation of mind that came from the alcohol in the beer.

"So," I communed with myself again, "beer will make me drunk, too. Well, there's nothing for me but total abstinence. I can see that."

Then I drank nothing but water and coffee for three years, and devoted myself to my work. I was pleased with the new habit. I slept better and was clear-headed. I did some good work on the newspapers and began to make a reputation. Then I took stock of myself again.

"Now," I thought, "I would just as soon be a drunkard lying in the gutter as a man who cannot take one drink of whiskey or wine or even beer. I'm going to try a little drinking and see if I can stop whenever I want."

I returned to drinking and drank everything, a little and only at night. I made it a rule never to drink in the daytime no matter what the temptation. And I found that I could achieve the balance between desire and caution. I was overjoyed when I found that I had gained self-control and could drink without getting drunk, but in the course of time I concluded there was little pleasure in drinking whiskey, and I seldom drink anything but wine or beer. That has been my habit for nearly forty years.

I decided to write this chapter, after much thought believing that I might help some other fellow who was irresolutely wondering whether or not he could master the craving for liquor that had control of him.

I think I have shown that this can be done, provided the man has a definite purpose in life which he knows he cannot attain while he is a drunkard.

And I have concluded that it cannot be done without a period of total abstinence.

Moreover, a man should train himself to be satisfied and to get real pleasure from drinking wine and beer, avoiding whiskey like poison.

There is no man in the world who can honestly say he drinks whiskey and has never been drunk.

In order to make these points I have had to keep the mind of my reader on drinking and to trace my experience through my entire life, putting aside for the moment all other incidents.

I will now go back to take up the thread of my story, telling the windup of my newspaper work in Albuquerque, Ouray and Denver in my final farewell to the frontiers of the Far West.

CHAPTER 15

Albuquerque Raw and Turbulent

A quiet Mexican town jolted into wildness by the coming of Americans... the danger of editing a reform paper on the frontier... bad men have fun with guns and a journalist... Wyatt Earp and Doc Holliday fleeing from a sheriff's posse bluff the town... former Senator Ross who saved President Andrew Johnson from impeachment goes on my payroll at fifteen dollars a week... the courage of Vinnie Ream.

ALBUQUERQUE, when I went down there in 1882 and founded *The Review*, was composed of two towns, about a mile apart. One, a straggling little Mexican adobe village, had been a small settlement when the Spaniards came in. They had built it up and had called it after the Duke of Albuquerque. The Rio Grande River, yellow and ugly, but supplying plenty of water for irrigation, flowed by the town, and the Mexicans raised excellent vegetables and fruits. Unlike Santa Fe, there were no rich people in the town, but they lived contented lives; had a church and weekly dances, with frequent fiestas, when business was stopped and everybody went in for merrymaking.

The Atchison, Topeka and Santa Fe railway ended at Albuquerque, and the Atlantic and Pacific railway, afterwards absorbed by the Santa Fe, began there and was then building west towards San Francisco, its goal. Both railways had headquarters and shops in the new town, which had begun to grow up along the railway. Buildings in the old town were of adobe; in the new town they were frame—a few of brick. Some hopeful man had organized a company and had started a streetcar line between the two towns, but the car ran so slowly that most people either walked or rode the distance on horseback or in buggies and buckboards. Most of the business was in the new town. One broad Street, called Railroad Avenue, connected the two towns. Usually the community numbered about 15,000, but on Saturday nights when the construction trains came in from the end of the tracks, loaded with men eager to get their pay and spend it, there were perhaps 20,000. The 5,000 wanted to drink and gamble and consort with women and the new town gave them all of that. Railroad Avenue was lined from the tracks for half a mile with saloons, gambling houses, hotels, which always had saloons and gambling rooms attached, and houses where women received the stranger. These amorous places usually centers of disorder, were distinguished by red curtains, and there were eleven on the street. The new town was always noisy and the old town quiet, and men with families usually lived in the old town. In the new town, during the week end, it was almost impossible to sleep. The shooting, shouts and screaming of women kept up nearly all night.

The town was not a resort of killers, but with all these rough men, of course, there were frequent murders and pistol fights on the street. The sheriff and his deputies were all Mexicans and they were always invisible when there was any trouble in the streets or in any of the houses. The sheriff owned the only wholesale liquor house in the two towns and sold nearly all the supplies to the places that cater to the public. He wanted to make no enemies.

I looked over the two towns for a week and then I picked out one of the few adobe houses in the new town as the place for the *Review*. It was in the very center of the town and therefore a good place for news. There was no street in front; just a sandy plain; but one could step out of the back door, go through a saloon, where a faro table was going most of the time, and be on Railroad Avenue, and in the thick of whatever was going on.

From the very first number of the paper, I insisted that Albuquerque was going to be a very large town and that it must clean up and become orderly. To begin with, I clamored for the removal of the red curtain houses from Railroad Avenue to some back street, and that demand got a large part of the population of the town down on me at once. The real estate men, the saloons and gamblers and the women themselves all wanted the places to stay where they were. It was so convenient. I was threatened by the railroad roughs as I walked the streets, women sitting at the windows of the red light houses laughed and jeered at me as I passed, and my friends remonstrated with me.

"Why should you try to run a reform newspaper in Albuquerque?" they said.

"It's a railroad town and it's got to be tough. You go ahead and give us the news and let the preaching alone."

My experience in Santa Fe, when the gambler had tried to kill me on the plaza, had made me cautious, and I never went out of the office without two double barrel Remington derringers, one in each pocket.

I tried to keep my hands on them as I walked the streets, but I usually forgot, not being a gun man, and the consequence was, that three times when my life was in danger and I needed the pistols, I was taken off my guard and couldn't get at them.

The journalism of that day was so personal that the younger newspapermen, impulsive and eager to expose injustice and wrong were constantly being attacked in their offices or on the street by desperados whom they had denounced.

In Socorro, a thriving little town near Albuquerque, the editor of the *Sun*, a courageous and earnest man named Conklin, was shot from ambush and killed one day, and although everybody had a very good idea who had killed him, nothing was ever done about it.

I sat in the front part of the *Review* building, facing the cases where the printers were setting type or running off the paper on the press, so I could see everything going on in the office. A window looking on the plain outside was behind me, and a curtain drawn halfway up hid me from the sight of anyone passing in front. I was not nervous, but I was too cautious to sit there exposed to a shot from an enemy.

Once, the Marshal of Albuquerque, a Mexican called Celso Guttierrez came into my office while I was bent over my desk and throwing a Colt .45 revolver down on me, announced loudly that he was going to kill me. I saw he was drunk, and asked him to sit down and talk over the matter. He was taken aback by the courtesy and at once holstered his pistol and began to explain.

"I shot up that house," said he, "because that man owed me $100 and wouldn't pay me, and when my wife went to get the money last week, he insulted her."

"Why didn't you tell me that, when I asked you about it before I wrote the article?"

"Because I was sore and thought it was none of your damn business."

"I'll print your explanation today," I said and he left the office, satisfied, even shaking my hand before he went out.

At another time, a deputy sheriff of Socorro County killed a prisoner whom he was taking to jail, seemingly just for fun. The man was handcuffed and was making no attempt to escape. I wrote an editorial demanding that this officer be removed, saying that we were not in Old Mexico where that sort of thing was done and justified under the *ley de fuga*.

Two days after that this deputy sheriff walked into my office and throwing a big Colt down on me, as I sat in my chair, announced, "I'm the fellow in Socorro you want removed from office. I'm going to kill you like Conklin."

15 | Albuquerque Raw and Turbulent

Three men were at the press, running off the paper, and they saw and heard, and with no weapons, started to my defense. The deputy drew another gun and covered the three.

"Get back there, and keep out of this or I'll get you all," he shouted and since it was plain that he could have got them all, they fell back. I had nothing but words to meet the glaring eyes of the man with the two guns and if ever I was eloquent, I was then.

I must have talked pretty well, but I don't remember a word that I said. He wavered from his murderous purpose and sat down by me, and told me the whole story of the killing.

"The man was a killer himself, and I was afraid if he got away, he would get me, so I had to get him first."

"Well," said I, "I will print what you say in tomorrow's paper."

"No, you don't. Just forget all about it. Now let's go out and have a drink."

We had several drinks and presently found ourselves in the roller skating rink, going around and around, hand-in-hand and falling down

The newspaper business was a dangerous occupation in the late 19th century. Angry subjects of articles often showed up with a gun to settle the matter. This engraving shows the news room of the Rocky Mountain News. *Note the employee's guns on the chair at the far left.*
From Albert Richardson, *Beyond the Mississippi*.

with each other in the most friendly way. Early in the morning, I left him at the Armijo House and never saw him afterwards.

The third time when I needed a gun, I got no chance to talk. Stung by my editorial articles, calling on the authorities to clean up Railroad Avenue, a Grand Jury pretended to investigate the conditions, and when I appeared before it I had to name a man who owned most of the houses where the unwary were drugged and robbed, enticed into them by women.

The next day, I was sauntering along the street, when this man came up behind me and knocked me down with a heavy stick. I grappled with him, pulled him down and we rolled around on the sidewalk, beating each other until we were separated. I got the stick and examining it, I saw that on its heavy knob, with which I had been struck, were carved the words, "I wrote that article."

"That's Tom Hughes' stick," said a bystander.

Hughes was the editor of the *Journal*, a very timid paper, who I supposed was a friend of mine. I went to see him with the stick in my hand.

"Why did you lend Ellis that stick? Did he tell you he was going to attack me?"

"Certainly not," answered Hughes. "Ellis told me he had a son just out of college in San Francisco, who was crazy to come out here and start a newspaper. Ellis didn't want him to come, and he said he intended to photograph that stick and send the picture to the boy to show him what a tough time editors out here really had."

"Well, I'll keep the stick, if you don't mind," I said, and I did.

The *Review* was an afternoon paper, and one morning, early in May 1882, I was writing furiously for the two fast printers we had, when the foreman rushed up to me excitedly, "Look out!" he exclaimed, "There are two bad man outside and they say they want to see you."

I got up and went outside. Two men sat on horseback in the street, with rifles strapped to their saddle flaps, pistol holsters at their sides, and one with a sawed-off shotgun lying before him on the saddle. Both had long mustaches and wore boots and sombreros, with the brims pulled down over their foreheads. They were young men, about thirty-five each; both were thin, but one was tall and one short. They were drooping in the saddle from long hours of hard riding, but they straightened up as I appeared, and bent steady eyes on me. The tall one with the shotgun spoke, "I'm Wyatt Earp and this is Doc Holliday. We're on our way to Colorado and we want to stop here today and rest our horses, and we don't want a damned word in your paper about our being here. Does that go?"

15 | Albuquerque Raw and Turbulent

"You bet it does," I answered. "There's a stable over there, and the Armijo Hotel is right around the corner."

Wyatt Earp and John H. Holliday, the consumptive dentist from Kansas, were the two best known killers of Arizona. I had been hearing for a year of the gunfights in Tombstone with Earp, who was a United States Marshal, his brothers, Morgan and Virgil Earp and Doc Holliday, on one side, and a band of outlaws, cattle rustlers and stage robbers on the other side, furtively supported by a crooked sheriff who hated the Earps. In these fights Morgan Earp had been killed and Virgil severely wounded, but Wyatt and Holliday had miraculously escaped the bullets.

When they left me, Earp and Holliday rode to the office of the *Albuquerque Journal*, the other newspaper, and got from Tom Hughes, the editor there, his promise to print nothing about their presence in town. Then they rode to the railway station and saw the agent, and he too gave them his word that he would send out nothing. At ease then, they put up their horses, and went to the Armijo House, where they ate their meals and Doc Holliday played billiards, Earp looking on. The people of Albuquerque paid no special attention to them.

After my paper went to press I went over to the hotel and sat by Earp watching Doc Holliday play billiards. He was not loquacious, but neither was he taciturn.

"We're going up into Colorado and ranch," said Earp, "if Doc can stand it. I don't know. He's got consumption bad. I may have to put him in a hospital. I'm sick of this gunplay, and I don't want to wear a star again, ever. They've got Morgan and Virgil and they'll sure get me if I keep it up. I've never killed a man except in self-defense and doing my duty as an officer. If you write anything about me, I want you to say that, and that goes for Doc Holliday, too."

I noticed that Earp did not carry his shotgun in the billiard room and ask him about it.

"I don't carry it," said he, "except when I'm riding. Doc hates 'em, but I like it sometimes, if more than one man is coming at you. It scatters buckshot, and it'll tear a man wide open. We had a fight coming over here and that gun did a lot of good."

I learned afterwards that two days before, in a battle with his enemies, Earp had almost cut a man I two with that shotgun. I asked him what weapon he preferred.

"Just my Colt here," he said. "I've got the feel of it and can handle it with my eyes shut."

I told him that I had known Billy the Kid, and he asked me many questions about him.

"Was he fast on the draw?" he asked. "I've heard he was slow."

"That's so," I said. "His specialty was catching a man off his guard." Earp nodded.

"Yes, I've heard that, too," he said, "but he could fight face-to-face when he had to. Now I'm slow with a gun, too, but I've got the best of many a faster man, just because I always aim to hit when I shoot, without thinking of what the other fellow is doing. If you do that you'll get nervous and your aim will wobble."

I showed Earp the pistols I carried, two little double-barreled derringers, one in each trouser pocket. He looked at the pistol tolerantly, and his set face relaxed in a smile.

"Well, that'll do for an editor," he said, "but not for a peace officer. Not enough shots, and it carries too big a ball for your aim. It would jerk up."

An Arizona sheriff's posse, composed of bitter enemies of the two, was scouring the country for Earp and Holliday at this moment. These pursuers were within fifty miles of Albuquerque, but they thought the two men were hiding in the mountains and had not the remotest idea that they would be bold enough to ride into a town with newspapers and a telegraph office, and stay there for the night. Had this station agent been treacherous and sent out word that Earp and Holliday were in Albuquerque, or had anyone else telegraphed, there would have been a battle in the streets of the town before morning. But the people of Albuquerque sympathized with the harried outlaws and they slept quietly and rode out towards Colorado at daybreak the next morning.

One morning, in 1883, I was busy with the shears and paste at my desk in the office of the *Albuquerque Review,* when I felt the presence of a stranger behind me. Looking up, I saw a man who my newspaper instinct told me was somebody. He was a small man; seemed to be about seventy years old; was bearded, and carried a stick; and he wore a frock coat, very strange attire for Albuquerque.

"You write all this paper?" he asked.

"Yes, I do, editorial matter and local news, and I edit the telegraph we get from Santa Fe."

"Don't you want somebody to write your editorial for you?"

"Yes, I do. I don't write good editorials and I know it."

"I'd like to do it for you. My name is Ross.⁵² I used to be United States Senator from Kansas. I suppose you can pay very little."

"Almost nothing," I confessed.

"I'll write a column a day for you for five dollars a week."

I learned afterward what a famous man was sitting at the rough desk in my adobe room, writing editorials for me at five dollars a week. Sometimes, indeed, he did not even get that, when advertising collections were slow and all of us went on half-pay. He was Edmund G. Ross, the courageous Senator from Kansas whose vote had prevented the impeachment of President Andrew Johnson in 1868, and who had been execrated and consigned to oblivion by the leaders of the Republican party for defeating their powerful plot.

Senator Ross worked for me for several months and I grew to respect and admire him greatly. He had suffered by that political act. He had gone to Washington a vigorous man of forty, with a promising political future, and he knew that his vote for the President would ruin him.

Edmund G. Ross posed for Matthew Brady. Photo Courtesy of Library of Congress.

During the impeachment trial, when the votes for President Johnson and against him were being listed, and the Republicans were bringing every kind of pressure on the Senators to get the thirty-six votes they needed to impeach, Ross was tortured by the threats he got from his party bosses in Kansas, who were afraid of him and distrusted

---

⁵² Kansas Senator Edmund G. Ross cast the deciding vote against convicting President Andrew Johnson from "high" crimes and misdemeanors in his impeachment trial. Ross was one of seven Republican Senators that did not vote for impeachment and the two-third impeachment vote failed 35-19. Why he did so is still a matter of debate, but the vote destroyed his political career. He was later one of the eight senators recognized by John F. Kennedy in his famous book, *Profiles of Courage*. After meeting Saunders, Ross moved to New Mexico where he spent the rest of his life.

his allegiance. He showed me his scrapbook and in it was a telegram sent to him, just before the voting began, signed by "D. R. Anthony and 1,000 others," saying that Kansas would repudiate him if he voted "Not Guilty" on the charges against the President. Anthony was the head of the Republican party in Kansas.

Ross answered the telegram, saying that he would vote as his sense of duty would tell him to vote, and he got in reply to that a most vituperative message from Boss Anthony, reading him out of the party.

But that was not all. As a last resort, Ross was threatened with a scandalous exposure of an intimacy between him and Vinnie Ream, the sculptress, who at the time of the trial was making a bust of Lincoln for the government and had a studio in the capital. This relationship did not exist.

"Vinnie Ream and I were very intimate friends," said Ross to me. "And I often dropped into her studio as she worked, and talked with her. She was also a friend of President Johnson, who got her several commissions. When I heard that the men who wanted me to vote for impeachment were whispering the story that Vinnie Ream was influencing me, I thought it over and then went to her and told her that there was danger they would get some paper to print the scandalous lie, and that would hurt her as well as me.

"I remember very well how she took this. She kept working on for a minute while she pondered. Then she came and sat down by me. 'If you vote against impeachment, and they print that story, my reputation will be injured, perhaps,' she said. 'But you will be ruined politically. Well, you vote as your conscience tells you, and don't think of me. If you can stand it, I can.'"

"They never printed the story, although it was hinted at in the press."

"President Johnson should have been very grateful to you," I said. "Did he offer you an office?"

"I was offered several offices," answered Ross, "but of course I could accept nothing. I voted against the impeachment because I thought it was wrong."

Senator Ross really had been driven out of Kansas by poverty, although he had remained there for ten years after the impeachment trial, trying to make a living. The Republican party was done with him and of course he made slow headway aligning himself with the Democrats. He had come to New Mexico with a little money, and hoped to build up a law practice.

He was really only fifty-two years old then. His appearance of age was caused by his mental worry, and he never recovered his physical strength. The lines of suffering in his face were always deep, but his clear gray eyes were always youthful.

Senator Ross wrote his last editorial for me in 1884. It was a strong argument for the admission of New Mexico into the Union as a state. In 1885 President Cleveland appointed him Governor of New Mexico, and that recognition restored his self-respect to a degree. He saved some money while he was governor and spent his last years in comfort.

Before he died he wrote a thorough and detailed account of the impeachment trial, which is in all the libraries, a most modest tale, saying nothing of his great part in the trial, except the report of his vote.

At the time I knew Senator Ross, Vinnie Ream was only the name of a sculptor of distinction to me, and I knew nothing of her work or her personal charm which made her famous. Years after, in 1905, I was floundering my way through a muddy gully in the unfinished grounds of the St Louis World's Fair, when I saw a woman trying to climb the slippery banks of the little ravine and went to her aid. When I had extricated her, and we were smiling at each other on the bank, we introduced ourselves. She was Vinnie Ream.[53]

A flood of memories rolled over my mind, and of course I begged her to let me be her cicerone for a while. We had lunch together and talked about Senator Ross. She was stout, and walking was hard for her, but her mind was full of the Washington history of which she had been a part, and our conversation was delightful. I could well imagine how she had fascinated men in the sixties.

"Senator Ross was a fine person," she said, "I wish that we had more men in the Senate like him now. We have a few, but there are never many like that anywhere. He had very high ideals and really lived for them. He was brave and honest, and his treatment by the Republicans of Kansas was a cruel thing. It ended his career and broke his heart."

---

[53] Vinnie Ream was an eighteen year old sculptress who lived in Washington, D.C. and is most famous for her bust and her life-sized statue of Abraham Lincoln which sits in the U. S. Capitol rotunda. Lincoln sat for her work in the morning for five months. She was the first woman to have a sculpture exhibited in the capitol. Ross boarded with Ream's family while the impeachment trial proceeded.

CHAPTER 16

A Lady Gambler Double-Crosses Us

Three Virginians who wanted to make fortunes... the luck of Frank Tilghman at faro... he explains to us the psychology of the game, the odds against the player... the crooked wheel and the woman who lured the suckers... the downfall of a frontier Lothario

VERY EARLY IN 1883, the Americans in Santa Fe suddenly went wild. Someone had discovered that this year was the 333rd anniversary of the founding of Santa Fe[54], and the *New Mexican* suggested a great celebration. Here was the opportunity to bring Santa Fe to the notice of the outside world, and the merchants, the saloon keepers, and the gamblers seized the idea with enthusiasm, raised the money for the first expense, and chose a committee to manage all the details.

There were no subcommittees to get in the way of each other. William T. Thornton, a leading lawyer of Santa Fe was at the head of everything. He advertised all over the United States; arranged that every county in New Mexico should have an exhibit of the things of which it was proudest; persuaded the Pueblo Indians to come and live in tents while they did their ceremonial dances; and—hardest of all—induced the Mescalero Apaches, with the consent of the government, to exhibit some of their war dances.

A great frame building was put up and five acres of land were fenced in. It was planned that the celebration should last three months, by the end of which time we thought everybody who could afford the railway fare would have seen the glories of Santa Fe, the merchants would all have become wealthy, the prospectors would have unloaded all their worthless holes-in-the-ground, and the gamblers and saloon keepers would have wrangled all the spare money away from the visitors.

---

[54] This was not the fact. Santa Fe was founded in 1610 and would have been 253 years old in 1883. The celebration was simply a promotional scheme that seems to have worked.

16 | A Lady Gambler Double-Crosses Us

The Santa Fe [rail]road, the only one running into the town, cordially helped, made low rates, and the show was such a success that it carried on for four months instead of three. Santa Fe was crowded all the time; the weather was good, and the people who came saw in the exhibits from the counties—gold, copper, silver ores, and fruits, and the highlights of Indian life—things that they talked about for a long time.

There were three newspaper men, all Virginians, in Santa Fe, who after the first two weeks of the celebration, thought they were not getting enough of the money being thrown around. One was Henry Brooke, who worked with me on the *New Mexican*, a first-class reporter with a keen sense of humor; another was Frank Tilghman of the Las Vegas *Optic*; the third was myself. So we all quit our jobs and opened an ice cream parlor. That is what we called it, but it was certainly a rough-and-ready parlor. The tables and chairs were of plain wood, there was no carpet on the floor, and the service, which was in the hands of two Mexican boys we employed, was abominable. But the people seemed to like this lack of style, and we made money.

Santa Fe and Las Vegas, like Denver, were then full of unhappy southerners, wandering about the country, looking for a fortune to drop into their laps. They had left their homes, like me, lured by the tales of fabulous gold discoveries; and finding these untrue, most of them had lost hope and were living by their wits. They brought derision on themselves by boasting of fine ancestry and aristocratic blood, and the Virginians were especially sinners in that respect, so much so that they were ridiculed openly. Once a section hand said to me, "F.F.V., he says he is. That means fighting for victuals, don't it?" [55]

And they talked so much about chivalry that this became a byword, and on the street, all the southerners, except those liked especially, were alluded to as "Chives."

"Oh, he's one of those damn chives," was a common characterization of a southerner who went about borrowing money that he never repaid.

This degradation of the Southerner on the frontier used to hurt my feelings, and when I went back to Virginia after years in the west, I spoke to my uncle, a fine old Virginia gentleman of Portsmouth, about it.

"You must remember," said he, "that these men out there with Virginia names who call themselves Virginians, are not all entitled to the distinction. In the days of slavery in Virginia, when we had white slaves, the bondman, when freed by purchases or otherwise, usually took the

---

[55] "F.F.V." stood for "First Families of Virginia;" i.e. socially prominent Virginia families with colonial roots.

name of the family to which he had belonged, although he may not have had a drop of Virginia blood in his veins."

Some of these good-for-nothing southerners, knowing that we were from Virginia, tried to attach themselves to us, but we gave them the cold shoulder. They ate ice cream once as our guests and never came back.

We three were not included by the opinion of the community as belonging to the professional southerners. We were working for a living, never borrowed money without paying and owed no one. We had earned our position as Santa Fe men.

Brooke and I were both good drinkers. We had innumerable acquaintances in Santa Fe and among the visitors from other parts of the country, so we found plenty of occupation in entertaining them. We did not try to guard the tenderfoot from capture by some unscrupulous chap from Los Cerrillos or the Sandia Mountains who wanted to sell him a mine; it would have been regarded as highly unethical if we had interfered in a matter like that, but we did tell our friends among the confidence-men to let this or that man alone if we saw them trying to get their money with the top and bottom trick or the knife trick or the lock trick. We advised our friends, too, as to the crooked and the square faro games in town.

We had a most extraordinary system with the ice cream place. It was closed at midnight. At that time, one or the other of us would go there and collect from the Mexican boys all the money they had taken in that day, lacking, of course, what they had stolen, give them five dollars for the supplies the next day, and then hunt up the other two partners and divide with them. We kept no books.

Brooke and I spent all our money in carousing with our friends. Tilghman, a thin, bright eyed youth of about twenty-five, the oldest of us three, never drank, but he had a passion for gambling and played for the highest stakes he could afford. He never played poker, but lost all his money at roulette and faro. I don't mean that he always lost. When he was winning he plunged. Once he came into the ice cream place, went into the back room where he knew Brooke and I were drinking with some friends, and threw $8,000 on the table.

"Won all that on the queen," he announced, exultantly.

That was another weakness of Tilghman—women. Brooke and I were free of that. Tillman thought and we believed that he was irresistible with women. He talked about his conquests very little, but we heard gossip that went to show that he had a sweetheart on every street in Santa Fe.

One day Tilghman burst in on us, as we sat.

16 | A Lady Gambler Double-Crosses Us

"Three men from Denver have got Harry Mottley's dance hall, and they are going to run it right. Every game in the world. The pick of the baile girls, and four bar keepers. They've got the biggest bankroll Santa Fe has ever seen!"

"Crooked games," said Brooke.

"Very likely. I'll see."

"See here, Tilghman," said a Silver City man, who was sitting with us, "they tell me you're a wizard at faro. Do you play a system?"

"I don't play a system, and I don't win, consistently," answered Tilghman, sitting at the table as if he were about to make a lecture, "System players don't win at any game, even poker, and that gives you the best chance for a system. The only way to win at faro or roulette is to press your luck when you're winning and quit when you see that you're losing. Don't press bad luck. I play faro more than any other game," went on Tilghman, "because it is the squarest game of all. The house has only two advantages. The player understands one of these, and is willing to buck it. That's the splits—but the other—and that's really the biggest advantage the game has—the player doesn't understand exactly. That is the principle that a gambler will always lose more than he will win. An ordinary player will quit the game when he is fifty dollars ahead, and go off and brag about it, but if he loses fifty dollars will he quit? Not on your life. He'll keep on playing till he loses his shirt."

Let me explain what the splits in faro are. If two of the same cards are drawn by the dealer out of the faro box, one after another, the game takes half of all the bets on that card, whether they are played to lose or to win.

"How much of that last big winning have you got there?" I asked.

"Not a damn cent," said Tilghman cheerfully, "and I lost it all in Shelby's game, too, the squarest game in town. My own fault. I won all that money betting on the queen to win, and the last 2,000 I won by calling the turn, queen, ace. What do you think of that? They can't take splits on the turn, you know. Now I go into Shelby's and I say to myself, "that queen can't win all the time. I'll bet on some other cards and copper the queen. "I played my roll heavy and in five minutes it was all over! I reckon that queen said to herself, 'so, he's going back on me. Well I'll just show him!' Anyway, Henry, I want to draw a little on today's receipts. I'm going down to Harry Motley's and try out those games."

The next day, Brooke and I were in the saloon of Ed Schwartz, on the plaza, listening to Ed sing as he polished his glasses. Ed was one of Santa Fe's most distinguished saloon keepers. He sold good liquor; ran a square faro game; and, when things were going right, he would come from behind the bar and sing sentimental songs in a lovely tenor voice of lyric quality. Ed, by the way, had two daughters whom he loved devotedly and when they grew up and began to know enough to be ashamed of their father's business he sold his saloon and moved to Phoenix, where he established himself as a dealer in Indian curios.

Frank Tilghman rushed in. "I've been hunting for you fellows all over the plaza," he exclaimed. "Come on down to Harry Mottley's. There's a girl down there running the roulette wheel, and she's a stunner!"

"Oh, get out of here, Frank," I said, "we want to hear Ed sing Molly Graeme. There's fifty girls down at Harry's and we don't want to see any of them."

"Say, this girl is different," insisted Tilghman. "She's from New York, and her name is Kate Fanshawe. She's the first girl I ever saw who could wear short skirts and not look like a dancehall girl."

So we went down, but we waited until Ed finished singing.

The games in Harry Motley's were going full blast, with a crowd around each table, but the roulette table was hidden by the men about it, placing their bets. Tilghman edged his way through, and we followed him, and saw the girl.

She was small, with black curly hair and brown eyes, and full of vivacity. She was dressed in a style unknown to Santa Fe, in a sort of

This illustration is of a Denver gambling hall. Almost any type of amusement was afforded in an attempt to get the customers involved.
Harper's Weekly, February 7, 1866.

16 | A Lady Gambler Double-Crosses Us

sailor jacket, short skirt, silk stockings, and slippers with silver buckles. Her hands and feet and ankles were all very small. I liked her effect. Simple but really smart.

She welcomed Tilghman with a warm smile, but did not address him especially.

"Faro is a good game, gentlemen, but this is a little faster," she said to the players. "Get your bets down and I'll do the rolling and give you action. Don't bet any more than you can afford. We don't want any crying here."

"My God," gasped Tilghman, "I just got to play. Got any money, either of you? You can take it out tonight."

We gave him what we had, and watched the wheel. He won and lost, but we were interested in seeing the play of his eyes with the girl's. They seemed to be falling in love, head over heels.

We left finally, and went about our rounds of places where we met our friends, and where the atmosphere wasn't so tense.

For the next week, Tilghman was moody and never spoke of either Harry Motley's or of the girl down there, but his face began to light up again soon, and he seemed happy. We judged that the affair was going well.

Then one afternoon, he dragged us out of a group on the plaza and took us into the back room of the ice cream parlor.

"If we could get $100,000 to divide, what would you choose to do?"

"I'd go home," I answered.

"So would I," said Brooke.

"Well, Kate and I are going to get married and take a trip to Europe," said Tilghman.

"Do you mean you've got a hundred thousand dollars?" I asked.

"Just as good as in my hands," answered Tilghman, "that wheel is crooked. Kate is going to throw the game to me and give me $100,000. But I've got to have $1,500 to start to play with, and I've got to get it right off."

"Well, Frank, before we talk about getting the money," I said, "suppose you tell us how that girl is going to throw the game to you and give you $100,000. I'm leery of the whole business, even if she is dead in love with you, and I suppose that's so."

Tilghman was so excited that he was trembling.

"Here's the idea," he said. "That wheel is wired! The sides of those slots where the ball falls are movable. They're controlled by wires that run down through the legs of the table to buttons on the floor, almost flat with the floor, so they can't be noticed. That's why Kate wears those thin little slippers so she can feel the buttons. She can shut all the red slots so the ball will roll into the black, and she can shut all the odd or the even slots, or the zero or the double zero, just as she pleases. The wheel is winning every night now because she shuts all the slots where the heavy betting is laid. I'm to come down there with $1,500, lose 500, and then win a hundred thousand on the red and the zero in three rolls of the wheel!"

"Those gamblers will raise hell when they find out they've been bilked," I remarked.

"Let 'em raise hell," said Tilghman. The boss of the outfit, Tom Ashton, is hated by every good gambler in Santa Fe, and they'll build bonfires if that game is busted. Now, the question is, where are we going to get the $1,500?"

"This place is only turning out about forty or fifty a day," said Brooks, "and we can't get the money from any bank. Our reputation's all right but everybody knows we haven't got anything. And we can't borrow from friends in such a hurry."

"Why not try to get it from Frank Manzanares?" I suggested.

That struck the other two as a good idea. Frank Manzanares was a Mexican gentleman, a very rich sheep raiser of Valencia county who had just been elected to Congress, and we three had helped him greatly, so much so that he had written us a letter after the election, saying that he felt that we had influenced the American vote largely. At that time there was only one delegate in Congress from New Mexico, and the post was one of great dignity and honor. The election had cost Manzanares nearly $100,000 but he felt that it was worth it.

We gave Tilghman all the day's receipts of the ice cream saloon and he went down to Los Lunas, the county seat of Valencia county, where Delegate Manzanares had his ancestral home. He came back with $1,500, and dashed down to Harry Mottley's to conclude the arrangements with his sweetheart.

Next evening, at midnight, we met in the dancehall. The long hall was crowded with dancers and with tourists in good clothes, cowboys and miners in the dress of the mountains and the plain, and a sprinkling of ladies seeking adventure, escorted usually by two gentlemen each. Most of the dancers were Mexican girls.

Two faro tables were doing a rushing business, but there was only one roulette table, and Kate was there with her most fascinating manner. We three stood and watched a moment. The wheel seemed to be losing, or at least only breaking even. The stakes were heavy. Fifty and one hundred dollar stacks of chips were shoved on the colors in the numbers, as fast as the little ball began rolling.

I saw Joe Stinson, the sheriff of the county, in the party at the table, making five dollar bets. "Hello," he greeted us. "Come down to give some nourishment to the Katydid? I'm winning. First time it ever happened. Somebody started a story that the girl was juggling the wheel and I came down to look it over—seems all right to me. That girl sure is a lulu! They say she was educated in the East and can talk French. Wonder how she came to fall for a crook like Ashton?"

"Fall for Tom Ashton? What do you mean?" I asked.

"Aston met her in Denver, in a dance hall," answered the burley sheriff, "she was capping for the roulette game there and she was simply great at getting other suckers to get stuck on her and then blow them against the wheel. Ashton brought her down here and she's been his girl ever since, but the other day they had a quarrel and she wouldn't make it up until he married her. I know because I found a priest for Ashton."

"Good Lord!" I said.

I looked for Tilghman. He was at the side of the girl, and the wheel was spinning. He had bought $500 worth of chips, and had bet them all on the red. The ball dropped on the black. As Kate gathered in the chips from the losers, flashing a smile at Tilghman, I shouldered aside the men between me and the wheel, intending to get near Tilghman and warn him, but at once I saw that Ashton had stationed four of his ruffians around Tilghman, the girl and the wheel, and I could not interfere without a deadly fight. So I stood there helpless and watched.

Tillman put $250 on the red and $250 on the zero. The ball dropped in black and 17.

Kate took in the chips. Tilghman sent her a quick and puzzled look, and she smiled.

He split the last $500 and covered the red and the zero. The ball dropped in black and 11.

Tilghman was broke. He stood dazed, looking at Kate, but she looked away and took the next bets.

"My God," broke out sheriff Stinson, standing by me. "What fool bets. Is he drunk?"

I made my way to Tilghman's side. "Kate is Tom Ashton's wife. That's a heavy dose for such a lady killer! We won't go home this year, and you won't take that trip to Europe. Now keep your mouth shut unless you want to be laughed at all over town, and come on up and we'll eat $1,500 worth of ice cream."

Brooke and I went back to the ice cream place, and by the time we got there we got over the worst of the incident and the humor of the thing struck us. We lay down on our cots in the back room and began to laugh.

Brooke said, "It wouldn't be so funny if you and I had got caught, but Frank Tilghman being fooled by a gambler woman is too much for me. Let's have a drink."

We drank. After an hour or so, Tilghman came in. At first we tried to respect his feelings, but presently Brooke chuckled, and that started us off again. We laughed so hard that it hurt.

"Go on, you fellows, laugh." said Tilghman finally. "Do you know what she did after you left? I guess she thought I was going to raise a row and she beckoned Tom Ashton and he came over to the wheel. I looked at her and said, 'Goddbye, Mrs. Ashton?' and she took this bouquet of pansies from her jacket and handed them to me. Fifteen hundred dollars for a bunch of pansies!"

Tilghman was not the same man after that. He moped around Santa Fe for a week or so, and then suddenly appeared to Brooke and me and announced that he was leaving town.

"I'm going to Australia," he said, "and go into racing there. Give me all the money you can spare and I'll hop a boxcar tonight and get on toward San Francisco."

I never saw him again.

CHAPTER 17

Back in Colorado, No Longer a Hero

The Utes are scattered, the Government having violated its treaty with them and opened the reservation to settlers... Sitting on blocks of ice in a freight car in January... Eugene Field and Bill Nye doing the lock step on the streets of Denver... My return to conventional life.

AFTER A WHILE, NEWSPAPER LIFE in Albuquerque irked me. I was not succeeding in the purpose of cleaning up the town, and I felt that the good human ruffians who controlled its affairs didn't care a hang what the newspaper said if they didn't get too personal. I wanted to see the Utes and the mountains and the mountain streams, and the great pine trees; the turbid waters of the Rio Grande nauseated me when I looked at the river. So, I left Albuquerque and went to Ouray again.

Although I had been lionized in Lake City and Ouray when I helped to rescue the Meeker women from the Utes, yet, when I returned to these mining towns four years later, I was not received as a hero. Nor did I think I would be. Four years in a mining camp was a long time and men were too busy getting gold and silver to live in the past. I was broke and my buckboard driver paid for my supper and my hotel bill in Lake City. I did not even take the trouble to look up the men who had been so eager to hear my story when I came there with the news of the rescue. I got breakfast and with no baggage, tramped the trail, thirty miles, to Ouray over the mountains.

Ouray, in the four years since I had seen it, had become a town of nearly a thousand people, full of prospectors and men with capital, willing to buy prospects and to mine. Both the papers, the *Times* and the *Solid Muldoon*, were doing well, but both of them had plenty of men to do their work and neither could offer me a place on its staff. I went to the hotel where I had lived and was offered a place as night clerk for my board. I took it with alacrity. This was in September—the snow was beginning to fly, and I must dig in for the winter.

In the few years that Saunders was away from Ouray, it continued to grow and to stabilize, although some of these Main Street businesses are still in log cabins.
P. David Smith Collection.

I made a very poor hotel clerk, I am sure. I felt myself almost a stranger in the town. Chief Ouray was dead. Our government, violating its treaty with the Utes, by which the great reservation and Colorado had been assured to them, had forced them to take $75,000 for the reservation, well worth seventy-five million dollars, and had scattered them in Utah and New Mexico, opening the reservation to settlement. Grand Junction, Delta and Montrose, three agricultural towns had been built on the reservation and were thriving.

Chipeta and my friends, Chiefs Shavano and Sapavanero, had been taken to Utah.

A profound melancholy oppressed my spirit, but I tried to shake it off, and forced myself to talk with the guests of the hotel since Dave Day, the owner of the *Solid Muldoon*, and the Ripleys, of the *Times*, both promised to buy from me any news I brought in, and I was in great need of money. I had been with the hotel about a month when one night, two young men, both black haired and slim, well-dressed, with warm clothing and white hands that showed they were not miners, dropped in as I was looking over the register.

"We are from Mississippi," said one of the two, "and this is Beach Chattin, my foster brother. We hear you are from the South, and we want to make your acquaintance. We came out here to practice law and we find there is none to practice. We're broke, and we've got to give up the room where we are. We're going to move down in a cabin on the side of the road a man here says we can have, and we thought that maybe you would like to throw in with us and live there during the winter."

"I think I will," I replied. "The landlady here gave me a strong hint today that I was eating too much. We won't have any freight wagons from Alamosa in the winter, and the town will have to live on what it has already. Food will be scarce. In the spring we can all go to Denver."

During the cold weather of the next three months we three lived in that log cabin about a mile below Ouray, on the bank of the Uncompahgre River. The cabin was banked in snow; the river was frozen, and we broke holes in the ice to get our water. We had plenty of bedding, fortunately, which was borrowed; and the cabin had an enormous fireplace, which we kept filled with logs. There were many fallen trees, which we had only to cut up for firewood. We had little money but now and then, not every day, I went up to town and turned in to the *Times* a lot of news which I got from the saloons and the stores, and the Ripley's paid me five or ten dollars or gave me an order for food on a store that advertised with the paper. Our larder was slim but we got enough to eat, living mostly on meat soups, bread and coffee. I made some money, too, by my letters to the *Denver Tribune*, but very little, and I wrote for a weekly magazine in Denver—frontier stuff.

As the cold-weather advanced, we found we were living in great discomfort. About the first of March, the weather became severe. It was below zero; the snow lay heavy on the ground; we were not well clad and we were cold all the time. The old chap who owned the cabin and the bedding, came down from Ouray one day and told us that he was going to Silverton and had to have his blankets.

We felt we simply had to get to Denver. My companions knew that they could find no employment in Ouray. There was no work there for anyone but miners, and these two southern youngsters could not work with their hands. The money I had got from the *Denver Tribune* was running low. So we sent Beach Chattin up to Ouray and gave him a dollar.

"See here, Beach," said Redding, "if you drink this up by yourself, we'll never forgive you, you've got to give the buckboard driver a drink and persuade him to stop on the road tomorrow and take us down to Montrose, where we can get in a box car and in some way get to Denver."

Chattin came back early in the morning, happy with many drinks, and jubilantly announced the success of his mission.

"He'll do it," he told us. "He's a good fellow, he has no passengers tomorrow and there's plenty of room."

So we got to Montrose the next day. We were ragged and unwashed and we had not a bit of baggage. Indeed we were tramps, and we looked no better than the other tramps, who coming from Utah, were lying around the railway yards, waiting for a good chance to jump a freight train. I still had about ten dollars, carefully hidden in my pockets. We had eaten everything we had in the cabin before we left that morning, so we went to the railway restaurant and by washing an enormous pile of dishes, got a dinner that was satisfying. Then, as dusk fell we set out to find a brakeman who would be friendly enough to take us on our way to Denver. We found one. He said he would take us to Gunnison, the end of his division for a dollar each. The train was to start about dark. When the engineer blew his whistle, we were to come to the third car from the end of the train and he would put us in. When we got there we found eight other tramps waiting. Each of them had paid the brakeman a dollar for the ride. The whistle blew; the brakeman came running; slid open the end door of the car and said, "Get in quick, damn you."

We got in quick, one after another, eleven of us. The whistle blew again; the brakeman slid the door shut and the train started, and we found that we were in a car of blocks of ice.

"My God!" shouted one of the tramps. "The son of a bitch."

How cold it was in that car I don't know. You may imagine. We were in there for six hours, and long before we got to Gunnison, we had all fallen into a stupor. After that first outburst of our companion, no one had said a word. Since we could do nothing to help ourselves, we had accepted our miserable situation, with the thought in the minds of us all, that if we ever met that brakeman again, we would kill him.

The train stopped at Gunnison. The brakeman came and threw open the door, calling to us, "Get out of here."

We did not kill him. We were too numb with the cold. We climbed out, stiff as wooden men, and made our way towards a light. It was the railway station. We entered the waiting room and there—praised be God—was an enormous cannonball stove, red hot and no one in the room. Some of us stood around the stove. Others lay down on the floor, as close to the stove as we could get without burning.

From Gunnison we walked and rode in boxcars to Denver. There Redding and Chattin got money by telegraph from their homes and went on East.

By promising to do Herculean labor I got a job on the *Republican*. And herculean it was. I undertook to write three departments of the paper—the railroads, the cattle and the police.

Denver was even a livelier town than it had been when I first saw it four years before. It had become famous all over the country as a health resort, and as a mining center. Colorado Springs was beginning to attract the sick and the people going there came to Denver first, to outfit and spend money. The streets and shops were lighted all night long and were crowded. Cowboys in their trappings rode along the streets, and they and the plainsmen thronged the hotels, the sidewalks and the saloons and gambling houses.

H.A.W. Tabor had made his strike in Leadville and was building his opera house. His wife had stopped taking in washing for the miners, to help Tabor and was wearing silks and diamonds, but poor woman, she was not happy. Tabor shamelessly divorced her as his money poured in and married a younger and prettier woman who helped to bankrupt him.

Miners in Arizona, New Mexico and Colorado, who made strikes, came to Denver to have a good time. When Ed. Schiefflin, the founder of Tombstone and the money backer of the *Tombstone Epitaph*, sold out his claims, he hastened to Denver, to enjoy himself. He spent money foolishly, and his idea of a good time was buying jewelry, looking at it for a while and then giving it away. He came into the Windsor Hotel, where he had a room, about two o'clock one morning, with both coat pockets full of gold watches, which he had been buying.

"Here's a beauty," he said the clerk. "I want to give this one to you."

He drew the watch from his pocket and it slipped from his fingers and fell on the tiled floor and shattered. Schiefflin looked down at it, but his balance was too uncertain for him to stoop.

"Never mind," he said, "let her lay, here's another one, just as pretty."

The *Tribune* was by long odds the best paper in Denver. Ottamar Rothacker, a slim, handsome man of thirty-five, with a long black mustache and curly black hair, a brilliant paragrapher, was the editor. F.J.V. Skiff was the city editor. He had been the city editor of the paper when I was first there. He was afterwards director of the Field Museum in Chicago and director of Exhibits of the St. Louis world's Fair.

Eugene Field was on the paper and was just then uncovering the vein of witty persiflage that made him famous afterwards in Chicago. Field hung many of his jokes on Wolfe Londoner a wealthy public-spirited and successful wholesale and retail grocer. Londoner liked the publicity and his generosity expanded under it. [56]

---

[56] Eugene Field became best known for his children poems, including the famous *Little Boy Blue* and *Wynken, Blynken and Nod*. In college he was better known for his outrageous pranks rather than his academics. He worked at various newspapers. He and Julia Comstock were married and had eight children that were the inspiration for many of his works. In the early 1880s he was managing editor for the *Denver Tribune*. He died in 1895.

Bill Nye was editing a little paper printed in long primer up in Laramie, Wyoming, called the *Laramie Boomerang*. Once every month he would come to Denver and he, Rothacker and Field would go on the streets and make a night of it. They would have a few drinks and then would do the lock step on the sidewalks. When they entered a saloon in this order, everybody there would shout with laughter and more wine would be poured out then could be drunk.

One evening, in the office of the *Tribune*, a man came in, the owner of a smelter, just built, to see a news story Skiff had written about it. Skiff handed him the sheets. He read it and was greatly pleased, and as he turned to leave his office, he laid a $100 bill on Skiff's desk. Skiff, without turning his head, rolled up the bill into a ball and tossed it at the man as he went out of the door. He turned, picked it up, saw the look on Skiff's face and went out without a word.

The work I was doing was interesting. The railroads were building extensions over and through the mountains and their plans gave me many a good story.

At the headquarters of the cattle men, I met the chiefs of that great industry and several times went out with them to watch a roundup of cattle.

In my police work I had to cover the office of the Rocky Mountain Detective Association. Dave Cook[57] managed that work. He was feared by every crook and bad man in the west, and he could have had a number of notches on his gun, but he had none. He didn't believe in that kind of ostentation. But he wanted credit for every arrest of a dangerous train robber or stage holdup that he made and so I got lots of front-page tales from him.

But, exciting as my work was, there was a sameness about it that made it pall on me. I was tired of the rough life, and I wanted to be among gentle people. Besides that, I could see that I was drinking too much whiskey. I would write until two o'clock in the morning; go to bed exhausted and get up about noon, so tired that I had to take several cocktails before I could eat breakfast and be steady.

So, one day, I gave up my desk in the *Republican* office and dropping into the office of the *Times*, I saw Tom Dawson, the editor, afterwards manager of the Associated Press in the press gallery of Congress.

"Dawson," I said, "do you remember the story I wrote for you about Aubrey's ride from Santa Fe to Independence? Was it worth ten dollars?"

---

[57] Dave Cook was a famous detective, Marshal and Sheriff in Denver, who was known for his absolute fairness and truthfulness with prisoners and the general public alike..

17 | Back in Colorado, No Longer a Hero

"Yes," said Dawson, "I'll pay you now."

"I'm tired of this wild and woolly west," I went on, "and I'm going down to Memphis and sit in the park and watch the squirrels and see the pretty women passing."

"I don't blame you," said Dawson, "I'd like to do that myself. Got any money?"

"I'm broke, but I don't mind that—I'll get something to do."

"Well, you don't look like a busted reporter," said Dawson, eyeing my cutaway shirt and high hat and patent leather shoes. I had equipped myself with these with the first money I had made.

I had my pocket full of railway annual passes, and I went to Kansas City, and then down to Memphis. I had no baggage but a small hand bag. I went to a cheap hotel in Memphis and for several days I enjoyed myself by walking on the levee and sitting in the park.

I doubt if I ever felt such sensuous satisfaction as I did during those few days. It was Spring and the weather was soothing. The park was full of birds and flowers and the agile squirrels, and in the afternoons well-dressed men and women walked there. The park gave me just what I had wanted to see and feel.

But one morning I woke up and found that I had only a little silver in my pocket—less than a dollar.

"Well, my dream is over," I said to myself. "Now I'll go to St Louis and get to work." I went to a pawnbroker and exchanged my high hat and my little bag for a cap and fifty cents, and on the way to St Louis I ate only ten cents worth of peanuts, shells and all. That was a trick that had been taught me by a veteran tramp, to stay appetite.

Epilogue[58]

AS HE DESCRIBED AT THE END OF HIS REMEMBRANCE, by 1888 Saunders was thirty years old and had become so jaded with reporting on the crime beats and such for the *Republican* and then the *Denver Tribune* that he wished to leave Colorado and the West. He also fully recognized that he had once more "fallen off the wagon" and was again drinking far too much. He knew he desperately needed to slow it down and thought he needed a major change in his environment to accomplish this. He thus abruptly resigned from the *Tribune*, and, though broke, tramped eastward toward Memphis, Tennessee. He emphasized how he was looking forward to forgetting the "wild and wooly west" and simply sitting in a park and watching the antics of the squirrels and the pretty women who might pass by him. From Denver the nearly broke young reporter traveled to Kansas City and on to Memphis. There he walked the levee and sat in the parks admiring nature as well as the well-dressed folks who strolled there. His time in the parks renewed his spirit and brought forth new energy and ambition in him. He subsequently cashed out what little he owned and headed for St. Louis, Missouri to again try his hand at reporting and a healthier lifestyle.

Saunders quickly found work as a reporter and over the next several years wrote for various papers, including the St. Louis *Globe-Democrat*, the *Chronicle*, and most notably, the *Post-Dispatch* with which he was

---

[58] Information for the Epilogue was gathered from Ancestry.com and from the *St. Louis Post-Dispatch* on-line newspaper files, and from a few extant copies of the *Santa Fe New Mexican* and *The New Mexican*.

long associated. He began making a name for himself in the community and in 1893 was appointed as secretary to the newly elected mayor of St. Louis, Cyrus P. Walbridge. In 1895 he was appointed the Republican member of the local Board of Election Commissioners. He held that post for three years until dismissed by a new political administration. He then became the assistant postmaster for St. Louis. He held that post until 1901 when he was made secretary of the city's Business Men's League—the precursor to the Chamber of Commerce which largely developed under his guiding hand. He held that position until about 1917. During this period he cultivated deep personal and political relations among the city's populace and particularly in its arts and business communities. He rose to become such a well-known St. Louis personality that his obituary in the *Post-Dispatch* on Monday, February 11, 1935 featured his photograph and life story of several column inches as front-page news.

Saunders was known as a skilled song writer and ballad singer and once was credited with a profusion of such efforts at the Annual Banquet of the Business Men's League. Saunders was particularly noted for the rousing tune "Boss Laciede," which was sung to the tune of the "Good Old

Undated Photograph of William F. Saunders, as pictured in his obituary that ran on the front page of the St. Louis Post-Dispatch *on Fenruary 11, 1935.*

Summer Time." While apparently still at the helm of the League he published a notable, but undated, book, *St. Louis Today* under the auspices of the Men's League. This was largely a book promoting the business potential offered by the city in its advantageous physical location on the Mississippi River which made it one of the major gateways to the West. It was likely published prior to 1917 and may have been associated with promoting the landmark 1904 World's Fair held in St. Louis. In that volume, Saunders wrote that St. Louis was *the great wholesale thoroughfare of the Southwest. On this avenue and adjacent streets are located the wholesale and jobbing houses devoted to the trade in dry goods, notions and related lines, carpets, boots and shoes, clothing, millinery, furniture, trunks and other branches. The business of the street is rapidly extending westward causing the erection of great warehouses and business blocks and the expenditure of enormous sums for modern structures.*

Saunders's book contained many photographs of the most notable businesses and commercial structures of the great city, which has through time—and in competition with Kansas City and Joplin—been commonly known as the "Gateway to the West." It seems a bit ironic that Saunders, after all of his youthful adventures out on the western frontier, would ultimately end his days at its very gateway!

The World's Fair, formally known as the "Louisiana Purchase Exposition," and which covered some 1,200 acres with 1,500 buildings of exhibits, ran for eight months in 1904 and attracted millions of visitors as well as exhibits from all over the world. Preparing for it was a major undertaking for the city and required the efforts of a great number of people for some years prior to its opening. This massive world class event was quite a "feather in its cap" for St. Louis and commemorated the city's role as the "Gateway to the West." From his post with the Men's League, Saunders handled many of the special duties relative to the planning, development and operation of the fair. Among these he organized tours and demonstrations relative to the "waterways movement," which involved a plan to develop a water shipping route from the Great Lakes to the Gulf of Mexico by way of the Mississippi River. He was then also the secretary for the "Lakes-o-the-Gulf Deep Waterways Association," which was promoting this project. These tours included one that took President Theodore Roosevelt down the Mississippi from St. Louis all the way to Cairo and Memphis. He also arranged a tour that took President Taft and a congressional delegation downriver all the way to New Orleans. Whether or not he accompanied the tours and mingled with these Presidents is not known.

Despite his difficult times in New Mexico, Saunders long retained warm feelings for the area and would return later in life to vacation there, particularly in 1907. At one point he pressed for historic preservation efforts to be undertaken at the "old adobe building" where the *Review* had been published under his hand. It was there that he had also been threatened by the gambling establishment with being burned at the stake, lynched/hung, "having his neck broken, being shot to pieces, or carved up with Bowie Knives etc." On his 1907 visit to his old haunts he noted the ruins of the decayed adobe Pecos church and believed the New Mexico Historical Society should obtain them and preserve them. On this visit he spent time with General Lew Wallace who was then governor and the author of the famed book *Ben Hur*. Wallace and Willie were apparently close friends.

Saunders long planned for development of the St. Louis Chamber of Commerce was finally realized in 1917. He then resigned as its secretary and secured the position of secretary of the Missouri State Council of Defense, headquartered in the state capitol at Jefferson City. Although he had by then risen to some prominence in Missouri he managed to get himself into a political pickle and was fired from that job. In the 1918 Senate primary campaign former Governor Joseph W. Folk was a candidate and he criticized the attitude of Missouri toward World War I. Saunders made a reply, apparently in the press, on the matter and rebuked Folk. That public action caused such a political flap that Saunders was forced to resign his post with the Council.

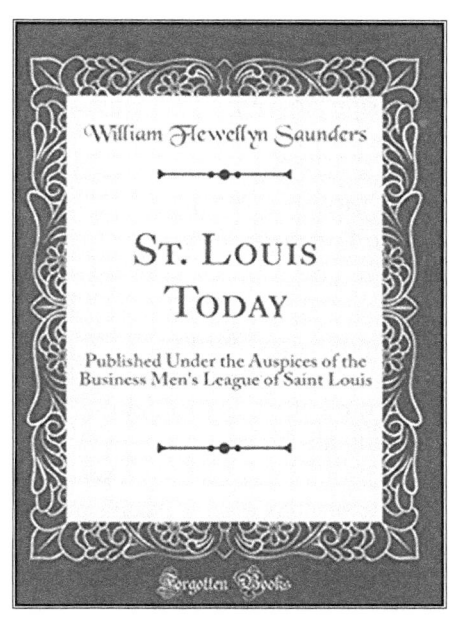

The cover of Saunders undated but important book St. Louis Today.

Saunders, who by then was about sixty years old, then headed out to Mexico City. Whether or not he was hiding out from the Missouri political fallout or just wanted a change of scenery will never be known. Perhaps he just wished to again simply sit in a park and watch the squirrels' antics and the pretty *senoritas* who might stroll by. He did, however, quickly find employment in Mexico as the secretary of the American Chamber of Commerce, likely with the help of some old acquaintance. He served in that post for the next ten years (until 1927). In this position his duties entailed obtaining the cooperation of American firms that might be interested in Mexico's future. In 1928, when he was seventy, he returned to St. Louis. Back home he remained a patron of the arts and was long an active member of the local Artists' Guild and Art League where he was in charge of dramatic productions and play-writing contests. Saunders was commonly known in St. Louis simply as "Willie." He was remembered as a notable former newspaperman, business organizer, and a political idealist.

On February 10, 1935, after an illness of several months, he, at seventy-four years of age, died of unlisted cause(s) in St. Louis at the home of his son, William Flewellyn Saunders, Jr. His substantive obituary was published in the *Post-Dispatch* the next day and shorter versions appeared in other regional papers. He was survived by his wife, Lillian Lincoln (Stone) Saunders (1869-1940) whom he had married in 1894, apparently in St. Louis. It is not known why he died at his son's home instead of with his wife at his family home in Ward 28. In addition to Lillian, he left two children, W. F. Saunders Jr. (1897-1969), who had been born in Paris, France, and a daughter, Nancy Lewis Saunders (1894-1969), who was born in St. Louis. He also left one sister, Nancy Inge Saunders ("Nannie") (1860-1941) who had been born in Norfolk, Virginia and ultimately married Dr. Crawford Howell Toy, one of Willie's old mentors. In his lifetime he was, of course, known to have visited not only all the places in the "Wild West" that he discusses herein, but also Europe—as a child and seemingly again as an adult and father, and again at least in 1905, Panama, and Mexico. Just what Mrs. Saunders was doing in Paris in 1897 when she delivered her son is not known, but the Saunders were obviously seasoned travelers and likely had been there together.

In 1905 or 1906 Saunders and his wife and children spent an extended period in Europe. All in all, however, he purportedly found that "his health and mind" were better restored by the long stay he made in New Mexico in the summer of 1907. On that visit he and his niece, a Ms. Durant of Minneapolis vacationed at the Valley Ranch on the Pecos River and from there he visited his old New Mexico acquaintances. At the time of William's and Lillian's "summer jaunt to Europe" together with his mother in June of 1905, the *Post-Dispatch* ran a short news brief. The author suggested that the party visit Wales before returning in order to "see the place where his weird middle name comes from!"

Index

Adams, General Charles—109, 111-123, 130, 131, 133, 136, 137
Alabama—9
Alamosa, Colorado—74, 75
Albuquerque, New Mexico—12, 181-190
Albuquerque Democrat—12, 182
Albuquerque Journal—188,189
Albuquerque Review—12, 146, 147, 181, 182, 184
Alcoholism—10, 168, 171, 181-184, 210
Alice (ex-slave)—45, 46
American School of Berlin—37-40
Anthony, D. R. (Boss)—192
Apache War—11, 12, 120, 137, 139, 148, 173, 174
Armijo Hotel—189
Arthur, Vice-President Chester—177
Ashland, Tennessee—58, 59
Ashton, Tom - 200-202
Atchison, Topeka, and Santa Fe Railroad—184
Avalanche (Mt. Sneffels)—85, 86

Bandelier, Adolph (Ad.)—146-148
Begole, "Gus"—84, 85
Berlin, Germany—38-41
Ben Hur—151, 152

Bible Selling—54-56
Billy the Kid (Henry McCarty)—9, 11. 153-160, 190
Black Warrior River—26
"Blind Tom"—28-30
Brooke, Henry—146, 168, 195-200
Burros—178-180

Camp Meetings (revivals) – 17-22, 44, 45, 54
Candle Making – 28
Carlsbad, New Mexico – 177
Chattin, Beach—204-206
Chesapeake Bay—46
Chicago Tribune—127, 128
Childers, Mr. and Mrs. J. B.—34-36
Chipeta—8, 9, 88-97, 100, 110, 125, 137-141
Chivington, Colonel John—115, 116, 136
Circuit Riders (ministers)—15, 16, 20, 27
Civil War—7-9, 24-30
Charley the Cook—178
"Chives"—195
Cleveland, President Grover—193
Cline, Captain Milton—112-125
Colorado (State)—7, 8, 138
Colorao (Colorado or Colorow) (Ute)—8, 98, 104, 111, 112, 126, 133, 135

Cook, Dave—208
Crawford, John Wallace (Captain Jack)—148, 149
Cuddigan, Mr. and Mrs. John (hanging)—82-84

Dawson, Tom—208, 209
Day, Dave—79
Deep South—15
Denver, Colorado—9, 10, 13, 70, 71, 139, 206
Denver Republican—13, 182, 206, 208
Denver and Rio Grande Railroad—75, 206
Denver Times—13, 182
Denver Tribune—112, 121, 127, 128, 205, 207, 208
Doc Holiday—188, 190
Dodge, Captain—106, 107
Doenhoff, Count—109, 114-118
Douglas (Quignant) (Ute)—88, 90, 113, 119-122, 133, 137

Earp, Morgan—189
Earp, Virgil—189
Earp, Wyatt—188-190
Elizabeth River—46
Ellis—188

Fanhawe, Kate—198-202
Faro (gambling)—197, 198
Ferguson, Jim—174-176
Field, Eugene—207, 208
F. F. V. (First Families of Virginia)—195, 196
Folk, Joseph W.—213
Furman, David—55-57
Furman, George—55
Furman University—51-54, 59, 60

Galt, Richard—43, 44
Gannon, John—171, 174
Garfield, President John A.—177
Garrett, Sheriff Pat—156, 159, 160
"Ghosts of the Pecos"—12
Gilbert—149, 150
Gildersleeve, Lieutenant—132
Gordon, John—106
Grand River, Colorado—116-118, 124, 126
Grant, President Ulysses—11, 161-166
Greenville, South Carolina—51, 52, 54, 58
Gunnison, Colorado—206
Guston Mine—81
Guttierrez, Sheriff Celso—186

Harvard University—68
Hayes, William S.—66
Hatch, General Edward—131-140, 152-156
Holiday, "Doc", John H.—188, 190
Hughes, Tom—188, 189

Ignacio (Ute)—90, 98, 102
Indian Wars—8

Jack (Ute)—98, 99, 104, 113, 119, 120, 133, 137, 138
Johnson, President Andrew – 191, 192
Johnson (Ute)—98, 99, 103, 113, 118-121, 133

Kansas City—209, 210
Kelly, John—84

Index

Keno (Gambling)—72, 73
Kistler, Russell—144
KKK (Ku Klux Klan)—9, 34-36

La Fonda Hotel—145,146
Lacey, Dr. John—87, 89-100, 102, 112, 126, 136, 137, 139, 140
Lake City, Colorado—10, 74-77, 128-130
La Placita—154
Las Vegas, New Mexico—143, 144
Las Vegas Optic—144
Lenore (of Edgar Allan Poe)—59
Lincoln, New Mexico—153
Lincoln County, New Mexico—158, 159, 174, 175
Los Cerritos—161
Las Vegas, New Mexico—195
Los Piños II (Uncompahgre Ute Agency)—78, 87, 89, 102, 108, 121, 126, 131
Louisville, Kentucky—10. 63, 66, 77
Louisville Age—10, 62, 64-69
Lucas, John—149

Manzanares, Frank—200
Mammy Lou—33
Manderfield, Billy—139
Martin, Bill—170,172, 173, 178
Meeker Captives Rescue—108-127
Meeker, Arvilla—123-125
Meeker, Father Nathan C.—101, 103, 107, 136
Meeker, Josephine—118, 122, 125, 141, 142
Meeker Massacre—9, 90, 101-108, 131

Memphis, Tennessee—209, 210
Merritt, General—106, 107
Mexican-American War—7
Mineral Farm Mine—84
Morehead—143, 144
Montrose, Colorado—141, 206
Mora, New Mexico—179
Mt. Sneffels—85, 86
Mount Chalchihultl—162
Motley, Harry—198, 199
Mullen, Sandy—106
Munn, Charles—101

Negro "Mammies"—32, 33
Negroes—19, 34-36, 49, 50, 53, 54, 60
Negro (Buffalo Soldiers)—107
New Mexico—10
New York Herald—128, 147
New Placer Mining Co.—162
Norfolk, Virginia—42, 46-49, 60, 61
Norfolk Women's College—44
Nye, Bill—208

Opelika, Alabama—30
Oregon Trail—8
Ouray's House—9, 98, 125, 136
Ouray, Chief—8, 87-110, 110, 111, 131-140
Ouray Times—10, 79, 87, 109, 125-127, 182, 203, 205
Ouray, Town of—9, 10, 12, 73, 74, 77-85, 100, 126, 127, 139, 182, 203-206

Palace of the Governors—155, 156
Page, Walter Hines—63-69
Pagosa Springs, Colorado—140
Paradise Lost—15
Payne, Captain—104-107
Persune—98, 99, 113, 119, 120, 123, 124, 133, 137, 138
Pecos River—173
Pietro—97
Piney Woods—15
Pines Wells—177
Pitkin, Governor Frederick W.—101, 129, 131, 138
Price, Mrs. and children – 122, 123, 125
Prospectors—81
Puerta de Luna—169, 177, 178

Quignant—See Douglas

Railroad Ave. (Albuquerque)—184, 185, 188
Rattlesnakes—171, 172
Randolph-Macon College—23, 58- 60
Rankin, Joe—105, 106
Rawlins, Wyoming—105, 106
Red Mountain Mining District—81
Revivals—See Camp Meetings
Ream, Vinnie—192, 193
Rio Grande River—184
Ripley, Henry & William (brothers)—79, 80, 126, 127, 204
Rome, Georgia—15
Ross, Edmund G.—193
Ross Chapel—30, 31
Rothacheker, Ottamar—207, 208

Sapavanero—98, 133, 135, 137, 140
St. Louis, Missouri—13, 182, 183
St. Louis Business Men's League—211
St. Louis Chamber of Commerce—213
St. Louis Chronicle—13, 182, 210
St. Louis Globe-Democrat—210
St. Louis Post–Dispatch—210
St. Louis Today—211-213
St. Louis World's Fair—212
Sand Creek Massacre—115, 116
Schieffin, Ed—207
Schwartz, Ed—197, 198
Santa Fe, New Mexico—11, 12, 139, 143, 145, 148-160, 167, 194, 195
Santa Fe New Mexican—11-13, 139, 146, 155-157, 167, 181, 194, 195
Santa Fe Railroad—144, 167, 195
Saunders, Lillian Lincoln (Stone) Saunders—214
Saunders, James—37
Saunders, Mary Joy Toomer—22-27, 39, 48, 74
Saunders, Robert Milton—16, 17, 23, 24, 39, 40, 44, 45, 51, 60, 74
Saunders Jr., William F.—214
Schurtz, Carl—90, 133, 197, 198
Shavano (Ute)—98, 99, 113, 114, 117-123, 133, 137, 140
Sherman, George—112
Solid Muldoon—79, 80, 84, 144, 203, 204
Susan (Shawsheen) (Ute)—119-124
Simpson, Harry—145, 146
Silver City, New Mexico—157, 158, 160
Shaw, John—169-180

Index

Slavery/slaves—19, 20, 28-31
"Soapweed Saunders"—172, 178
Stanley, Agent William—109, 111, 126, 133
Socorro, New Mexico—186
Stoddard, Billy—81
Stenson, Sheriff Vincent Joe—201
Stuffed ham—67
Surveying—11, 167-181

Tabor, H.A.W.—207
Tegel, Germany—40-42
The Fair God—151
Thornburg, Major T. T.—103-105, 114, 130
Thornton, William—194
Tilghman, Frank—195-202
Toomer, James H.—22, 23
Toomer, Sally—3, 30
Toomer, Sheldon—26, 27
Townsend, John—132, 133, 135, 136
Toy, Crawford Howard (Cousin Crawford)—10, 24, 37, 51, 57, 58, 62, 63, 67, 68
Toy, Nancy Saunders—10, 68, 69
Treaty of 1881 (Ute)—131-139
Tuscaloosa, Alabama—15, 23, 24, 27
Tuscaloosa Women's College—23, 25, 26, 36, 37

Uncompahgre River—81
Utes (General)—9, 94, 95, 98-100, 103, 110, 115, 130-136, 140, 147, 204
Ute War—11
Ute Indian Agency (Uncompahgre)—87
Utes, Southern 140

Utes, Tabeguache—9, 88
Utes, Uncompahgre—9, 101, 132, 138, 140
Utes, White River—99-103, 110, 113, 120, 133, 140

Valois, Lieutenant—132, 136
Victoria, Chief (Apache)—152

Walbridge, Cyrus P.—211
Wallace, Lew—151-156, 159
Washington, D. C.—136-139
Wetumpka, Alabama—23
Whitewater Creek—116
White River Ute Agency (See also Meeker)—129, 130

Yankee Girl Mine—81

Zuni Indians—146-148

www.ingramcontent.com/pod-product-compliance
Lightning Source LLC
Chambersburg PA
CBHW070550160426
43199CB00014B/2441